MILLIONAIRES [illegible] HUGE FEES FOR [illegible] THAT IS YOURS IN THIS BOOK

One of the best kept secrets about taxes is how remarkably easy it is to reduce the amount you have to pay—while staying well within the law.

Even less known is the fact that these tax shelters are not just for the upper one percent of income earners, but can be used by middle-income Americans.

Now a successful tax attorney gives you all the details of all the many kinds of tax shelters readily available to you—including their tax benefits, potential profits, possible pitfalls, and the very latest laws dealing with them.

It is your duty to pay taxes. It is your established right not to pay more than you have to. Now this complete guide enables you to exercise that right by pinpointing all the money-saving, money-making ways to cut your taxes legally. We can only urge you to use it.

A COMPLETE GUIDE

ROBERT AND CAROL
TANNENHAUSER

Revisions with the assistance of
Bryan J. Tomasek

REVISED EDITION

PUBLISHER'S NOTE
This publication is designed to provide accurate and authoritative information in regard to the subject matter covered. It is sold with the understanding that the publisher is not engaged in rendering legal, accounting or other professional service. If legal advice or other expert assistance is required, the service of a competent professional person should be sought.

NAL BOOKS ARE AVAILABLE AT QUANTITY DISCOUNTS WHEN USED TO PROMOTE PRODUCTS OR SERVICES. FOR INFORMATION PLEASE WRITE TO PREMIUM MARKETING DIVISION, THE NEW AMERICAN LIBRARY, INC., 1633 BROADWAY, NEW YORK, NEW YORK 10019.

Published by arrangement with Crown Publishers, Inc.

SIGNET TRADEMARK REG. U.S. PAT. OFF. AND FOREIGN COUNTRIES
REGISTERED TRADEMARK—MARCA REGISTRADA
HECHO EN CHICAGO, U.S.A.

SIGNET, SIGNET CLASSICS, MENTOR, PLUME, MERIDIAN AND NAL BOOKS are published by The New American Library, Inc., 1633 Broadway, New York, New York 10019

First Signet Printing, January, 1980

Seventh Printing (Revised Edition), October, 1982

8 9 10 11 12 13 14 15

PRINTED IN THE UNITED STATES OF AMERICA

To David and Emily,
with love
In memory of Ana Horowitz

Contents

Acknowledgments

Writing a book, we discovered, in addition to being exciting and gratifying, can be a long, lonely, and demanding experience. In our case, many people made both tangible and intangible contributions to help lighten the burdens. For their careful and concerned readings and comments, we'd like to thank Bertha Blanck, Albert Blanck, Mae Tannenhauser, Max Tannenhauser, and Michael Tannenhauser. For their expert opinions and advice, we are grateful to Robert Bernstein, Eric Rosenfeld, Peter Fischbein, Steve Ellsworth, Sharon Mahoney, Meyer Lieber, and David Lesser. We are eternally grateful to Ginger Hanlon for her help in organizing the manuscript.

Our publisher, Bruce Harris, was unquestionably the conceiver of and guiding force behind the book; we'd like to thank him for recognizing the need and convincing us that we could properly satisfy it. Special thanks to Susan Petersen, a constant source of encouragement and wisdom—a very special person. Thanks also to our editor, Marcy Posner, and to our good friends and family for the understanding and patience they displayed during this long and preoccupied period. Last, and most of all, we thank each other.

R.F.T./C.E.T.
June, 1982

Authors' Note

This book was written to make the subject of tax shelters comprehensible to the average investment-oriented layperson. Because of the complex and technical nature of the material, it was necessary to generalize and simplify many of the tax and legal concepts. Do not rely solely on the information presented here. Before investing, it is absolutely essential to consult an expert to determine how the many facets of the law apply to your specific circumstances.

PART I
A General Discussion

Introduction

You do not have to pay the maximum in federal income taxes. It is not your moral, legal, or patriotic obligation to do so. Judge Learned Hand put it succinctly in a 1934 United States Court of Appeals decision, when he wrote, "Any one may so arrange his affairs that his taxes shall be as low as possible; he is not bound to choose the pattern which will best pay the Treasury . . ."

Yet, most people do just that, yielding to the most conservative methods of computing their returns; watching silently, year after year, while exorbitant sums are withheld from their salaries; feeling lucky if they don't have to pay any additional taxes—blessed if they receive a refund, however small.

Why are so many people—successful people with sizeable incomes, obviously proficient and aggressive in their fields—so passive when it comes to managing their personal affairs, so willing to pay top tax dollar? There are many reasons, but two of the most common are fear and lack of understanding.

Everyone is afraid of the IRS. The most elusive criminals and illustrious politicians have fallen before its enormous power. No one wants to take his chances in an audit, where many fear their motives will be questioned, their deductions disallowed, or worse. Inevitably, a discussion of tax shelters finds its way to the question, "Are they legal?"

The answer would be obvious if tax shelters were more commonly understood. For tax shelters, as they are meant to be, are unquestionably legal. In fact, they are sanctioned, even encouraged, by Congress, largely because of their social and economic benefits. In oil and gas exploration, for example, the incentive for investment through tax shelters is one way of providing the funds necessary for exploration, thus stimulating domestic production and reducing dependence on foreign oil.

People also fear being swindled or losing everything in a "surefire" deal that falls apart at the seams. It can happen. Even seasoned investors have been stung in highly-publicized financial fiascos that have helped give tax shelters their questionable reputation. But in most cases, it happens because the investors are not diligent or knowledgeable enough to understand and evaluate the investments they are making. Tax shelters are complicated entities and few, if any, explanations of them exist in laymen's terms. Hence, this book.

Finally, many people miss out on tax shelter investments simply because they do not realize they are in a position to benefit from them. Contrary to popular belief, tax shelters are not just for the very rich. In fact, there are countless kinds of tax shelter investments suitable for a broad range of taxpayers in an equally broad range of financial situations. The key is recognizing what you need and which kind of investment can provide it. We hope in this book to offer the information to help you make those determinations and realize that you too can lower your tax rate—and make money at the same time.

CHAPTER I
Tax Shelters: An Overview

In recent years, the subject of tax shelters has become increasingly popular in the media, political forums, and among inflation-weary taxpayers seeking to get off the treadmill of higher earnings/higher taxes. Unfortunately, many of the discussions are based upon misinformation and misunderstanding. For tax shelters are the by-product of one of the most complex and ever-expanding bodies of federal law. With hundreds of sections, each more complicated than the last, the Internal Revenue Code of 1954 is an enigma to all but the most carefully schooled tax practitioners—and even they approach it cautiously.

To make things more complicated, the Tax Code is constantly being revised according to the objectives of the President and Congress. Since this book was first written, four years ago, there have been three major tax reform acts: the Revenue Act of 1978; the Windfall Profits Tax Act of 1980; and, most recently, the Economic Recovery Tax Act of 1981. All of these actions have had far-reaching consequences for tax shelter investors, and this book has been revised and updated to reflect these changes in the tax law as they relate to tax shelters.

It is our purpose to demystify those portions of the Internal Revenue Code relevant to tax shelters, so they may be understood and applied by those people they affect most: ordinary taxpayers. No attempt will be made to sell tax shelters, only to explain, in the simplest terms possible, how they work and to provide guidelines for evaluating the advantages and risks of the major types of shelters available. This chapter will deal generally with those questions frequently asked about tax shelters by interested laymen. In addition, it will provide the fundamental concepts and definitions necessary to understand later, more specific material.

What Is a Tax Shelter?

A tax shelter is an investment, generally one of two types. The first is an investment in which the profits earned are tax-free. These are usually individual investments, the most common of which are the recently created All Savers Certificates, which will be discussed in detail later, and municipal and other tax-exempt bonds. In essence, the purchaser of a municipal bond is lending money to a city or other municipality. The bond is the city's I.O.U., evidence, much like a promissory note, of its obligation to repay the amount listed on the bond—with interest. What sets this loan apart from others is the fact that the interest earned by the investor is exempt from federal income taxes. Barring unusual circumstances such as the 1975 New York City fiscal crunch, these can be relatively safe investments.

The second type of tax shelter investment, the kind with which this book is primarily concerned, provides the investor not only with fully or partially tax-free returns, but with enough excess deductions and credits to reduce his current tax bill. The most common vehicle for these investments is the limited partnership, but they may also take the form of individual investments or stock ownership in subchapter S corporations. Their activities include coal mining, cable TV, real estate, records, oil and gas, farming, equipment leasing, cattle, movies, books, research and development, Individual Retirement Accounts (IRAs), and many more. All these will be explained fully in later chapters.

Who Can Benefit from Tax Shelters?

People seek tax shelters for many different reasons. Certainly profession is not the common denominator, for if you check the roster of tax shelter investors, you will find a broad spectrum of individuals, ranging from brain surgeons to ball players, politicians to plumbers, lawyers, publishers, professors, salespeople, entertainers, and others. All share a common desire to decrease their tax bite and increase their wealth through investment. Each will benefit differently from a tax shelter, depending upon his financial position and other variants, such as age, health, type of income, future earnings, and expenses. Undoubtedly, the overriding factor is income, but here again the range is great and so are the ramifications. A taxpayer earning $25,000 per year won't get the same benefits as a taxpayer earning $60,000, but he can still benefit, as demonstrated by the following simplified example:

Tom, Dick, and Harriet filed joint federal income tax returns with their respective spouses for the year ending December 31, 1982. If they had not become involved in a tax shelter, after subtracting all deductions, exemptions, credits, etc., Tom would have been left with a taxable income of $25,000; Dick with a taxable income of $40,000; and Harriet with a taxable income of $95,000. Based upon these figures and the federal income tax rate schedule for 1982, Tom would have owed the federal government $4,153 in taxes; Dick would have owed $9,195; and Harriet would have owed $35,249.

However, on January 1, 1982, Tom, Dick and Harriet invested in the Domestic Drilling Company, a tax-oriented oil and gas drilling venture. Domestic Drilling, a partnership, was formed to drill for oil in Texas. Each of the three investors put in $5,000, entitling each to a one-third share of the venture.

On January 1, 1982, Domestic Drilling borrowed $30,000 from a local bank for the purpose of drilling the wells (Tom, Dick, and Harriet each guaranteed one-third of the loan, which was to be repaid over a 5-year period). With the proceeds of that loan and the trio's $15,000 investment, the drilling was completed by the end of 1982. In the process, $30,000 was spent on drilling costs, interest, and other business expenses that, according to the Internal Revenue Code, are deductible for federal income tax purposes. Because each partner owned a one-third share of the venture, each was entitled to utilize one-third of these deductions, or $10,000, to reduce his or her 1982 taxable income. In addition, if the drilling is successful, beginning in 1983 each investor can expect to receive an annual distribution of $400, which presumably will result from income exceeding operating expenses. These distributions will be partially tax-free.

As a result of his investment, Tom has reduced his taxable income from $25,000 to $15,000, and has correspondingly reduced his tax bill from $4,153 to $1,823. This constitutes a net tax savings of $2,330. If we subtract that $2,330 savings from the $5,000 he invested in Domestic Drilling, we can say that Tom's investment really cost him only $2,670. For that $2,670, beginning in 1983, he will be receiving a partially tax-free annual distribution of $400, which is the equivalent, approximately, of a 15% annual return on his investment. Obviously, that is a substantially greater return than would be received if the same $2,670 were put in a savings account earning only 6% interest.

Now for his slightly more affluent friend. As a result of Dick's investment, his taxable income has been reduced from $40,000 to $30,000, and his tax bill from $9,195 to $5,607, for a net tax savings of $3,588. If we subtract the $3,588 he saved in taxes from his $5,000 investment in Domestic Drilling, we can say that Dick's investment really cost him only $1,412. For an investment of $1,412, Dick will be receiving $400 per year, which represents the even greater annual rate of return of 28%.

Harriet, by investing in Domestic Drilling, has reduced her taxable income from $95,000 to $85,000, and her tax bill from $35,249 to $30,249, for a net savings of $5,000. If we subtract from the $5,000 she invested in Domestic Drilling the $5,000 she saved in taxes, we find the cost of her investment to be zero. Add to that the $400 per year distribution and the benefits of tax shelter for her are unmistakable.

Tom, Dick, and Harriet have reduced their tax bills and acquired potentially profitable investments. Obviously, Harriet, the highest income earner, has gained the most since, in essence, her investment cost her nothing. However, Tom and Dick have also benefited by acquiring property that can provide them with a high rate of return on their money, paid for in part by the government.

How Do Tax Shelters Work?

Tax shelters work because the Internal Revenue Code allows for certain tax deductions and credits for money spent in the conduct of trade, business, or activities engaged in for profit. Most tax shelters are designed to use available dollars in a way that will maximize the tax benefits that flow through to investors, while at the same time meeting the financial needs of the venture. One of the most effective ways of doing this is by using "leverage," or borrowed funds, to help pay for deductible items. The Domestic Drilling venture used leverage to the obvious advantage of Tom, Dick, and Harriet. Each was able to claim deductions based not only on the expenditures made with his or her $5,000 investment, but also on those made with the funds provided by the bank loan. Although, as we shall see in later chapters, the 1976 Tax Reform Act severely limited the use of leverage in providing tax benefits, it is still an important aspect of many tax shelter deals.

In the early years of operation, the tax deductions and other tax benefits generated by such a business venture will usually exceed the income derived from it. The result is a tax loss, which the investors can share and then use to offset their income from other sources. In some cases, such as real estate, these so-called excess deductions are spread over a number of years. In others, such as oil and gas and coal, they generally occur only in the first year of operation.

If the venture is successful and makes money, the investors will be entitled to their share of the cash generated. This is known as the "cash flow" or "cash distribution" from the venture. The benefits of cash distributions are greatly enhanced in tax shelter situations because, as we shall see later, they will often be tax-free.

It is important to point out, especially to those who question the propriety of tax-oriented investments, that tax shelters generally do not provide for the permanent avoidance of tax—rather, the deferral until a future time, perhaps upon retirement, when the investor is in a lower bracket or better able to absorb the liability. This is because, as the venture develops, a greater portion of its expenditures will become non-deductible, and certain tax allowances will gradually diminish. This will have the effect of increasing the taxable income from the venture—of which each investor must claim a share—while the cash distributions remain constant. For example, in the first year of our Domestic Drilling venture, the proceeds of the $30,000 bank loan were used to pay expenses that in turn provided tax deductions. However, over the next five years the loan must be repaid, and loan payments, except for interest, are not tax-deductible. Therefore, as the Domestic Drilling venture earns the $30,000 to repay the loan, each partner must claim his share of the income and pay his share of the tax due on those earnings, without receiving any additional cash distributions. Thus, while in the first year the investors receive deductions for more money than they actually spend, in the later years, as the loan is repaid, they will be taxed on more than they receive.

In a sense, a tax shelter is really the sum total of many separate deductions and credits. The deductibility of each expenditure made by a venture is of prime importance and will affect the overall tax results to the investors each year. Whether an item is deductible and in what manner is determined by the Code, interpretive Treasury Regulations, and federal case law.

Some expenses are "currently" deductible, which means they may be "written off" in the year paid or incurred. Others must be deducted over a period of time or are flatly non-deductible.

Generally, the Code provides that "all *ordinary and necessary* expenses paid or incurred during the taxable year in carrying on any trade or business" are currently deductible. A profit motive seems to be the criterion for qualifying as a trade or business. Unfortunately, there are no concrete guidelines for determining what is "ordinary and necessary." Usually, items such as labor, management, supplies, insurance, advertising, repairs, rents, telephone, travel, etc., will be allowed if reasonable in amount. Ordinary and necessary expenses vary greatly with different types of business activities and will be discussed in detail with the individual shelters.

In addition to ordinary and necessary expenses, the Code permits allowances for certain specified items, such as real estate taxes, interest charges, business losses, bad debts, intangible drilling costs, research and experimental expenses, and a host of others to which it devotes pages and pages of rules and limitations. Perhaps the most significant from a tax shelter point of view are: the allowances permitted under the Accelerated Cost Recovery System (ACRS), which was added to the Code in 1981 to replace the depreciation deduction; the allowances for the "depletion" of certain mineral properties; and the "tax credits" permitted on the purchase of certain types of business property. Because these are key elements of many tax shelter deals, we will consider them in detail later.

Understand that business ventures should not be created solely to provide tax benefits; business ventures should be formed for profit, and structured and used as tax shelters only after it is determined that they are economically sound. Tax shelters work if, when, and because they make good business sense and conform to the specified and intended rules and limitations of the tax laws.

Are Tax Shelters Legal and Proper?

Legal, without question. As we shall see in Chapter III, ACRS deductions and the tax allowances for depreciation, depletion, and business expenditures are not only sanctioned by Congress but created by it, as a means of stimulating investment in different segments of the national economy. This was freely acknowledged in the *Tax Shelter Training Manual* prepared by the IRS for its agents, which stated:

> Many tax shelters result from congressional intent for legislation, assuring certain social-economic benefits. The audit effort is not directed against these legitimate shelters.

However, the Manual also cautioned that, in some cases:

> Investors engage in transactions, individually, or through partnerships, with little or no promise of gain apart from the anticipated income tax benefits. The manipulations of many promoters and investors are at the brink of acceptability, for tax purposes, and are to be scrutinized. The Commissioner has expressed interest in the tax shelter program and his concern for those shelters ". . . stretching, bending, or breaking the provisions of the tax law."

There is no question that some promoters do try to stretch the Code beyond its legal limits. Unfortunately, investors in such ventures, innocent or not, will suffer as a result of such abuses. It is therefore imperative for potential tax shelter buyers and their counsel to question aggressive tax positions, and to ensure that any venture they consider is well within the intent and provisions of the law.

What Can Go Wrong?

Many things can go wrong, potentially expensive things that can result in loss of investment and loss of anticipated tax benefits. The state and federal securities laws require that most tax shelter offerings, public or private, fully disclose, in prospectus form, all major aspects of a venture—including the risks. Rather than be accused of incomplete disclosure, these sections can be prohibitively expansive and complex, containing pages of "boiler plate" discussion capable of curing the most acute case of insomnia. Tax shelter investors, however, should not stop short of fully understanding the venture they are entering. They should do their own investigating, looking beyond the promoter's projections, which are just that—projections. What is said on a neatly typed prospectus and what actually happens on a construction site, at an oil field, or before the IRS can be drastically different.

Economic Risks

The first area of risk to consider is economic. It cannot be overly stressed that tax shelter ventures must be economically sound to deliver the tax benefits they promise. Usually, these ventures involve the operation of a complex business enterprise, which means a host of interacting factors to go right or wrong. Since tax shelter investors are almost always passive investors, with no say in the actual running of affairs, they must depend on the manager of the venture for success or failure. In effect, they are investing in his experience, reputation, and expertise. If his track record in similar ventures is not available for scrutiny, it could be non-existent or of questionable merit.

The first point then is to know or investigate the people you are entrusting with your investment. Consider the financial condition of the manager. If he is under pressure, he may not have the time or resources to ensure the success of the venture, or to respond in damages in the event of wrongful failure to perform. Banking and other financial references are easy and important to check.

It is also advisable to inquire about the manager's other business interests, to determine whether they are in conflict with the activities of the venture or its investors. If he is involved in similar competing ventures in the same area, he may be tempted to give preferential treatment, or devote substantial time and resources, to them at the expense of the venture you are considering.

As for the businesses themselves, their risks are as varied as their activities. In real estate, for example, construction costs can soar or there can be prolonged difficulty in renting. Accidents and strikes can beset coal mines; oil wells can come up dry. One common point is that all businesses require adequate capital to succeed; capital to meet not only projected costs but also the unforeseen contingencies that frequently arise.

On the other hand, there is the risk of over-financing. If leverage is used and the loan is too large or the interest payments are too high, a financial burden could be placed on the venture that its operations would be unable to support. That raises the possibility of default and foreclosure.

Foreclosure, for whatever reason, can be disastrous. Although many loans to tax shelter ventures are "non-recourse," which means the investors are not personally liable for repayment, the effects of default and foreclosure can still be costly. Not only does the venture lose its interest in the property and the investor his investment, but often the investor must pay tax as well. If the unpaid balance of a foreclosed loan exceeds the cost of the property, less any ACRS deductions taken with respect to the property, the difference will be considered taxable income to the investors. Thus, they will have a tax liability without having received any cash. Here is an example:

Sandi K. borrowed $1,000,000 to purchase a shopping center. In the next two years, she took ACRS deductions totaling $140,000, and paid off $20,000 of the loan, leaving an unpaid balance of $980,000. Then she defaulted on the non-recourse loan, and the bank foreclosed. At that time, she would have had a taxable gain of $120,000, computed as follows:

Unpaid balance of the loan	$980,000
Minus cost less ACRS deductions [$1,000,000 - $140,000]	–860,000
Equals gain	$120,000

Tax Risks

In addition to economic risks, there is the possibility with tax shelter investments that any or all of the anticipated tax benefits will not be realized. This can happen for two reasons: the tax deductions or credits do not conform with the letter or spirit of the tax laws; or, the laws are amended, revised, or otherwise changed.

If the IRS determines that a deal is constructed, a transaction completed, or an investment made solely for the purpose of avoiding or evading federal income taxes or that deductions or credits are unjustifiably inflated, those deductions and credits will be reduced or disallowed. Basically, the IRS might question the true economic goals of a venture. The Code specifically states with certain exceptions that "*if [an] activity is not engaged in for profit, no deduction attributable to such activity shall be allowed* . . ." In other words, don't go into business for tax benefits alone. On that basis, they could be denied.

The IRS might also challenge certain judgments or estimates made by a venture, affecting tax allowances. Or it could question whether certain expenses are, in reality, "ordinary and necessary," such as managers' and promoters' fees, which are sometimes inflated to increase deductions from the venture. If an error is determined, some portion or possibly all of the tax benefits could be disallowed.

Underlying every tax shelter deal is the possibility that the Code will be changed. Tax reform is an emotional and effective political issue, as intrinsic to campaigning as smiling and shaking hands. Sometimes, however, it goes beyond rhetoric, as was the case in 1976, when a major tax reform bill was enacted that cut right through to the core of tax shelters. One of its main thrusts was to limit the tax allowances available to investors in many ventures to the amount they actually invested or risked. Not only did this restriction on the use of non-recourse borrowing require new structuring innovations for shelter deals, but since it was in part retroactive, it severely and adversely affected the investors in many already-existing ventures.

As we mentioned earlier, since then tax shelters have also been significantly affected by the Revenue Act of 1978, the Crude Oil Windfall Profit Tax Act of 1980, and the Economic Recovery Tax Act of 1981. The effects of these legislative actions will be discussed in detail later.

Conscientious firms—legal, accounting, or otherwise—involved with tax shelter deals are undoubtedly aware of the latest tax trends, proposed or enacted legislation, Treasury Department rulings, court decisions, statements by government officials, and other tax-related happenings. It is their business to stay current and informed, which makes it good business to consult an expert when considering a tax shelter deal.

CHAPTER II
Profiles

The following profiles introduce the major types of tax shelter investments and the kinds of needs that bring people to them. Don't be discouraged if a term or phrase eludes you. This is merely an overview, a chance to see what is available and what can happen. Later chapters will explore the important concepts and major types of shelter in detail.

Real Estate

For a long time, Ken and Jane S. have had a desire to do something about their taxes. Ages 35 and 33 respectively, married for 8 years with 2 small children, both are on the professional rise, he as an electrical contractor, she as a bank executive. Between them, their joint taxable income is approximately $45,000 per year after all deductions, exemptions, and credits. They anticipate their income will at least remain stable and probably increase over the next few years, along with their tax bill, which already exceeds $11,000 annually to the federal government alone.

Ken and Jane are more inclined to moderate-return, moderate-risk investments than high-return, high-risk ventures. They are looking for an investment that will provide them with a return on their money, as well as a reduction of their tax bill for the next few years. Knowing this, their accountant suggests a real estate tax shelter that is currently being offered. Real estate, he explains, when successfully rented and properly managed, can be a stable, predictable investment that will often provide, at least in the initial years, tax deductions greater than the investor's cash commitment.

Ken and Jane soon receive a lengthy and rather tedious prospectus (offering memorandum), explaining what appears to be every possible fact and risk connected with the proposed investment. They read the prospectus with great difficulty, but are able to extract that they would be purchasing an ownership share or interest in something referred to as a "limited partnership." They would be joined by nineteen other equal investors.

This particular partnership was formed to purchase a specified parcel of land in Houston, Texas, and to construct and operate a garden apartment complex on it. Their investment, as well as that of each of the other investors, would amount to $5,000 per year for the next 4 years. The partnership would use these funds, together with borrowed money, to buy the land, construct the apartments, and meet expenses until sufficient rental income was generated.

As a result of his investment, each partner would be entitled to a share of the partnership's income and losses. In the early years of the venture, until all the apartments were completed and rented, the operating expenses and "ACRS deductions" (the "losses") would probably exceed the income and provide Ken and Jane and their partners with tax deductions, which could be used to reduce their tax bills for the year. Additionally, once the apartments were rented, and income began to exceed expenses of operation, they could also expect to receive annual cash distributions, which could exceed 7% of their investments. For several years, those distributions would be tax-free.

That is how the investment would work under ideal conditions. The prospectus also goes on for pages and pages, describing the economic and tax risks of this type of venture. Construction costs could outstrip available funds; strikes could delay materials; apartments could go unrented. Still, according to the prospectus, the managing or general partners of the partnership have already entered into contracts with apparently reputable and experienced builders and managers. They have thoroughly researched the rental market and trends in that area of Houston and found them to be quite good. Ken and Jane are convinced. They decide to go ahead and invest. The venture proves successful and the bottom line to them is a reduction of their tax bill and a potentially profitable investment.

Oil and Gas

Charles G. is in approximately the same income bracket as Ken and Jane this year, but his financial needs and goals are very different. Sixty years of age, married, a homeowner, he has for

20 years been employed as the Sales Manager of a used automobile concern in northern Los Angeles. He earns, and expects to continue earning, $40,000 per year.

Early this year, unexpectedly, Charles received a bonus of $15,000. After the initial excitement, his thoughts turned to taxes. Unlike Ken and Jane, Charles is not particularly conservative in his investments and is willing to take higher risks in return for potentially greater gain. He is not a foolish investor, but one who enjoys an educated gamble. With enough money set aside in savings accounts and his employer's profit sharing plan to provide for his retirement, he can afford to have this attitude.

Since Charles does not anticipate receiving such an extraordinary bonus next year, he has little interest in real estate ventures, which spread deductions over a period of years. Charles is interested in an investment that will provide the bulk of its tax benefits in the first year.

His stockbroker shows him a prospectus on a limited partnership formed to explore for and, if successful, commercially exploit oil and gas reserves in Louisiana. Charles would be required to invest $10,000, all this year. The partnership would use the investors' funds to finance exploratory drilling for oil and gas reserves at 7 designated locations. A sizeable portion of the money spent in the drilling activities would be tax deductible, thus providing each investor with a share of deductions that could almost equal his investment. In Charles's case, there would be enough to substantially reduce the income tax payable on his bonus.

The drilling operations are being supervised by the managing partner of the partnership, who, according to the prospectus, is an experienced drilling contractor with a track record of successes. The geologist hired by the managing partner has chosen the drilling sites after careful analysis of the relevant geological data available. If the exploration and development prove successful, Charles can expect to receive cash distributions which could be quite substantial, depending upon the extent of the reserves discovered. These distributions would be, in part, tax-free, due to certain depletion deductions allowed by the Internal Revenue Code.

Before Charles starts counting his profits, however, let him be warned that oil and gas can be elusive. While the growing energy shortage places a high premium on these minerals, the odds of striking potentially exploitable reserves are not generally favorable. If the venture fails to find oil and gas, Charles will lose his investment and will have to console himself with his tax deductions. The risk may seem worth it, however, when Charles considers that he's gambling partly with money that would have been paid in taxes.

Coal

Dr. Sara M. is not new to tax shelters. A 53-year-old pediatrician earning about $70,000 per year, she has for some time been investing in real estate shelters to reduce the taxes on the upper levels of her income. This year, thanks to the mixed blessing of a sale of stock acquired on a tip, those levels have risen; she has a $25,000 short-term capital gain.

Sara is obviously interested in an investment that will generate deductions this year to reduce the tax resulting from her stock sale. She is not inclined to invest in oil and gas and chance losing her investment if the wells turn up dry. Real estate does not suit her needs either, since most real estate shelters provide for deductions and investments over a period of years and her concern is with tax relief for this year alone.

Sara's lawyer sends her a prospectus on a coal tax shelter. Like oil and gas, coal ventures can provide sizeable deductions in the first year. Unlike oil and gas, however, the location, quantity, and quality of coal can be quite predictable and so it is a lower risk and generally lower return investment. This particular venture offers interests in a partnership which has just acquired the mineral rights to property in Kentucky containing 800,000 tons of high-quality coal. The managing partner of the venture, an experienced coal miner, has arranged for the purchase of necessary mining equipment, as well as for the sale of the coal to a local utility company. The partnership has agreed to pay the owner of the property a royalty payment of $1 for each ton of coal mined. It has also agreed to a minimum royalty payment of $75,000 per year, even if little or none of the mineral is extracted. This year, the partnership will use the investors' funds to make the minimum royalty payment, a deductible expense that will provide them with the excess tax deductions they seek.

Once the mining operations are successfully under way, the investors should begin to receive cash distributions, part of which will be tax-free, thanks to the depletion deductions allowed. Sara can thus shelter her capital gain and, at the same time, acquire an investment with the potential for a moderately high return.

Equipment Leasing

Michael T. would like to branch out. However, as the proprietor of a small electronic toy manufacturing corporation that is steadily but slowly increasing in value, he seems to pay in taxes whatever excess capital he might have used to expand his corporate activities. He wants an investment that will both reduce his corporate tax bite and enable him to use the tax savings to finance expansion of his business.

Michael consults a law firm that specializes in finding and structuring tax deals. They explain that certain types of ventures, such as equipment leasing, can provide a corporation with substantial early deductions and credits to be applied against its taxes. If properly managed, they can also become lucrative business enterprises.

Michael's corporation could, for example, purchase new manufacturing equipment, using borrowed funds as well as its own capital. It would then lease the equipment to other companies at a rental rate designed to repay the loan and return a profit. A combination of the investment tax credit and ACRS deductions available to purchasers of new business equipment would provide the corporation with tax savings nearly equal to the cash invested. In other words, a good portion of the venture would be financed by the deductions and credits it generates. The corporation's backer in the equipment leasing business would be the federal government.

Movies

It's been the kind of year every tennis pro dreams of for aging star Peter B., 32, who, until a streak of superb playing won him several major titles and more than $300,000, was earning most of his sizeable income from a posh tennis camp.

A flamboyant fellow with money to spend and now, money to shelter, Peter has always been fascinated with movies, and so when his business manager suggests a movie tax shelter, he is intrigued and ready to go. For a moderate down payment and a 10-year pay-out of the balance, his manager arranges the purchase of a new, unreleased mystery thriller. At the same time, he enters into a contract with a film distributor, recommended by the producer of the movie, to promote the film and arrange play dates in theaters across the country.

By purchasing the film, Peter is eligible for certain deductions and investment credits, which could result in tax savings substantially greater than his down payment, enough to slice a considerable amount from his tax bill. With his income tax crisis averted, he could then turn his thoughts to the performance of the film which, if successful, would mean substantial profits for him. The odds of a box office hit are not great. Still, the investment has a certain attraction: Peter's tax deferral is sizeable, and besides, more than one sleeper has been known to make it big. This could, of course, send him off in search of additional shelter.

Research and Development

A research and development (R&D) tax shelter is what Alice G. chose this year, when unusual circumstances left her with a greatly inflated taxable income. A competitor offered to buy Alice's lucrative real estate brokerage firm, for a substantial amount of cash and the promise of adequate income for a period of time in return for consulting services. Alice was elated, until her accountant tallied the tax tab for profits reaped from the deal.

Not just a purveyor of bad news, the accountant told her about an R&D tax shelter that one of his other clients was syndicating. For a lower investment than Peter's movie deal, Alice could participate in a partnership that was attempting to develop a way of mass-producing interferon through genetic engineering. Like Peter, she would receive certain deductions that would provide her with substantial tax savings in the first year of her investment; not as much as Peter, but enough to satisfy her particular needs. With her tax problem handled, she could turn her attention to the progress of the research, which, if successful, could mean a nice return on her money.

Trouble

They heard it from their patients, at dental seminars, from suppliers and friends: "Tax shelter, tax shelter, tax shelter . . ." Norman M. and Jay R. were itching to get in on it. Partners in a thriving dental practice, their incomes certainly merited it, but their business naïveté held them back. Where do you get it? How does it work? What is it, anyway?"

Opportunity knocked. Norman's father-in-law, a prominent criminal lawyer, told them about a cable TV deal recommended to him by one of his clients. What matter if they knew nothing about the field or Norman's father-in-law's connection? The tax benefits were phenomenal, cable TV was a hot item, the deal was a sure thing. And so they invested, becoming partners in a venture formed to construct, install, and operate a cable TV system in northern Maine.

The deal seemed a little unusual. In order to circumvent a provision of the 1976 Tax Reform Act, which limited tax deductions from most partnerships to the actual dollars invested or at-risk, the promoters arranged to buy Treasury Bills and required each investor to assume a portion of the liability for the loan used to purchase them. Thus, the "at-risk" amount for each investor was conveniently inflated. It seemed, at best, contrived; after all, there was not much risk in Treasury Bills. Still, according to the promoters of the deal, this kind of thing was done all the time, and besides, remember those deductions . . .

For more than a year, Norman and Jay glowed each time they thought about their tax savings. Then, in one sickening instant, the lights went out. The IRS challenged the structure of the deal, saying they could find no capital at-risk in the Treasury Bill purchase, and thus disallowed a large portion of the deductions. Norman and Jay would have to reimburse the government, with interest, for the disallowed deductions they had already claimed.

Panic-stricken, they called the promoter, who informed them that taxes were the least of their problems. The venture was out of money. The creditors had foreclosed on all its property. The deal was bust. It seems the developer of the project knew as little about the cable TV business as Norman and Jay. He had vastly underestimated his cash needs, failing to allow for such things as increases in equipment costs and interest charges. In plain English, the venture went broke. For Norman and Jay, it meant not only a complete loss of investment, but a costly I.O.U. to the federal government.

Where did they go wrong? First and foremost, they plunged into a tax shelter knowing absolutely nothing about the subject, totally unqualified to competently and judiciously evaluate an offering. Second, they let themselves be blinded by the promise of superb tax benefits, ignoring any economic considerations of the deal and their own instincts, which told them the structure was shaky. Third, they put their money in a business totally foreign to them, in the hands of people they knew nothing about. They hadn't even bothered to check the promoter's track record or something as simple as bank references. Fourth, they failed to call in a professional to advise them, help them evaluate the venture, or suggest alternatives. In short, they overlooked the safeguards, ignored the warnings, and never really understood the concepts and factors that make tax shelters work or fail. These are common mistakes that often cause investors either to miss out on good shelter opportunities or to get burned in bad ones.

This book attempts to fill the information gap, to provide a foundation of understanding for those interested in tax shelters. From general considerations to the most specific aspects of every major type of shelter available, from the benefits to the risks, we will try to be as clear and simple as possible.

CHAPTER III
Depreciation and ACRS Deductions, Depletion, and Tax Credits

While the business activities of tax shelters vary widely, most ventures involve the acquisition and ownership of property. Whenever tangible business or investment-related property is involved—whether you're dealing with buildings, cows, movies, mines, etc.—certain tax allowances and incentives are available. Three of these—depreciation deductions (known as ACRS deductions since the passage of the Economic Recovery Tax Act of 1981), depletion deductions, and tax credits—emerge repeatedly as important sources of tax benefits in most shelters. These allowances are actually quite simple in theory, but are obscured by countless methods for computing them and limitations on their use. We will now examine these important tax allowances in detail, as a foundation for future discussions. Later we will show how they apply to each type of shelter.

Depreciation and ACRS Deductions

Theoretically, business assets become obsolete with the passage of time or wear out with use and must be replaced. Therefore, the Code provides for "a reasonable [annual] allowance for the exhaustion wear and tear [including a reasonable allowance for obsolescence] [1] of property used in trade or business, or [2] of property held for the production of income." This allowance enables a taxpayer to deduct or "write off" the cost of these properties over a period of years, since he is not permitted to do so at the time of purchase or payment.

The Economic Recovery Tax Act of 1981 substantially rewrote the rules governing computation of allowable depreciation, now known as ACRS deductions. However, the types of assets that qualify for the deductions have not changed, and the new rules generally apply only to tangible property acquired after January 1, 1981. (In some cases, property acquired after that date will continue to be subject to the "old" depreciation rules.) First, a brief look at some of the general rules that still apply, and an example of how depreciation was computed on property acquired before 1981. Then some highlights of the most important changes made by the 1981 Act.

The principal kind of business or income-producing property subject to the depreciation (and now the ACRS) allowance is property with a useful life of more than 1 year, such as buildings (not including the land), machinery, automobiles and trucks, office furniture, and other such equipment. Personal assets, such as a family residence, clothes, or a car used solely for pleasure, are not eligible. There are countless rules limiting the use of the deduction, and several methods for computing its annual allowance. The following is an example of how this important tax benefit worked prior to the Economic Recovery Tax Act of 1981:

On January 1, 1978, Al B. bought a piece of machinery for use in his business. The cost of the machine was $15,000 and Al estimated that after 10 years it would have to be replaced due to wear, tear, and obsolescence. The 10-year period was referred to as the "useful life" of the machinery, or the period over which it might reasonably be expected to be of use to Al in his business.

Al further estimated that, at the expiration of its useful life, the machinery would be worth $3,000. The $3,000 was referred to as the "salvage value" of the asset. The cost of an asset minus the salvage value equaled the "basis for depreciation." This was the amount that could be deducted over the useful life of the property. In this case, the $15,000 cost, minus the $3,000 salvage value, equals $12,000, to be deducted over the 10-year useful life. If Al deducted the $12,000 in equal portions over the useful life of the machinery he would be entitled to a $1,200 depreciation deduction per year. The annual rate of depreciation of his machinery would thus be 10%.

The Code provided more than one method for computing the annual depreciation allowance. A taxpayer could choose any permissible method, as long as it was used consistently for each particular asset. In the above example, Al chose the "straight line method," by which the basis for depreciation is deducted in equal annual amounts over the useful life of the asset. The Code also allowed certain "accelerated methods" of computing depreciation, which offered greater deductions in the early years of ownership. With few exceptions, these accelerated methods could be used only with respect to property that was new.

One of the most frequently used accelerated methods was the "declining balance method," which gave the greatest depreciation allowance in the first year and a gradually smaller allowance in each subsequent year. A taxpayer motivated by an immediate need for larger deductions might have chosen this method. In certain activities, he would be permitted to use a rate of depreciation up to 200% or twice the rate determined under the straight line method. However, each year his basis for depreciation would be re-computed, by subtracting from the original cost of his asset (without regard to salvage value) the total of all the previous years' depreciation deductions. Thus, the uniform depreciation rate would be applied to a smaller, or declining, balance each year, and his deductions would diminish with time. The following chart illustrates the difference in the depreciation allowances for each year of the useful life of Al's machinery under the straight line and the declining balance methods:

200% Declining Balance Method

Year	Basis for Depreciation	Rate	Deduction	Deductions Under Straight Line Method
1978	$15,000	20%	$3,000	$1,200
1979	12,000	20%	2,400	1,200
1980	9,600	20%	1,920	1,200
1981	7,680	20%	1,536	1,200
1982	6,144	20%	1,229	1,200
1983	4,915	20%	983	1,200
1984	3,932	20%	786	1,200
1985	3,146	20%	146	1,200
1986	3,000	20%	-0-	1,200
1987	3,000	20%	-0-	1,200
	TOTAL		$12,000	$12,000

The reason the deduction in the declining balance column in 1985 is limited to $146 is that the Code stipulates that an asset could not be depreciated below its salvage value.

This example illustrates not only how the use of an accelerated depreciation method could increase early tax benefits, but also how important the concept of "useful life" was. What if Al's machinery had had a "useful life" of 20 years? Obviously, his depreciation deductions in the early years of ownership would have been much lower. What if the useful life had been 5 years?

The increased tax benefits in such a case are readily apparent.

In an attempt to encourage investment in certain segments of the economy, the Economic Recovery Tax Act of 1981 changed the rules for computing depreciation deductions in a number of ways. In general, the '81 Act significantly reduced the time required to fully deduct the cost of business assets. The new system is officially referred to as the "Accelerated Cost Recovery System," or ACRS. Among the most important changes are:

Useful Life—The concept of the "useful life" of an asset has been largely eliminated. Instead, depreciable assets are "assigned" lives of 3, 5, 10, or 15 years by the Code, depending upon the type of property. These assigned lives are referred to as "cost recovery" periods.

Salvage Value—Salvage value is now disregarded in computing ACRS allowances and in determining the "basis" for the ACRS deduction. The basis is simply the cost of the property.

Methods of Computing ACRS Allowances—Generally, all ACRS allowances are computed using accelerated methods, unless the taxpayer elects otherwise.

New versus Used Property—The same accelerated methods for computing ACRS allowances are now available whether the property is new or used when acquired.

Perhaps the most graphic way to illustrate the effects of the '81 Act is to look again at Al's machine and assume it was purchased on January 1, 1981. Under the 1981 Act, the machinery would be assigned a cost recovery period of 5 years. The rate for each of the 5 years would also be set forth in the Act, based upon when the property was placed in service. As a result, the depreciation deductions over the machine's actual 10-year life would be as follows:

Year	**Basis for ACRS**	**Rate**	**Deduction**
1981	$15,000	15%	$2,250
1982	$15,000	22%	3,300
1983	$15,000	21%	3,150
1984	$15,000	21%	3,150
1985	$15,000	21%	3,150
1986			-0-
1987			-0-
1988			-0-
1989			-0-
1990			-0-
		100%	$15,000

As you can see, the deductions in the early years are now substantially greater than they would have been even using the 200% Declining Balance Method.

By combining the concept of leverage (borrowed funds) with accelerated depreciation, and now ACRS deductions, we can see how tax benefits can be maximized. Both depreciation and ACRS deductions are based upon the cost of the asset; the greater the cost, the greater the deductions. Since leverage is often used to acquire assets, as in the case of real estate when a bank extends a mortgage loan, costs will frequently far exceed the actual cash outlay of the investors. Yet the borrowed funds are included in computing the basis for the ACRS or depreciation allowance. Thus, a relatively small investment can be leveraged into a large amount of deductions.

It is important to note that many of the tax benefits derived from depreciation and ACRS deductions can be lost upon premature sale or foreclosure of the property. If this happens, the owner will be taxed on the gain. Gain is the difference between the amount he receives for the property and his "adjusted basis," which is his original cost less all depreciation or ACRS deductions taken. Generally, the gain will be subject to tax at the favorable capital gains rate. However, under certain circumstances a portion of the gain may be taxed at the generally less favorable ordinary income rates. The taxation of gain at ordinary income rates by reason of depreciation or ACRS deductions is referred to as "recapture" since, in essence, the tax benefits from these deductions are being recaptured by the Treasury. Recapture will be discussed at length as it applies to the various kinds of shelter.

The Depletion Deduction

Many tax shelter investments involve the exploration for, and extraction of, mineral reserves. When the owner of a mineral property extracts the minerals from it, he is depleting his reserves, and thus decreasing the value of his property. To compensate, the Code allows as a deduction *"in the case of mines, oil and gas wells, other natural deposits and timber . . . a reasonable [yearly] allowance for depletion."* Actually, like the ACRS deduction, which allows the owner of a business asset to deduct the cost of the asset over a period of time, the depletion deduction allows the owner of a mineral property to deduct the cost of the property, and frequently more, as the minerals are extracted from it.

The Code provides two basic methods for computing the "reasonable allowance" for depletion: "cost depletion" and "percentage depletion." It further stipulates that the higher of the two allowances must be applied.

Under the cost depletion method, the owner of a mineral property is permitted to deduct his cost per unit (e.g., barrel, ton, etc.) of the mineral for every unit he sells. For example: Max T. purchases, for $600,000, the mineral rights to property estimated to contain 300,000 tons of coal. Max's cost per ton of coal is therefore $600,000/300,000 tons, or $2.00. In accordance with the rules of cost depletion, Max can deduct from his taxable income $2.00 for every ton of coal he sells. If he sells 10,000 tons of coal in the year, he is entitled to a $20,000 depletion deduction.

In 1926, a special method for computing the depletion allowance was adopted in an effort to stimulate exploration for, and discovery of, vitally needed new mineral reserves. Called "percentage depletion", this method allows substantial deductions, often in excess of cost depletion and sometimes in excess of the original cost of the property. Percentage depletion is computed by applying a fixed percentage to the gross income (total annual sales, before expenses) derived from the mineral property. The percentage depletion deduction may not exceed 50% of the taxable income from the property. Taxable income is generally the gross income, less allowable deductions, such as mining costs and selling expenses.

The fixed percentage of the gross income allowed by the Code for coal properties is 10%. Assume in the above example that Max sold the coal for $25.00 per ton, for a gross income that year of $250,000. Assume again that his mining costs and other deductible expenses were $202,000, leaving him with a taxable income of $48,000 ($250,000 – $202,000). Under the percentage depletion method, Max would be entitled to a $24,000 depletion deduction, computed as follows:

$250,000 (gross income) x 10% (fixed percentage) equals $25,000. However, since the depletion deduction cannot exceed 50% of the taxable income, and Max's taxable income was $48,000, his depletion deduction is limited to $24,000.

Ordinarily, the percentage depletion deduction is greater than the cost depletion deduction. Additionally, since the total of deductions allowed by percentage depletion is not limited by the cost of the property, it is not uncommon for the deductions to continue after the full cost has been recovered. If Max continues to mine the same amount of coal each year, to sell the coal for the same price, and to incur the same expenses, at the end of 30 years, when all the coal has been mined, he will have taken a total of $720,000 in percentage depletion deductions—$120,000 more than his original investment in the property.

Tax Credits

There is an important distinction between a tax deduction and a tax credit. Simply, a tax deduction reduces a taxpayer's taxable income before his tax is computed, thus, indirectly lowering the amount of tax due. A tax credit is subtracted directly from the amount of tax due. For example Domestic Drilling investor Harriet had a taxable income of $95,000 and a tax liability of $35,249. In the year that she received a tax *deduction* of $10,000, that amount was subtracted from her taxable income, lowering it to $85,000, and thereby reducing her taxes to $30,249. If, however, instead of a deduction, she received a tax *credit* of $10,000, it would have been subtracted directly from her tax liability, lowering it from $35,249 to $25,249.

There are many types of tax credits, but the ones most important to tax shelters are the "investment tax credit" and the "energy tax credit." The Code allows an investment tax credit in connection with the purchase or construction of certain kinds of property. Generally, in order to be eligible for the investment credit, property must (1) be business or income-producing property; (2) be tangible, personal property, which includes machinery, equipment, and any other tangible property, except land, buildings, and the structural components of buildings; (3) have a certain minimum useful life; and (4) be placed in service by the taxpayer during the year the credit is claimed. There are some exceptions to these general rules. For example, the expenses incurred in rehabilitating a building to be used in a trade or business may qualify for an investment credit. To the extent that these exceptions have become the focus of tax shelters, they will be dealt with in later chapters.

Like depreciation, the computation of the investment tax credit was significantly affected by the Economic Recovery Tax Act of 1981. Prior to the passage of the '81 Act, computation of the allowable investment tax credit was based on the estimated useful life of the asset involved. Now, computation of the credit has been simplified and the amount allowed depends upon the "recovery period" assigned to the asset. However, as with depreciation, prior law will continue to apply to certain property and many of the basic concepts remain unchanged. For these reasons, we will look first at how the investment tax credit worked before the '81 Act.

Generally, before the passage of the Act, an amount equal to 10% of a taxpayer's "qualified (not actual) investment" in eligible property was the allowable investment credit. "Qualified investment" was determined by taking a specified percentage of the cost of the property based on its useful life. According to the Code:

If property has a useful life of:	The qualified investment was:
3 to 5 years	33⅓% of the cost
5 to 7 years	66⅔% of the cost
7 or more years	100% of the cost

Thus, hypothetically, qualified investment could be computed as follows:

Cost of Property	Useful Life	Applicable Percentage	Qualified Investment
$200,000	4 years	33⅓	$66,666
$200,000	6 years	66⅔	$133,333
$200,000	8 years	100	$200,000

The 1981 Economic Recovery Tax Act retained most of the ground rules for determining which types of property qualify for the investment tax credit. However, as with depreciation, the actual useful life of eligible property has become irrelevant. For property assigned a 5-, 10-, or 15-year life ("cost recovery period") for ACRS purposes, a full 10% investment credit is now allowed. For 3-year property, 60% of the amount invested is considered the "qualified investment." (In other words, for property with a three-year cost recovery, only a 6% investment credit is allowed.) Under the 1981 Act, the qualified investment in the above example would now be computed as follows:

Cost of Property	Cost Recovery Period	Applicable Percentage	Qualified Investment
$200,000	3 years	60	$120,000
$200,000	5 years	100	$200,000
$200,000	10 years	100	$200,000
$200,000	15 years	100	$200,000

Again, as you can see, the incentive for investment is greater.

It would be simple if all there remained to do now to determine the investment tax credit was to take 10% of the qualified investment. However, simple is not the nature of the Code. First of all, the total amount of investment tax credit available to one taxpayer in any one year may not exceed the sum of $25,000, plus 90% of his tax liability in excess of $25,000. (However, the excess may be applied back to earlier years, or carried forward to be used in later years.)

Second, the above formula applies only to property that is new. In the case of used property, the costs to which the above percentages are applied may not exceed $125,000, which means the investment tax credit on used property may not exceed $12,500 (10% of $125,000). Beginning in 1985, however, by provision of the '81 Act, the allowable cost for used property will be raised to $150,000.

Let's see how all these methods and limitations come together. The following is an example of the computation of an investment tax credit:

Harris K., in October 1982, purchases and places in service in his mining business a new piece of mining equipment. The equipment costs $400,000 and has a "recovery period" of 5 years. Assume that Harris's tax liability for the year is $40,000.

Since the equipment has a 5-year recovery period, Harris's qualified investment equals 100% of the cost, or $400,000. Ten percent (10%) of that amount is $40,000. However, Harris's investment tax credit for the year is limited to $38,500, which is $25,000 plus 90% of his tax liability in excess of $25,000. Once again, slowly:

$25,000 plus 90% of $40,000 (tax liability) minus $25,000
OR $25,000 plus 90% of $15,000
OR $25,000 plus $13,500
EQUALS a $38,500 investment tax credit.

The second major type of tax credit that has become particularly significant to tax shelters is the "energy tax credit," created by the Energy Tax Act of 1978 and the Crude Oil Windfall Profit Tax Act of 1980, in an attempt to reduce this country's consumption of oil and gas. It was the intent of Congress to foster the development of "alternate energy sources" and to curtail the overall growth of the country's energy requirements through tax incentives. Thus, the energy tax credit applies to investments in a wide variety of properties designed to produce energy from sources other than oil and gas, or to reduce the consumption of those minerals. For example, the credit may be available on investments designed to produce energy from solar or hydroelectric facilities, or for certain commuter vehicles.

The energy tax credit is discussed in detail later in the book. However, several points about it are worth mentioning now. First, the energy tax credit applies *in addition* to the investment tax credit. The allowable amount of the energy tax credit ranges from 10% to 15% of the cost of eligible property. Building a windmill, for example, could yield an energy tax credit equal to 15% of the windmill's cost, as well as an investment tax credit of 10% of the amount invested. In addition, the energy tax credit can be used to offset all of a taxpayer's tax liability, not merely $2,500 plus 90% of tax liability in excess of $25,000, like the investment tax credit.

As in the case of the depreciation and ACRS deductions, the use of leverage together with tax credits can yield valuable tax benefits. However, also like those other allowances, tax credits are subject to recapture upon premature sale or disposition of the property.

Depreciation and ACRS deductions, depletion deductions, and tax credits are three of the major items used to provide tax benefits in tax shelter investments. Others, equally effective but not quite so broad in application, also exist, such as intangible drilling costs for oil and gas shelters, and advanced minimum royalties for coal. These will be discussed fully as they arise in treatments of the various activities.

Next, a discussion of the different types of vehicles for tax shelter investments.

CHAPTER IV
Investment Vehicles: Limited Partnerships, Subchapter S Corporations, and Individual Investments

Every business venture, and so every tax shelter, requires a form or a structure—a vehicle for raising capital and managing its affairs. Generally, the type of vehicle chosen, be it a partnership, a corporation, an individual investment, etc., is determined by the nature of the enterprise; the amount of capital available or needed; the number of investors; the economic risks; and, of course, the tax considerations. In the case of tax shelters, there is the added need for a vehicle that can filter tax benefits through to its investors, which they can in turn use to offset their other income. Additionally, since most tax shelter investors are passive investors (they do not participate in the management or control of the business), there is strong incentive to limit their liability to the amount that they invest.

Several business structures fulfill one or the other of these needs. Obviously, an individual investment or sole proprietorship, where the investor buys and runs a business in his own name, provides unlimited tax benefits. However, it also exposes the investor to unlimited liabilities. Similarly, a general or ordinary partnership—loosely defined as an unincorporated association of two or more persons [a corporation may also be a partner] who carry on a business as co-owners for profit—offers generous flow-through tax advantages. Since a partnership is not viewed as a separate entity for federal income tax purposes, each of its partners must directly and individually claim his share of the partnership's gain and deduct his share of the losses. Again, however, just as the tax benefits of a general partnership pass through to its investors, so do the claims against it. The partners—all of whom may actively participate in the management of the venture—are also fully and personally responsible for any debts or obligations it incurs.

This is not the case with shareholders of a corporation. Though their say in business management is usually limited to the election of directors and officers, so is their liability limited to the amount that they invest. However, since corporations are viewed as separate entities for federal income tax purposes, the tax consequences of their activities remain at the corporate level. As "taxpayers," corporations report and pay their own taxes directly and are the sole recipients of any tax allowances they generate. This lack of flow-through benefits in all but sub-chapter S corporations (which will be discussed later in this chapter) restricts their appeal for tax shelter purposes.

Only the limited partnership, hybrid of the general partnership and the corporation, provides both the flow-through tax advantages and the economic protections needed by tax shelter investors, with a minimum of restrictions and conditions. Like a general partnership, it is not viewed as a separate entity for income tax purposes, and so the tax attributes are passed on to its investors. Like a corporation, it offers limited liability to an investor who qualifies as a "limited partner." Prohibited from participating in the management of the venture, limited partners still enjoy the same generous tax benefits as general partners, but without opening themselves to any greater financial loss than the amount of their agreed-upon investment. For this reason, the limited partnership has soared to prominence in the past decade as the most popular, flexible, and one of the most effective vehicles for tax shelter investment.

Limited Partnerships in General

Actually, the limited partnerships is not a new kind of business structure, created just to meet current financial needs. In fact, evidence of it exists as far back as the Middle Ages in countries such as Italy, France, Switzerland, and England, where "they seem to have been devised to enable persons to engage in mercantile business without being known or named, [and they] became the most frequent combination of trade, and in large degree contributed to the commercial prosperity which the above named countries afterward enjoyed." *[Moorhead v. Seymour, 1901, 77 N.Y.S. 1050.]* Introduced to American statute by New York in 1822, they have become one of the most important means of raising capital in certain areas of investment.

Limited partnerships are created in accordance with the laws of the state in which they are formed. Most states have limited partnership statutes that conform, with some variation, to the

Uniform Limited Partnership Act (U.L.P.A.), which was adopted in 1916 by the Commission on Uniform State Laws. However, limited partnerships are *regulated* on two levels: state law governs the rights, duties, and liabilities of the partners to each other and to third parties, such as creditors; and federal law controls the relationship of the partners and the partnership to the federal government for income tax purposes. Unfortunately, the two governmental levels do not always agree. It is possible for a limited partnership to exist according to state law, but not for federal tax purposes. Conversely, it may be considered terminated under state law, while it continues to exist for federal tax purposes.

Because many tax shelter ventures depend upon the limited partnership structure for their economic protections and tax benefits, it is essential that they meet both state and federal standards. Among the most serious risks to tax shelter investors is that the structure of their deal will be termed either a general partnership by the state, thus exposing them to unlimited liability; or a corporation by the federal government (reclassification as a general partnership would not affect their tax status), thus denying them flow-through tax benefits.

In order to assuage the anxiety of investors in tax shelter limited partnerships, the promoters normally obtain opinions, from an attorney of the state in which they are formed and from tax counsel, as to classification of the organization. However, considering the consequences, it is still wise to check. Potential investors should have a clear understanding of the legal status of the limited partnership, and the requirements, of both levels of government, for achieving this status.

State Law—Rights, Powers, Liabilities, and the Limited Partnership

The Limited Liability Factor: As we noted, state law governs the formation and operation of a limited partnership, and the rights, duties, and liabilities of its members. State courts have the power to reclassify as a general partnership any limited partnership they determine to be improperly formed, structured, or managed, and to strip the protective mantle of limited liability from any limited partner who has overstepped the legal boundaries established.

Limited Partnerships Defined: According to the U.L.P.A., "A limited partnership is a partnership formed by two or more persons . . . having as members one or more general partners and one or more limited partners." A limited partnership usually may carry on any type of business.

Rights, Powers, and Liabilities of a General Partner: A general partner in a limited partnership has the exclusive right to manage the property or business of the partnership. He cannot, however, without the consent of the limited partners, do anything which would make it impossible to carry on the business of the partnership. Nor can the general partner violate the terms of the certificate of limited partnership, which will be discussed in detail later.

Of key significance: "A general partner is subject to all the liabilities of a partner in a partnership without limited partners." A general partner is fully and personally responsible for any debts or obligations incurred by the venture, except, of course, in the case of non-recourse loans.

Rights of a Limited Partner: A limited partner does not have the right to take part in the control of the business. He does have the right, just as does a general partner, to inspect the books and records of the partnership, and to receive complete information about the partnership's activities and regular accountings of its affairs.

As for compensation, a limited partner has the right to his share of the profits and other distributions stipulated in the certificate, provided that when they are paid, sufficient assets remain to cover the partnership's liabilities.

Liabilities of a Limited Partner: "A limited partner shall not become liable as a general partner unless, in addition to the exercise of his rights and powers as a limited partner, he takes part in the control of the business." It is hazy as to what degree of participation will subject a limited partner to unlimited liability. Some states, such as Delaware, are quite liberal in their provisions, allowing limited partners to exercise broad rights and powers, as long as they are set forth in the certificate. For the most part, however, states do not offer adequate guidelines, so limited partners who mix in business matters are taking their limited liability in their own hands. This uncertainty about permissible powers is dealt with in the Revised Limited Partnership Act, adopted by the Commission on Uniform State Laws in an effort to bring the 60-year-old statute up-to-date with the current range and magnitude of limited partnership activities. However, as of this writing, the Revised Act has been formally adopted by only 11 states.

Although limited partners are not liable to creditors, they are personally liable to the partnership to the extent of any distributions they receive which are needed to meet partnership obligations. In other words, if the cash the limited partner receives is needed to pay debts incurred by the partnership before this cash was distributed, the cash must be returned to the venture.

Distribution of Assets Upon Dissolution of a Limited Partnership: When a limited partnership is dissolved, the assets must generally be used first to repay creditors. Any remaining property, unless otherwise stipulated, is distributed first to the limited partners, and then to the general partners. As you can see thus far, the creditors come first in every situation.

The Certificate of Limited Partnership: Like corporations, but unlike general partnerships, limited partnerships, as a condition of formation, are required by state law to file certificates, usually with the Secretary of State's Office. If a certificate is not filed, a partnership may be formed, but it won't be a limited partnership, and it won't offer limited liability. It would probably be considered a general partnership. The main reason for this requirement, aside from providing certain information and setting guidelines for operation, is to let all those dealing with the partnership know which partners have the right to act on behalf of the partnership (general partners), and which have limited liability (limited partners). Essential to attaining state qualification as a limited partnership, the certificate must be signed and sworn to by all the partners and is generally required to include the following information:

(1) The name of the partnership: Generally, the partnership's name cannot include the surname of a limited partner. If it does, that limited partner may be subject to liability as a general partner. Some states require the name to include the words "Limited Partnership," or the abbreviation "L.P."

(2) The character of the partnership's business: For example, to own and operate residential real estate for profit.

(3) The location of the principal place of business of the partnership: This is often the general partner's address. It is not necessary for any partner to reside in the state of formation, nor is it theoretically required for the partnership to maintain its business operations there. Some states do require that an office and agent be designated and maintained within the state.

(4) The name and residence of each partner, general and limited partners being respectively designated.

(5) The amount of time for which the partnership is to exist: Unlike corporations, partnerships do not have perpetual existence. General partnerships dissolve automatically when a partner either dies, sells his interest, or otherwise withdraws from the partnership. Limited partnerships dissolve either upon the death, retirement, insanity, etc., of any of the general partners (unless otherwise stipulated), or after the date or period of years set forth in the certificate. At that time, the limited partnership ceases to exist.

If the certificate does not specify either a date of dissolution or a term after which the limited partners can expect to have their investments returned, any of those partners can demand his capital back simply by giving prior written notice (usually at least 6 months). Because such an unexpected demand could place a premature financial burden on a limited partnership, most set forth a termination date.

(6) The investment of the limited partners: The U.L.P.A. provides that, when acquiring an interest in a limited partnership, "the contributions of a limited partner may be cash or other property, but not services." The amount, value, and nature of the contribution of each limited partner must be set forth in the certificate. A general partner is not required to make a cash or property contribution in exchange for his partnership interest. He generally receives his interest in return for the services he provides.

(7) Additional contributions of the limited partners: Frequently, the capital contributions of a limited partner are made in installments over a period of years. When this is the case, the certificate must specify the amount of, time for, and, if they are contingent, the events that will trigger, the future payments. Often, security, such as a letter of credit, is required from the limited partners to discourage defaults, which could undermine the financial structure of the deal.

(8) The time, if agreed upon, when the contribution of each limited partner shall be returned: If no time is set, upon dissolution of the partnership, any assets remaining after the creditors have been paid will be used to repay the limited partners first.

(9) The share of the profits, or other compensation, which each limited partner shall receive by reason of his investment.

(10) The right, if given, and the terms for substituting limited

partners: According to the U.L.P.A., "A limited partner's interest is assignable," but only if the right to do so is set forth in the certificate. If it is, a limited partner can assign his interest to either a "substitute limited partner," with all the rights and powers of the original, or an "assignee," entitled to the original partner's share of the profits, distributions, etc., but none of his other rights, such as voting. Most tax shelter limited partnerships restrict the rights of limited partners to substitute. This will prevent a change in 50% or more of the partners which, as we will see later, would cause the partnership to be terminated for federal income tax purposes.

(11) The right, if given, of the partners to admit additional limited partners.

(12) The priority of limited partners: If one or more limited partners is to have priority over the others with respect to contributions or compensation, the right to, and nature of, the priority must be stated.

(13) The right, if given, of the remaining general partner or partners to continue the business upon the death, retirement, or insanity (bankruptcy in some states) of a general partner: Normally, this right is granted as a safeguard against premature dissolution. If it is not, should any of the above events occur, the partnership would automatically terminate, unless all the partners agree to its continuation.

(14) The right, if given, of a limited partner to demand and receive property instead of cash in return for his investment.

It is important that all the information on the certificate of limited partnership be accurate. Among other things, if a third party loses money because of reliance on a statement later shown to be false [such as the amount of invested funds available], all the partners are liable to him without limitation, if they knew the statement to be false or, possibly, if they merely should have known. To avoid costly repercussions, the opinion of counsel should always include a review of the certificate, and investors should be certain that, to their knowledge, everything it says is correct.

The Limited Partnership Agreement: In essence, the statutory provisions and certificate furnish the broad guidelines for a limited partnership's operations and internal affairs. Clearly, in as complex a business transaction as a tax shelter operation, far more comprehensive provisions are necessary. Often, a limited partnership will require its members also to become parties to written partnership agreement. The agreement fleshes out the details of the transaction, expanding upon or limiting the provisions of the law.

It is possible for a provision of an agreement to deal or conflict with a matter set forth in the statute or certificate. That provision may be unenforceable or worse, may result in loss of limited liability. It is wise, therefore, to have the agreement scrutinized by counsel, not only to be sure it conforms to the laws of the state, but also because these long and often complicated documents control a partner's rights and obligations.

Federal Law—Taxes and the Partnership

For federal income tax purposes, it doesn't matter whether you have a general or limited partnership; all partnerships are tax conduits that pass their gains and losses on to their investors. What matters is that you are not treated as a corporation which, as we have seen, except for a subchapter S corporation, retains its own tax attributes, leaving the tax situations of its shareholders unaffected. Because this is such a crucial distinction, one that can make or break a tax shelter deal, let us first consider how to avoid corporate treatment and achieve status as a partnership for federal income tax purposes.

As we said earlier, the question of how a business organization is taxed falls under the sole jurisdiction of the federal government. An organization duly qualified as a partnership or limited partnership for state purposes might not be considered such for tax purposes. The determination is based upon provisions of the Code, interpretive Regulations issued by the Treasury Department, and federal case law. Fortunately for tax shelter investors, the existing guidelines make it relatively easy to be classified as a partnership.

It is interesting to note that these guidelines were originally established before the proliferation of tax shelters, in an effort to prevent unincorporated entities, such as medical and other professional partnerships, from qualifying for corporate tax treatment, and the greater pension benefits available to corporate employees. To this end, the government issued Regulations making it easy for an unincorporated organization to qualify as a partnership and difficult to qualify as a corporation. Ironically, since that time, the state laws prohibiting professionals from have been changed, but the federal Regulations ed the same (to the joy of tax shelter syndicators). ne IRS, in recent years, has shifted its emphasis toward classifying organizations as corporations.

Qualifying as a Partnership: Basically, the Code defines a partnership as a business entity that is not, among other things, a corporation. It then provides that the term "corporation," for tax purposes may include certain unincorporated associations. Case law and the Regulations have interpreted these provisions to mean that, under certain circumstances, a partnership may be considered an association and thus, taxable as a corporation. The determination is made primarily on the basis of 4 specified corporate attributes. If an organization possesses at least 3 of these, it is, for tax purposes, a corporation. If it lacks at least 2 of the attributes, it is taxable as a partnership.

The 4 characteristics used to distinguish between corporations and partnerships are: (1) continuity of life; (2) centralization of management; (3) limited liability of the owners; and (4) free transferability of interests.

Continuity of Life: The Treasury Regulations provide that an organization has continuity of life if it continues to exist despite a change in its membership. This is true of a corporation, which has perpetual existence separate and apart from its shareholders. It is not true of a limited partnership organized in a state whose laws conform to the U.L.P.A., which states that the death, resignation, insanity, bankruptcy, etc., of a general partner will usually result in the dissolution of the partnership. Although a partnership can avoid dissolution if a remaining general partner continues the partnership's business with the consent of the other partners, the mere possibility that it may be dissolved is enough to prevent it from having continuity of life.

Centralization of Management: Centralization of management, according to the Regulations, is "a concentration of continuing exclusive authority to make independent business decisions on behalf of an organization which do not require the ratification of its members." Centralization of management exists in a corporation because the elected officers and directors act as representatives of the shareholders. General partnerships lack this trait because any of their members may act on his own behalf and his action will bind the partnership. Limited partnerships, true to form, fall somewhere in between. They seem at first glance to possess centralized management, since control of the business rests solely in the hands of the general partners. However, if a general partner has a substantial economic interest in a limited partnership, his decisions might be considered as made on his own behalf and not in a representative capacity, [as with corporate officers]. What constitutes a "substantial" enough interest to avoid centralization of management is not clearly defined. Therefore, if the general partners own only a minimal share of the partnership, centralization could be considered to exist.

Limited Liability: The Regulations state that an organization will lack the corporate quality of limited liability if at least one of its members is personally responsible for its debts and obligations. This is a simple matter for a general partnership and, it would seem, for a limited partnership as well, since both structures have general partners with unlimited liability. However, the Regulations indicate that, in the case of a limited partnership, if the general partner does not have "substantial assets" aside from his partnership interest, and is merely a "dummy" acting as an agent for the partnership, his liability will be considered limited. Again, there are no concrete guidelines as to what constitutes "substantial assets" or a "dummy" general partner, so if confronted with a general partner with few assets in relation to the size of the venture, or holding a small partnership interest, you could lose this point also.

Free Transferability of Interests: Free transferability of interests means that a member of a business organization has the right to substitute in his place, and confer all the attributes of his interest upon, someone else, without the consent of the other members. Since it is a simple and common matter for a tax shelter limited partnership to restrict this right, this corporate characteristic is easily avoidable.

As you can see, it is not difficult to structure a tax shelter limited partnership to lack at least 2 of the above corporate attributes and thus qualify for partnership tax treatment. Most tax shelter offerings include assurances of this, in the form of an opinion of tax counsel or, less frequently, an advance ruling from the IRS. If an opinion is offered, be sure it reviews current IRS positions and developments, since the issue of partnership tax status could be radically changed at any time. In January 1977, for example, the IRS promulgated proposed amendments to the Regulations that would have seriously affected and limited the classification of future and existing partnerships for tax purposes. Although the proposal was quickly withdrawn before becoming effective, there are no guarantees that it will not reappear in the same or a slightly altered form in the future.

Of course, an advance ruling from the IRS—made on the basis of facts submitted by the syndicators of a deal—is the best assurance of partnership tax treatment. However, advance rulings are not always sought or available. The IRS has refused to rule on limited partnerships when, as is often the case, the general partner is a corporation, unless the corporate partner has a specified net worth, owns at least 1% of the partnership, and is not itself owned in excess of 20% by the limited partners. The IRS has also refused to rule when, in the first 2 years of operation, the losses of a limited partnership exceed the amount invested by the partners.

Partnership Taxation: At the close of its fiscal year, every partnership is required to file an "information tax return," setting forth the tax consequences of its activities and each partner's share. For example, a partnership's activities may result in excess deductions, which means its deductions exceed its income. Or it may have excess taxable income, if its income exceeds its deductions. Taxable income should not be confused with cash flow, which results when the cash received by the partnership from its operations exceeds its cash expenditures.

Since the partnership itself does not pay taxes, each partner is required to report on his personal tax return his share of taxable income from the partnership's operations; the gains from any sale of partnership property; losses, deductions, and other tax benefits. Partnership taxable income and gains are added to a partner's taxable income and gains from other sources, increasing his tax liability. Conversely, partnership losses, deductions, and other benefits will reduce a partner's overall tax liability.

Tax Basis: The ability to provide tax losses that can offset an investor's other income and lower his tax bill is a major advantage of a tax shelter partnership. However, there is a ceiling on the amount of losses a partner can claim each year. The partnership sections of the Code provide that a partner can use his share of partnership losses only to the extent of the "adjusted basis" of his interest in the partnership. The higher his adjusted basis, the larger the amount of losses he can claim. As we will see later, adjusted basis also affects the tax consequences of cash distributions from the venture.

Fluctuating from year to year along with the operations of the business, adjusted basis is generally the amount of a partner's initial investment, plus his share of the partnership's taxable income, less his share of partnership losses and cash distributions.

By following the progress of Petersen H.'s investment in a real estate limited partnership, we can illustrate the computation of adjusted basis. Petersen's initial investment, made in 1981, was $20,000, for which he received a 10% share of the partnership. In that year, the partnership operated at a loss, generating excess deductions, of which Petersen's share was $10,000. In 1982, the partnership operated profitably, resulting in taxable income, of which Petersen's share was $2,000. The cash flow however was somewhat less than the taxable income, therefore he received cash distributions of only $1,000. His adjusted basis would be computed as follows:

1981

Initial contribution	$20,00
Minus losses	-10,000
Equals adjusted basis	$10,000

1982

Adjusted basis (carried from 1981)	$10,000
Plus taxable income	+2,000
Equals adjusted basis prior to distribution	$12,000
Minus distribution	-1,000
Equals new adjusted basis for 1983	$11,000

Suppose in 1983 Petersen's share of losses was $12,000. His adjusted basis would permit him to claim only $11,000 that year. However, the Code allows him to carry the additional $1,000 in losses over to a subsequent year, when his adjusted basis may be large enough to use them. This ability to carry unused losses into other years is one of the reasons partnerships are a favored vehicle for tax shelter investments. As we will see, the subchapter S corporation, one of the other commonly used vehicles, lacks this attribute.

Adjusted basis was one of the items hardest hit by the Tax Reform Act of 1976. Prior to the Act, a partner could increase his adjusted basis to the extent of his share of partnership liabilities—including both those for which he was personally responsible and those for which no one was ("non-recourse loans''). Since non-recourse loans are frequently much greater than the amount of equity invested by the borrowers, this arrangements gave partnerships—especially limited partnerships—the ability to increase a partner's basis (and so, the losses he could claim) far beyond his actual investment, or capital at-risk. For example:

In 1982, Lauren B. invested $15,000 for a 10% interest in a coal mining limited partnership. To operate its mine, the partnership secured a $100,000 loan, for which none of the partners was personally liable. Lauren's adjusted basis for 1982 is $25,000, computed as follows:

	1982
Initial investment	$15,000
Plus 10 % share of non-recourse loan (10 % x $100,000)	+$10,000
Equals adjusted basis	$25,000

If Lauren's share of the partnership losses for 1982 was $20,000, under the old rules she would be entitled to use them, even though her investment was only $15,000.

Now, however, as a result of the 1976 Reform Act, a partner may only use liabilities for which he is personally responsible, for the purpose of increasing allowable deductions. Non-recourse loans can no longer be included to provide investors with losses in excess of their investment, or economic risk. This restriction applies to all partnerships, except for those engaged in real estate. Basically, the 1976 Reform Act limited the amount of deductions an investor can claim to his actual ''at-risk'' investment. The meaning of the term ''at-risk'' will be discussed fully in the next chapter. Suffice it for now to say that real estate is the only remaining partnership activity that can offer investors deductions in excess of the capital they stand to lose.

One more point: just as a partner in a real estate venture can increase his basis by his share of non-recourse debt, so will his basis be reduced if there is a reduction (repayment) of the loan. As we will see in the next section, this could result in unfavorable tax consequences to the investor.

Taxation of Partnership Distributions: The Code provides that only the portion of a partner's share of cash distributions that exceeds his ''adjusted basis'' will be taxed. Theoretically this is because his adjusted basis includes his share of undistributed partnership income, which has already been taxed but not distributed. Therefore, distributions equal to, or less than, adjusted basis are treated either as previously taxed income or as nontaxable returns of money invested. Only those portions of distributions that exceed adjusted basis are subject to tax. For example:

Adam G. is a limited partner with an adjusted basis in the beginning of 1981 of $1,000. That year, Adam's partnership operated at a profit, of which his share is $5,000. In 1982, Adam's share of partnership taxable income is $2,000, and he also receives a cash distribution of $10,000. The results to Adam in 1981 and 1982 are as follows:

1981

Beginning adjusted basis	$1,000
Plus share of partnership taxable income	+$5,000
Equals end of year adjusted basis	$6,000

1982

Beginning adjusted basis	$6,000
Plus share of partnership income	+$2,000
Equals adjusted basis prior to distribution	$8,000
Distribution	$10,000
Minus adjusted basis prior to distribution	–$8,000
Equals amount of distribution subject to tax	$2,000

Thus, Adam's total 1982 taxable income from the partnership is his $2,000 share of the taxable income, plus the $2,000 by which his distribution exceeds his adjusted basis. His adjusted basis after receiving the distribution is reduced to zero. (By the way, adjusted basis can never be less than zero.)

There is another element to taxation of distributions, one that unfortunately involves "paper" distributions, or "phantom income," which is income the investor has not received. If a partnership has liabilities for which the partners are personally responsible, or a real estate partnership has a non-recourse loan, each partner may increase his adjusted basis by his share of them. If such a liability is reduced, each partner will be treated as having received a cash distribution equal to his share of the reduction. If his share is less than his adjusted basis, the partner will not be taxed. But if it exceeds his adjusted basis, he will be taxed to the extent of the difference. For example:

In January 1981, as a result of prior years' losses, the adjusted basis of Susan P.'s interest in a real estate limited partnership was $6,000, including her share of non-recourse liabilities. The partnership had a $75,000 non-recourse loan, of which Susan's share is 10%, or $7,500. In December, 1981, the partnership paid off the loan, reducing it to zero. As a result, Susan is deemed to have received a $7,500 distribution, with the following result:

	1981
Adjusted basis	$6,000
Minus distribution (Susan's share of the repaid loan)	–$7,500
Equals adjusted basis	$-0-
And Taxable gain	$1,500

Susan is taxed on a distribution that she never received.

Allocation of Partnership Income and Losses: Partnership agreements generally allocate partnership income, gains, losses, deductions, and credits in a manner consistent with the economic interests of the partners. Thus, a limited partnership might be structured like this:

Four people invest $10,000 each to become limited partners in a coal mining limited partnership. The general partner invests $60,000 to bring the combined total of the partners' contributions to $100,000. The economic interest of each of the limited partners in the partnership is therefore 10% and the general partners' economic interest is 60%. In order for each partner's share of the partnership income, gains, losses, deductions, and credits to be consistent with his interest, each limited partner must be allocated 10% of these items, and the general partner must be allocated 60%.

Assume that in the first year of operation the venture reports no income or gains, a $50,000 loss, and a $10,000 investment credit for the purchase of mining equipment. Each of the limited partners would be entitled to a $5,000 deduction (10% of $50,000), and a $1,000 investment credit (10% of $10,000), to offset his other income and reduce the amount of his taxes. The general partner would be entitled to a $30,000 deduction, and a $6,000 investment credit.

Special Allocations: Suppose that in the planning stage

of the deal, to encourage the 4 limited partners to invest, the general partner agreed to allocate to them 100% of the first year's losses and 40% of the investment credit. Each of the limited partners would then be entitled to a 25% share of the losses, or a $12,500 deduction, and a 10% share of the investment credit, or $1,000. These allocations, which are clearly disproportionate, are commonly called "special allocations." Special allocations are permitted by the Code in limited circumstances.

The 1976 Tax Reform Act provides that if a partnership agreement does not specify a partner's share of the tax consequences of the partnership, or if the allocation provided in the agreement does not have "substantial economic effect," it will be disregarded, and each partner's share will be determined according to his interest in the partnership. The Code does not specify when special allocations will be deemed to lack "substantial economic effect." However, Congressional Committee reports indicate that the intent of Congress in enacting this provision was to eliminate the use of special allocations for tax avoidance purposes without disturbing their use for legitimate non-tax purposes. If there is a special allocation in a venture you are considering, question its propriety. The IRS might.

Retroactive Allocations: Prior to the 1976 Tax Reform Act, many tax shelter partnerships were structured so that partners could enter late in the year and still be allocated a full share of the year's deductions, losses, credits, etc. This practice, known as "retroactive allocations," was based upon a 1972 Tax Court decision, the *Rodman Case,* in which the IRS was attempting to tax a partner on a share of partnership income earned during a period of the year prior to his admission. They won what soon became apparent was a pyrrhic victory. Tax shelter promoters seized upon this decision to justify allocating a full year's share of losses, deductions, and credits to partners entering partnerships as late as December 31st.

The 1976 Reform Act put an end to retroactive allocations, stating that an incoming partner is only entitled to claim a share of tax benefits arising after his entrance into the partnership. Ironically, in the same year the Reform Act passed, the *Rodman* decision was reversed on appeal, thereby destroying the case law foundation for retroactive allocations. One way or another, they were eliminated.

Sale or Redemption of Partnership Interests: If a partner sells his partnership interest, or has it redeemed (repurchased) by the partnership, he is subject to tax on the gain. Gain is the amount by which his selling price exceeds his adjusted basis. If the interest was held for the required period of time and the rules of recapture do not apply, he will generally be taxed at the more favorable long-term capital gains rate.

When, in connection with the sale or redemption of an interest, a selling partner is relieved of any partnership liabilities, he will be treated as having received a cash distribution equal to his share of the liability. For example, if the partnership is engaged in real estate and has a non-recourse loan, the selling partner will automatically be considered relieved of his share, and taxed to the extent that it exceeds his adjusted basis. Thus, the sale or redemption of a partnership interest might work out like this:

Jon T. has an adjusted basis for his partnership interest of $5,000, and a share of partnership non-recourse liabilities equal to $10,000. He sells his interest for $6,000, for a taxable gain computed as follows:

Consequences of the Sale

Amount received for his interest	$6,000
Plus share of liabilities relieved	+$10,000
Equals	$16,000
Minus adjusted basis	-$5,000
Equals taxable gain	$11,000

As we can see, Jon's taxable gain from the sale exceeds the amount of cash he received for his interest, probably because his adjusted basis was reduced by prior years' losses and distributions. We must hope that Jon took advantage of those losses when he needed them, and made his sale only when he could afford the increase in his tax liabilities.

Termination of the Partnership: Just as the Code has its own definition of a partnership, it has its own guidelines for determining when a partnership is terminated for tax purposes. "A partnership shall be considered terminated . . . if—no part of any business, financial operation, or venture of the partnership continues to be carried on by any of its partners—or [if] within a 12-month period there is a sale or exchange of 50 percent or more of the total interest in partnership capital and profits." Should either of these events occur, each of the partners will be treated as having received a distribution of his share of the partnership property, whether or not it is actually distributed. In the case of a 50% sale of interest when the business operations are continued, each remaining partner will be considered to have recontributed his distribution to a new partnership—with unfavorable tax consequences, as the following example illustrates:

Loren K. has a 25% interest in a partnership, and an adjusted basis of $2,000. The partnership has $20,000 in cash and new business equipment. Unexpectedly, one of his partners sells her 50% interest, with the result of terminating the partnership for tax purposes. Each of the remaining partners is treated as having received a distribution equal to his share of the partnership property and then contributing it to a new partnership formed with the purchaser of the interest. Loren suffers the following results:

Cash distribution ($20,000 x 25%)	$5,000
Minus adjusted basis	–2,000
Equals taxable gain	$3,000

In an effort to avoid these adverse consequences, many limited partnership agreements prohibit the transfer of partnership interests. It should be noted that the admission of new partners by reason of expansion of the partnership will not result in a termination, even if the new partners own more than 50% of the partnership. A partnership will only be considered terminated if 50% of its *existing* interests are transferred.

Partnership Tax Returns: As we mentioned earlier, a partnership is not a taxpaying entity. However, it is required to file an information tax return each year. This return summarizes all the financial transactions of the partnership for the year and the tax consequences of these transactions. Attached to the return is a Schedule K-1 for each partner (a copy of which is generally also furnished to the partner). The K-1 sets forth the partner's share of the partnership's tax consequences, which he must then report on his own tax return for the year.

Tax Audits: The IRS has recognized the importance of a partnership as a vehicle for tax shelters and, in keeping with its policy of attacking abusive shelters, the Commissioner has instituted a program of increased audits of partnership tax returns. If an audit results in a determination that an error was made on the partnership return, each partner will be required to adjust his own return to reflect his share of the change, or to litigate the issue with the IRS. While this increase in pressure is not directed at legitimate, properly structured tax shelters, prospective investors should, with professional assistance, carefully evaluate the projected tax consequences of any venture, to insure compliance with the provisions of the tax laws.

Subchapter S Corporations

The exception to the general rule that corporations are not suitable vehicles for tax shelter investments is the Subchapter S Corporation. Named for the segment of the Code that creates and regulates it, this form of doing business has all the attributes of an ordinary corporation except one: it is ordinarily not a taxpaying entity. For the most part, it passes the tax consequences of its activities on to its shareholders.

Actually, a sub S corporation (as it is commonly called) is an ordinary corporation whose shareholders have filed a form electing to be taxed at the shareholder level, rather than the corporate level. Otherwise, it retains its corporate identity, which means, among other things, it has shareholders, officers, and directors, none of whom is personally liable for its debts and obligations.

Despite this combination of the availability of tax benefits and limited liability for all members, sub S corporations have been greatly overshadowed by limited partnerships in the tax shelter field. This is primarily because they are subject to certain tax and other limitations that do not (or, as we shall see, did not) affect the partnership structure. Most significantly, sub S corporations are limited with respect to (1) the number and type of investors they may have and thus, indirectly, the amount of money they can raise; (2) the type of activities in which they may engage; (3) the type and amount of losses they may pass on to shareholders, and the way in which those losses can be allocated; and (4) the use of non-recourse financing to provide shareholders with tax benefits in excess of their investments. However, since the 1976 Tax Reform Act has also cut back the use of non-recourse financing by many partnerships, sub S corporations may well come into their own as tax shelter vehicles, especially when you consider their added advantage of allowing investors to participate freely in the control of a business without losing their limited liability.

For our purposes, the most meaningful way to approach sub S

corporations is from a tax point of view in relation to partnerships. First, however, let us consider how sub S status is achieved.

Qualifying as a Subchapter S Corporation

A sub S corporation is formed in the same manner as a regular corporation, that is, by filing a certificate of incorporation with a designated state agency. In order to qualify for the special tax treatment it must also fulfill the following requirements:

(1) It must have no more than 25 shareholders (a husband and wife owning stock jointly are considered one shareholder);

(2) The shareholders of a subchapter S corporation generally must be either individuals, estates, or certain trusts. Corporations may not be investors in a sub S corporation, as they may be in a partnership. This exclusion of corporations seeking tax shelter is another reason for the limited appeal of the sub S corporation in the field;

(3) A subchapter S corporation may issue only one class of stock. The voting and dividend rights of shareholders may vary only by reason of the amount, not type, of stock they own;

(4) The corporation must be a domestic, as opposed to a foreign, corporation, whose members are all U.S. citizens or residents, rather than non-resident aliens.

In addition to these requirements, during the first 75 days of the taxable year (or during the year before) the corporation must file an election to be taxed as a subchapter S corporation, together with the written consent of each of its members. A late filing will disqualify the organization, unless it is formed in the middle of the year, in which case the election must be filed within 75 days of formation. Once an election is made, it will continue to be effective from year to year until it is terminated. Once terminated, a new election may not be filed for at least 5 years without the special consent of the Commissioner of the IRS.

Revocation of Subchapter S Status

Sub S status and tax treatment will be terminated if, at any time, any of the above conditions is not maintained, or if any of the following events occurs:

(1) A new shareholder, within 60 days of acquiring his stock, notifies the IRS that he does not consent to subchapter S status. Since such a refusal could radically alter the tax treatment of

other shareholders, many sub S corporations will by agreement forbid the transfer of stock to parties who refuse to consent;

(2) All the shareholders consent to termination of subchapter S status. This does not necessarily mean the end of the corporation; it may continue to exist, but it will do so as a taxpaying entity;

(3) In any year more than 20% of the corporation's gross receipts are considered "passive investment income," except during the first year provided the passive income does not exceed $3,000. From a tax shelter point of view, this is a major limitation. Passive investment income includes royalties, interest, and rent, which means the subchapter S corporation cannot be used for most rental real estate ventures;

(4) In any year, more than 80% of the gross receipts are derived from sources outside the United States.

Taxes and the Subchapter S Corporation

Like the partners of a partnership, the shareholders of a subchapter S corporation generally can use their share of corporate losses to offset their other income and reduce their taxes. However, despite this similarity, a subchapter S corporation is still a corporation, not a partnership, and there are significant differences in tax treatment that should be considered.

Tax Basis: Shareholders, like partners, are limited in the amount of losses they can claim to the adjusted basis of their stock. A shareholder's adjusted basis includes the cost of his stock, plus his cumulative share of undistributed corporate income, plus any loans made by him to the corporation. Notably, it does not include any portion of the corporation's liabilities, which means a shareholder cannot take advantage of non-recourse loans, as may a partner in a real estate partnership. A shareholder's adjusted basis is reduced by prior years' losses, but only ordinary losses, since, as we shall see, capital losses do not pass through a subchapter S corporation.

If a shareholder does not use certain losses because of insufficient basis, he may not carry them over to a year in which his basis is increased, as may a partner in a partnership. However, since adjusted basis, as well as the amount of corporate losses, is determined at the end of the year, it is possible for a shareholder to make an investment or loan money to a subchapter S corporation right up to the last day, in order to obtain sufficient basis to use his losses.

Tax Losses: The losses of a subchapter S corporation are allocated on a per diem basis. In other words, in any given year, the net losses of the corporation are divided by the number of days in the corporation's tax year, then allocated to each shareholder according to the number of days he owned stock and the amount of stock he owned. Unlike partnerships, there is no opportunity to allocate losses only to those who owned stock at the time the losses occurred. In fact, there is no opportunity for special allocations at all in a subchapter S corporation. The items comprising corporate losses do not retain their individual character, and therefore cannot be specifically or disproportionately assigned to certain shareholders, as they can be in a partnership.

Another significant point: as already stated, capital losses do not pass through a subchapter S corporation, as they do a partnership. Shareholders cannot use the corporation's capital losses to offset their capital gains from other sources. Instead, capital losses remain with the corporation to reduce future corporate capital gains.

Taxable Income and Gains: Unlike losses, which are allocated on a per diem basis, the undistributed income and gains of a subchapter S corporation are allocated to the shareholders on the last day of the taxable year, in direct proportion to their stock ownership at that time. This raises the possibility that a shareholder, by selling stock in a bona fide transaction prior to the end of the year, may be able to avoid taxable income or gains.

Cash Distributions: Since the shareholders of a subchapter S corporation, like the partners of a partnership, are taxed on income even if it is not distributed, later distributions of this previously-taxed income are generally tax-free, to the extent that they do not exceed adjusted basis.

Sale of Stock or Liquidation of Subchapter S Corporation: Upon sale or redemption of stock, or liquidation of the corporation, the shareholders of a subchapter S corporation are generally taxed in the same manner as the shareholders of a regular corporation. They are taxed at capital gains rates to the extent that the amounts they receive for their stock exceed their adjusted basis.

CHAPTER V
"At Risk": The 1976 Tax Reform Act Loss Limitations

Prior to the Tax Reform Act of 1976, shelters in many areas could offer investors tax savings far greater than their actual investment, or risk of economic loss. The shelters used non-recourse loans to help finance the ventures and generate excess deductions and credits. Unfortunately, the quest for "paper losses" sometimes ended in abuse. Since many of these non-recourse loans were made by the sellers of the tax shelter property, the costs of the property and the size of loans could be arbitrarily inflated without additional risk to the investor (remember, no one is personally liable for a non-recourse loan). This would have the effect of driving up depreciation (now ACRS) deductions and investment credits (the "paper losses"), which rise proportionately with the cost of property, while at the same time increasing an investor's basis, or ability to use the losses. It was a tempting package, and it lured many investors into deals lacking the profit motive required by the Code.

Richard B. was such an investor. A high-priced corporate executive with a taxable income in 1975 of $50,000, he would have paid approximately $20,000 in taxes, if he had not become involved in a movie shelter that developed in the following way:

The seller of the picture originally asked for $25,000, payable as $5,000 in cash and $20,000 over the next five years. The $20,000 was to be a non-recourse loan, secured by the film and repaid from its proceeds. The operations of the venture would entitle Richard to a depreciation deduction in the first year equal to 20% of the cost of the film, or $5,000, and an investment credit of 10% of the cost of the film, or $2,500. That would mean that, for a cash investment of $5,000, Richard would save $5,300 in taxes.

But perhaps there was a way for him to save even more. Richard's advisor urged him to negotiate a $50,000 price for the film, payable $5,000 in cash and $45,000 as a non-recourse obligation, due from the film's proceeds over the next 10 years. This would inflate Richard's allowable depreciation deduction in the first year to $10,000 [20% x $50,000], and his investment credit to $5,000 [10% x $50,000]. Thus, for the same $5,000 cash investment, and no additional risk, he would now save approximately $11,000 in taxes. The seller wouldn't object, since he stood to make even more on the film. And Richard certainly didn't, since he would gain enough in tax savings to make the investment profitable, whether or not the film succeeded. Indeed, so attractive were the tax benefits that Richard ignored the fact that, considering the loan and distribution fees, the film would have to gross the unlikely figure of $5,000,000 before he would begin to receive a cash return on his investment.

It was to discourage investments like this, made primarily for the purpose of avoiding taxes, that Congress included in the 1976 Tax Reform Act certain provisions aimed at limiting the amount of losses investors can claim to the amount they are actually "at-risk" in connection with the investment.

The "At-Risk" Activities and Partnership Loss Limitations

The first provision added to the Code, by Section 465 of the 1976 Tax Reform Act, approached the issue directly, specifying 4 business activities that were to be subject to the "at-risk" limitations on losses. This provision applied to investors in the following 4 activities, regardless of the investment vehicle: oil and gas; motion pictures and video tapes; personal property leasing; and farming. The second provision, which was contained in Section 704, approached the issue indirectly, broadly restricting partnership use of non-recourse loans (loans for which no partner has personal liability) to increase a partner's basis and thus the amount of losses he could claim from the partnership's activities. This provision did not apply in the case of real estate partnerships or partnerships engaged in the activities covered by Section 465.

The Revenue Act of 1978 expanded the "at-risk" rules so that they now generally apply to all activities (not just the enumerated 4) engaged in by individuals (including partnerships), subchapter S corporations, and closely held corporations (corporations in which five or fewer individuals are deemed to own 50% or more of the stock). Investment in real estate is the only activity which is exempt from the "at-risk" provision.

Determining the Amount "At-Risk"

As a result of the above legislative actions, the Code now states that an investor can use losses available from an at-risk activity only to the extent that he is actually economically at-risk in connection with the activity. This applies to partners of a partnership, shareholders of subchapter S and closely held corporations, and individual investors. An investor will be considered at-risk for all the money and other property contributed by him to the venture, plus any loans for which he is personally liable, and any property he pledges to secure such loans. Obviously, nonrecourse loans are out. So are loans for which the lender's only security is the investor's interest in the venture or property connected with it, and loans from related parties or parties with an interest in the capital or profits of the venture other than as creditors. An investor will also not be considered at-risk for any amount which he protects from economic loss, either by insurance or by such arrangements as guarantees or stop-loss agreements.

An Illustration

In 1982, Louis H. purchased a new computer from its manufacturer for $100,000. He paid $10,000 at closing, and agreed to pay $90,000 to the manufacturer from the proceeds derived from leasing the computer to other companies. The loan was due within 7 years of the date of purchase. Louis delivered $15,000 worth of IBM stock as security for the loan, and agreed to be personally liable for $20,000 more if the leasing revenues were not sufficient. The manufacturer agreed that if there was still a balance at the end of 7 years, after selling the IBM stock and collecting the $20,000, his only recourse would be to reclaim the computer, which Louis also pledged as security. Based on these facts, in 1982, Louis would be considered at-risk for $45,000 computed as follows:

His $10,000 down payment, $15,000 worth of IBM stock, and $20,000 personal obligation would all be included in his at-risk amount. The value of the computer pledged as security would not, since property used in the activity is excluded from the calculation.

That year, Louis could use losses, generated by the purchase of the computer, of up to $45,000. The losses he claimed would be subtracted from his at-risk amount for the following year. If the available losses were greater than $45,000, Louis would be permitted to carry the excess over to the next year, when his at-risk amount might be increased, either through additional investments or through personally guaranteed loans. One last point for clarification: at-risk is computed solely for the purpose of limiting losses. It does not affect an investor, as does basis, for other purposes, such as taxation of distributions. When at-risk and basis both apply (for example, in an oil partnership), the lesser of the two calculations generally determines the amount of losses allowed.

Recapture

The Revenue Act of 1978 contained a provision requiring a taxpayer to report income in any year in which the amount he is at-risk is reduced below zero. In our above example, let us assume that Louis utilized his $45,000 in losses in 1982, and thus, the amount he was considered at-risk was reduced to zero that year. If, in 1983, his IBM stock, worth $15,000, was returned to him, his amount at-risk would correspondingly be reduced to below zero by $15,000. In 1983, Louis would be required to report that $15,000 as income. The Code provides that the amount subject to "recapture," as it is called, would be limited to the extent that the losses previously deducted from the activity exceed any amounts that have already been recaptured. This recapture provision applies only to losses incurred after December 31, 1978. Furthermore, to the extent that losses are recaptured by reason of this provision, they may be deducted in subsequent years in the event that the amount at-risk is increased.

"At-Risk" and Tax Credits

The Economic Recovery Tax Act of 1981 generally expanded the coverage of the at-risk rule to include tax credits. For example, if a piece of equipment is purchased in 1982 for $100,000, $10,000 payable in cash and the balance over 10 years pursuant to a $90,000 non-recourse note, the "qualified investment" when the equipment is first placed in service is limited to $10,000. In later years, as payments are made on the non-recourse note, the "qualified investment" can be increased by the amount of these payments. Again, real estate is not subject to the at-risk rules, so that tax credits available as a result of the rehabilitation of real estate are not subject to these provisions (the rehabilitation credit will be discussed further in later chapters). Additionally, an investor will be considered at-risk even with respect to non-recourse loans, provided they are obtained from "qualified lenders" such as banks, insurance companies, unrelated third-party lenders, federal, state, or local governments, etc. He must also be at-risk for at least 20% of his interest in the property, and the property must be acquired from an unrelated party.

In the case of the energy tax credit, certain qualified energy property is exempt from the at-risk provision provided the investor is at-risk with respect to at least 25% of the property and the terms of the loan require repayment in substantially equal payments.

Loopholes

New tax legislation, such as the at-risk provision and the restriction on partnerships using non-recourse loans, tends to deal narrowly with existing abuses and inequities. Very often, because the Code is so complex, the closing of a loophole may create others as a result of incomplete, inconsistent, or conflicting provisions. Even before the Tax Reform Act of 1976 officially became law, new structuring innovations and forms for tax shelter investment started to emerge. Some have independent economic significance and are quite legitimate; some are questionable; and some are clearly abusive, complying with the letter of the law while neatly eluding its spirit. The ill-fated venture of Norman and Jay in the second chapter was an example of such maneuvering. Here is a closer look at a similar situation:

Paul K. was a promoter with the opportunity to acquire potentially valuable mineral rights and set up a coal mining operation in Kentucky. To get started, he needed $500,000 capital, which he hoped to raise by offering investors attractive tax benefits. He knew he could generate tax deductions and credits far greater than the invested funds, by using loans and other financing, but he needed to find a way to pass the losses on, without substantial risk, to the investors.

Paul also realized that investors are wary of exposing themselves to personal liability on loans, especially in a limited partnership, where they have no control of management. He needed to arrange financing in a way that would make the investors personally liable, without really exposing them to great risk of loss.

His advisors offered a suggestion: have the partnership, on the last day of the taxable year, purchase $100,000 worth of U.S. Treasury Bills on margin, perhaps paying $10,000 down, and securing the balance with the Treasury Bills themselves and with each partner's personal guarantee for a pro rata share of the loan. With such a low-risk investment, backed by the federal government and easily sold for full value at any time, there would be little danger to the investors and each could use his share of the liability to increase his tax deductions.

Technically, it seemed to work. The partners were personally liable for the Treasury Bill loan and thus, should have been able to use their share of the liability to increase their adjusted basis. However, the actual risk of loss was negligible and the whole transaction seemed to produce a result not contemplated, and certainly not intended, by Congress. First, considering the stability of the collateral, couldn't the loan be considered a non-recourse liability, or one that offered the kind of protection, like a guarantee or stop-loss agreement, that exempted it from being at-risk. Second, even if it was not a non-recourse liability, since it was essentially a separate activity engaged in by the partnership, could it be used to increase allowable losses from the coal mining operation? Section 465 specifically states that an investor must be at-risk in connection with the activity generating the losses to be used.

It was possible that the incompleteness of the at-risk provision had created a loophole through which the Treasury Bill purchase might have passed. The IRS didn't think so. Late in 1977, in a case similar to our example, they ruled that partners could not increase their basis as a result of the Treasury Bill loan. The Commissioner indicated that he did not consider the investors liable for the loan, since the value of the collateral was obviously equal to, or greater than, the debt. He added that "it would be quite artificial to allow a liability incurred in the passive activity of investing in government securities to affect the amount considered to be at-risk in a wholly unrelated activity. Congressional intent should not be so easily thwarted." Still, the IRS ruling is not the final word on the Treasury Bill issue. Rulings, which are usually sought prior to the consummation of deals in order to be sure of the tax consequences, are not law. They simply represent the conclusion of the IRS as to the tax effects of certain given situations. They may be amended or revoked at any time, although they usually are not.

Assume in the above example that Paul K. disagreed with the interpretation set forth in the IRS ruling and decided to go ahead with his transaction, using the Treasury Bill loan. If his return is not audited, there will be no problem. If it is audited, and the IRS takes the same position it took in the ruling, Paul will be faced with the choice of either paying the disputed tax or contesting the IRS position, usually in tax court. If he chooses the latter, the court will then finally decide which intrepretation of the partnership at-risk provision becomes law.

Bear in mind when considering a tax shelter with an aggressive or untried structure, or one (like Paul's) in which the IRS has taken an adverse position, that litigation can be expensive. Even if the desired tax consequences are eventually upheld in court, legal fees could significantly detract from the victory, just as they could increase the damage if the case is lost, as could interest charges and penalties.

We have thus far considered tax shelters in general, investment vehicles, and relevant tax law. We will now turn our attention to the specific kinds of business activities commonly offered in today's tax shelter market. The next chapter is devoted to real property, or "real estate," the one activity exempted by Congress from the at-risk provisions. Even if real estate is not your particular interest, it would be worthwhile to read that chapter first, since many of the economic and tax concepts discussed in detail apply to the other activities as well.

PART II
Real Estate Shelters

CHAPTER VI
Real Estate

"Buy land, they ain't making any
more of the stuff."
—WILL ROGERS

General Discussion

The law of supply and demand is not the only reason Will Roger's advice is still as sound as ever in today's investment market. In addition to providing a hedge against inflation, investments in well-located, well-developed real estate can be a source of significant tax benefits.

In the previous chapter, we noted that real estate is the only business activity in which an investor can engage unrestricted by the at-risk limitations. That means a real estate venture can still use non-recourse financing to increase allowable losses. Congress never fully revealed why real estate was given that privilege. Perhaps it was the result of effective lobbying, or social and economic objectives, or perhaps Congress believed that real estate is less susceptible to abuse than most other tax shelter activities. Whatever the reason, many now contend that the tax laws have made real estate "the only game in town." While the remainder of this book will offer evidence to the contrary, there is no denying that it does possess some definite advantages.

Black's Law Dictionary defines real property as "land, and generally whatever is erected or growing upon or affixed to land." For the purposes of tax shelter investment, that usually means land upon which buildings are constructed for rental purposes, such as apartments, office buildings, motels, warehouses, and shopping centers. These projects generally pass through similar stages of development, each having its own economic and tax considerations and consequences. Because we believe that all ventures should first be analyzed from an economic point of view, we will present an overview of the development of a typical real estate deal, before we consider the tax aspects.

Development and Financing

A real estate venture usually begins in the mind of a developer who senses a need or demand for a particular type of project in a certain area. After locating a parcel of land suitable for what he intends to build, he either enters into a contract to purchase, obtains an option to purchase, or leases it. Next, he commissions an architect to design the project, after which he compiles estimates of what his construction costs will be. Then, armed with plans and projections, he seeks financing for the venture.

The first objective is a commitment for a long-term or "permanent" mortgage loan. To obtain one, the developer either applies to a lending institution dealing in this type of financing, such as a banking institution, insurance company, pension fund, etc., or engages a mortgage broker to do it for him. The permanent loan will be secured by a first mortgage interest in the property. A first mortgage, or "deed of trust" as it is called in some states, assures the lender of first priority in the event the borrower defaults on repayment of the loan or any of the conditions required by the loan agreement (i.e., maintenance of adequate insurance, proper upkeep of the property, etc.). Should a default occur, the first mortgagee has the right to foreclose on the property, sell it, and use the proceeds to repay the loan. Such action could extinguish the rights of any subsequently acquired interests in the property or any claims against it, such as a second mortgage or other lien. All those dealing with the borrower are notified of this risk by the filing of the first mortgage in a public recording office.

Obviously, a real estate venture should take advantage of its ability to use a non-recourse permanent loan, and thus to enable investors to claim deductions in excess of their capital at-risk, without assuming personal liability for repayment. Ideally the amount of the loan will be equal to, or greater than, the projected construction costs, although this happens infrequently. Typically, the loan will be repayable in monthly installments over a period of time exceeding 10 years. The monthly payments will consist of interest payments, based upon a fixed interest rate, and amortization payments, or payments to reduce the loan principal. A loan may either be "self-amortizing," which means that if all the monthly payments are made, the loan will be fully repaid by its due date, or "partially-amortizing," which means that on the due date there may be a sizeable balance outstanding. In the latter case, the borrower would have to dig into his own pocket to make up the difference or, as is commonly the practice, seek "refinancing" of the loan.

At this point it seems appropriate to note that the interest portion of the monthly loan payment is tax deductible, whereas the amortization portion is not. Since the monthly interest payment is calculated by applying the fixed interest rate to the unpaid balance of the loan, the interest is highest at the start of the venture, before the loan has been substantially reduced by amortization payments. This is one of the reasons shelters often provide their greatest advantages in the early years. For example:

On January 1, 1982, a limited partnership owning an office building obtains a $100,000 loan, with an annual interest rate of 16% and a term of 10 years. For the sake of illustration, assume that instead of monthly payments, the loan provides for one payment of $20,000 to be made at the end of each year. At the end of 1982, since no payment had yet been made, the unpaid balance was still $100,000. Interest at 16% was therefore $16,000 [16% x $100,000], leaving $4,000 [$20,000 – $16,000] of the payment to go toward amortization. Thus, in 1982, $16,000 of the $20,000 payment made to the lender by the partnership was tax-deductible.

At the end of 1983, however, the unpaid balance of the loan has dropped to $96,000 [$100,000 – $4,000 amortization payment in 1982], reducing the interest portion of the 1983 payment to $15,360 [16% x $96,000] and raising the amortization portion to $4,640 [$20,000 – $15,360]. As the years pass, unless the loan is refinanced, more and more of the loan payment will thus become non-deductible.

As the permanent loan negotiations with the developer near completion, the lender will have an appraisal made of the property and proposed development plans. If satisfied, the lender will then issue its written commitment for the loan, specifying the terms and conditions under which it will be made. Often, the conditions will include completion of construction and achievement of a certain occupancy and/or rental income level within a given period of time. It is not uncommon for the commitment to provide for a portion of the loan ("floor") to be paid ("funded") when construction is completed, and the remainder ("ceiling") when the specified rental or income level is reached.

The permanent lender will generally charge a fee for issuing the commitment and arranging to make the funds available. Along with this "commitment fee" go closing costs and various other charges in connection with the loan, sometimes referred to as "points." These fees and charges are similar to those encountered in the purchase of a private home and may each equal as much as 1% or 2% of the loan. The points and closing costs may only be deducted in equal annual amounts over the term of the loan. However, there is some authority for deducting a portion or all of the commitment fee when paid, although this issue is not free of doubt.

Since a permanent loan usually will not fund until construction is completed, the developer must seek another loan to cover the actual costs of construction. This is appropriately referred to as a "construction loan," and is usually obtained from an institutional, or "construction lender." Until the permanent loan is funded, the construction loan will be secured by a first mortgage interest in the property. However, it will have a relatively short term, presumably just long enough to allow the builder to complete construction and achieve whatever rental or occupancy level is required for the funding of the permanent loan. Assuming this is accomplished, the money from the funding of the permanent loan will be used to repay the construction loan.

The interest on a construction loan is usually based on a sliding rate set a few percentage points above, but geared to fluctuate with, the prime rate of interest. Prime rate is the rate charged by a lending institution to its best credit borrowers. If the prime rate rises during construction, so will the interest on the construction loan. This is a possibility the developer must consider when estimating his construction costs. In the early seventies, and again in the last two years, many developers failed to do so, and when the prime rate rose quite suddenly and dramatically, they were left with insufficient funds to complete construction after paying the large interest costs on their loans. This resulted in many foreclosures and "work-out" situations, in which developers struggled desperately to avoid foreclosure, complete construction, and repay their debts. Many were forced to take in additional partners to raise more money and to induce lenders to temporarily modify either the terms of the loans or the interest charges. Others resorted to less prudent measures, like those employed by a certain developer of an apartment complex. This developer was involved, or rather, overextended, in several construction projects at the same time. The prime rate soared and almost doubled the anticipated interest rates charged on his construction loans. Short of cash and desperate, he used the loan proceeds from one apartment to meet the expenses of another. When the construction lender finally inspected his apartment site, it became apparent that a good portion of the loan proceeds had never reached it. The lender decided to pull the plug and foreclose. The investors who had been backing the developer had a problem: the developer was penniless and, therefore, a lawsuit against him would be fruitless.

Before leaving the discussion of construction loans, we should note that many states have so-called "usury laws", which set different limits on the amounts of interest that may be charged on loans to individuals, partnerships, and corporations. These laws generally allow a higher rate to be charged to corporations than to individuals or partnerships. Since the interest rate on construction loans may fluctuate, many construction lenders will lend only to corporations, in order to avoid violating the usury laws. Because investors in corporations (other than subchapter S) cannot use the corporation's tax benefits, partnerships and individuals sometimes enter into arrangements with a "nominee" corporation to take out a loan on their behalf. As we will see later when we discuss nominee corporations, this could have adverse tax consequences, depending upon the arrangement made between the corporation and the partnership or individual.

Ideally, though not usually, the construction loan will be large enough to buy the land; pay the commitment fee, points, and other costs of obtaining the permanent loan; complete construction; pay its own interest charges; meet operating expenses until the property is rented; and provide a profit for the developer, if he is able to keep his construction costs low. Usually, the loan will be funded in installments, or "draws," as construction progresses and monies are needed for labor, materials, and other expenses.

With the permanent and construction loans arranged, the developer will enter into the construction contracts (plumbing, roofing, electrical, etc.) necessary to complete the project. At this point, he might decide to attract investors by structuring the venture as a tax shelter. What he can offer are sizeable tax deductions generated by the project, which usually will not be fully offset by rental income until the project has been completed and rented for a number of years. For his own purposes, the developer might want investors for any of a number of reasons:

(1) If he is unable to obtain a construction loan large enough to meet all anticipated or contingent costs, he could obtain the additional funds from tax shelter investors.

(2) If the permanent loan is too small to repay the construction loan, again investors could provide the difference, filling the gap.

(3) If the permanent loan commitment provides for the funding of the floor upon completion of construction, with the ceiling funded upon rental achievement, if the floor is too small to repay the construction loan, invested funds could be used.

(4) If the developer is not interested in holding the project as a long-term investment, a pre-completion sale, or "pre-sale," would almost certainly assure him of a profit. Although he could probably command a better price if he completed and rented the project, a pre-sale would still provide him with a "bird in the hand" and probably save him some headaches.

(5) If the developer is involved in a number of projects, he may simply have more tax benefits available than he can use in the foreseeable future. By bringing in the tax shelter investors, he can "sell" some of his tax benefits for cash.

Whatever the reason or combination of reasons, if the developer is interested in attracting investors, or "syndicating the deal," he will now probably seek the assistance of a "syndicator."

Syndication

Generally, a syndicator is a person or group that specializes in organizing ventures such as real estate partnerships, structuring them to provide tax benefits, and locating and attracting investors. In a sense, the syndicator is the investors' representative, the middleman between the partnership and the developer. The investors depend upon his skill and experience in evaluating the property, negotiating the deal, and often overseeing its progress. In turn, the syndicator will want assurances from the developer that construction will be completed in a timely manner within the projected budget; that sufficient funds will remain to carry the venture until rental income is generated; and perhaps, even that the projected cash distributions will in fact be made.

The syndicator and the developer (who may be the same

person) together determine the amount of money to be raised from the investors, when and how it will be used, and what the investors will receive in return. Often, if the developer has not sold his entire interest in the venture, the two will serve as co-general partners, an arrangement that could offer important protection for the investors. Since the developer has undertaken certain obligations to the investors and the partnership, they can only benefit by having his actions checked by someone more inclined to represent their interests. As a general partner, the syndicator would be in a position to act quickly on their behalf, in case of a default or other problems.

If he is not himself an attorney, the syndicator will employ legal counsel for tax advice, to prepare the necessary agreements and prospectus ("offering memorandum"), and to file the documents required to comply with state and federal securities laws. An accounting firm might also be engaged to prepare the projections of the syndicator and developer as to the anticipated economic and tax results of the investment. The syndicator will then offer the limited partnership interests to prospective investors through a variety of channels including registered brokers, accountants, lawyers, business managers, financial consultants, or simply personal references. It is not uncommon for these people to receive fees or commissions, often in excess of 5% of the total investment, in return for producing or representing an investor. This, of course, raises the possibility that the investor's representative could have a conflict of interest. However, in most instances, state and federal laws require that representatives fully disclose any commission or other compensation they receive.

When the prospective investors have been located, they will be required to sign a subscription agreement or similar document, in which they not only agree to purchase the interest at the required price, but also declare that they have the ability to analyze the investment (or have consulted with someone who has the ability) and the requisite net worth to afford it. They will then be required to sign the certificate of limited partnership and the partnership agreement and usually to make a down payment on the investment and furnish promissory notes covering any future payments. Since real estate shelters often provide excess deductions over a period of years, the syndicator will attempt to match those payments with the deductions. However, this must be tempered by the financial needs of the venture for which the funds are earmarked.

If an investor should default on a future payment, the partnership could find itself short of funds to meet its obligations. Therefore, investors are usually required to provide security to the partnership with respect to future payments. Security can take the form of bonds, marketable stocks, or savings accounts, but letters of credit are probably the most common. A letter of credit provides that, should it become necessary, the banking institution that issued it will make the required payment on behalf of the investor at the time it is due. To obtain a letter of credit, the investor might have to pay the bank 1% or 2% of the amount in question and also furnish security to protect the bank, in case it is called upon to pay on the letter of credit.

The investors' capital is usually paid to a bank or law firm to be held in a separate trust or escrow account and used only for specified purposes. In order to protect the investors and to make sure the developer performs, the syndicator will often arrange for the disbursement of all or part of the invested funds in installments, based upon the progress of the venture. For example, if all the partners' payments and capital contributions total $1,000,000, the agreement between the syndicator and the developer might provide that $300,000 be paid upon completion of construction, $300,000 upon funding of the permanent loan, and the remaining $400,000 upon achievement of the specified rental or income level.

That completes financing. With the permanent loan, the construction loan, and the invested funds committed, the ground can be broken for construction.

Construction

The developer, general partner, or general contractor (all of whom may be the same person) now asks the construction lender to begin funding the construction loan. As we said, construction draws are usually paid as the project progresses to certain levels set and monitored by the lender. The first draw is often the "land draw," providing the funds needed to complete the purchase of the property. It may also cover interest charges, commitment fees, points, and other costs. Subsequent draws are made at various stages of development with a certain portion of the loan withheld for contingencies.

During the construction period, the venture is in the hands of a general contractor upon whose skill, experience, and financial strength the partnership must depend. He is responsible for purchasing material and hiring, firing, supervising, and coordinating the many subcontractors. He must assuage the harried electrician who is on a tight schedule but cannot begin work until the plumber is finished, when the plumber is delayed on a previous job due to material shortages, strikes, or bad weather. Situations like this can delay construction interminably, draining the resources and undermining the carefully balanced financing of the venture. It is essential that construction be completed expeditiously, for reasons such as the following:

(1) *Interest costs*—The longer the construction period, the longer the constrution loan is in effect. The longer the construction loan is in effect, the higher the interest costs and the less money available for construction and contingencies.

(2) *Terms of the construction loan*—Construction loans usually have relatively short terms, providing only enough time to complete construction and meet the requirements for funding of the permanent loan. If construction drags on and the due date passes, it could mean a default by the partnership and foreclosure on the property. On the other hand, it could simply mean an extension of the due date.

(3) *Loss of the permanent loan commitment*—Since permanent lenders must take provisions for having funds available to meet their obligations, most permanent loan commitments require that the conditions for funding be met within a specified period of time. If construction is delayed beyond that time, the partnership could lose its permanent loan commitment. This would probably be viewed as a default under the terms of the construction loan or, at least, would place the partnership in the position of having to get a new loan commitment. That means more commitment fees, etc., and less money for completion of construction. It could also mean a higher interest rate or shorter term on the permanent loan that is finally obtained.

(4) *Loss of tenants and rental income*—Often, in the case of real property such as office buildings and shopping centers, part of the space is "pre-leased," or rented prior to completion. However, it is generally agreed that tenants may terminate these leases if the project is not completed by a date agreed upon. Therefore, construction delays could mean the loss of tenants. They would also postpone the time rental income begins.

Clearly, the project must be completed quickly, but it must also be constructed well. If the contractors cut corners, skimp on quality, and fail to build according to plans and specifications, the consequences could be serious. First of all, they would probably violate the terms of the construction loan, the permanent loan commitment, and perhaps even local building codes. This could result in a default on the loan or could force the contractors to backtrack to correct the deficiencies, thus wasting more time and money. Poor construction also inevitably means higher repair, replacement, and maintenance costs, and could even result in rejection by the tenants—all of which would lower or eliminate future profits.

No matter how skillful and diligent the general contractor, he is still only human. Therefore, certain safeguards on his performance are often available to the partners. As we said, the construction lender will usually keep a close watch on the project, conducting inspections as draw requests come in, to determine whether the required progress has been made. Progress might also be monitored by the syndicator, architect, permanent lender, and tenants. Additionally, for a fee, the developer and/or general contractor might offer personal guarantees that construction will be properly completed, no matter what contingencies arise. If they are financially sound and responsible, this could mean they will supply any extra cash that is needed. In some cases, they may be bonded, which means their performance will be guaranteed by an independent bonding company. The mere fact that a bond can be obtained is some evidence of their financial stability.

In the event of a problem, someone must be in a position to act on behalf of the partnership, either to solve it or to enforce the guarantees. If there is only one general partner, and he is also the developer and general contractor, a conflict of interests would clearly exist. The general partner, especially if financially pressed, would be reluctant, to say the least, to enforce obligations against himself. If he defaults, who would then replace him, seek redress, and see the job through? Certainly not the limited partners, who usually have neither the experience nor inclination (this could also end their limited liability). Ideally, the syndicator will have the ability and commitment to act, which is all the more reason for him to be a co-general partner unaffiliated with the developer.

As a further safeguard, ventures can be structured so that invested funds, or some portion of them, are not disbursed until completion occurs. That way invested money is not placed at-risk and can serve as a "contingency fund" to help deal with any problems.

Let us assume construction is completed. With the project ready for tenants, the venture now enters into its rent-up and operating period.

Rent-Up and Operation

All efforts are now directed at renting the available space. Once again, speed and quality are the objectives. Speed is necessary to reach the rental or income levels required to fund the permanent loan and repay the construction loan. Also during this period, the partnership will be running up bills for items such as payroll, advertising, real estate taxes, insurance, maintenance, utilities, etc., and the early receipt of rental income could help alleviate financial pressures and permit a more selective and profitable rental program. In the case of commercial properties especially, this would mean the signing of "quality" tenants (for example, well-known chain and department stores or major corporations) who would be unlikely to default and who might attract other prospective tenants.

The success of the rental program depends both on the quality and location of the project and the effectiveness of its management. At this point, the general partners might decide to bring in a manager or management company to supervise the renting, day-to-day operations, and maintenance of the property. For an annual fee usually based on a fixed amount, a percentage of the gross rental income, commissions for leases signed, or some combination of these, the manager would direct the rental program, hiring and firing personnel, paying bills, collecting rent, making repairs, purchasing insurance, and keeping the books and records for accounting and tax purposes. The manager may or may not be affiliated with the general partner, general contractor, or developer but, as you can probably guess, we suggest that if he is not independent, one of the other general partners be unaffiliated with him and experienced in real estate ventures. This is particularly important if the manager is involved in potentially competing ventures in the same area. In many instances, for a fee, he will refrain from competing for a period of time.

As in the construction phase, the expenses during rent-up could substantially exceed the income and perhaps even the financial resources of the partnership. To protect against this, it is possible (again, of course, for a fee) to obtain the personal guarantees of the developer and/or manager to provide any additional funds, either as a loan or contribution, needed to meet the expenses of the period. If they are financially sound or if part of their compensation is withheld, this could mean significant protection for the partnership.

While the skill of the manager in renting the space and keeping expenses low is critical, success is also a function of the location, price, quality, special features, and amenities of the project, compared to those of other ventures in the area. Sometimes, no matter how competitive the property is, it may be necessary to grant rent reductions and concessions to attract initial tenants.

If the rent-up program is successful, rental income should exceed expenditures, leaving a reserve fund for contingencies and a cash surplus, or "cash flow," for distribution to the partners. As you recall from our discussion of partnership taxation, to the extent these distributions do not exceed adjusted basis, they may be tax-free. Assuming the property is well maintained and efficiently managed, cash flow should continue for many years. As the property increases in value and the mortgage loan is amortized, at some point the partnership will be faced with a decision: either take advantage of the inflated value of the property by selling it for a profit, or stay in business and seek refinancing of the permanent mortgage loan.

Sale or Refinancing

A real estate shelter must be viewed as a long-term investment, for both tax and economic reasons. Tax-wise, many of the early benefits could be lost, or "recaptured," if the property or partnership interest is sold prematurely. Economically, it will be a long time before the entire investment, or even a major portion of it, is recouped, even though shortly after completion and rent-up the investor in a successful venture should begin receiving tax-free distributions.

On the other hand, as the years pass, real estate tends to increase in value, while the mortgage debt decreases. These factors make it possible, approximately 10 to 15 years into the lifetime of a venture, to raise the funds for a return of investment, and even sizeable profit, by selling the property, refinancing the permanent mortgage loan, or perhaps selling a partnership interest.

Sale of a partnership interest is probably the least viable

alternative. First of all, to preserve the character of the partnership, most partnership agreements restrict the right of the limited partners to sell without the consent of the general partners. Even then, with the majority of the tax benefits utilized by the investor in the early years, the marketability of the interest is diminished, and the tax consequences of the sale could be serious.

Sale of the property for an amount greater than the outstanding mortgage loan is a much more attractive possibility. Such a sale could leave the partnership with enough money, after repaying the balance of the loan and other debts, to make a substantial cash return to the investors. Naturally, the gain on the sale would be taxable income to the partners, but a portion (or all) of it should be taxed at the more favorable capital gains rate. Sale of the property, however, would terminate the partnership's business activities and the partnership would be dissolved.

An alternative to sale is refinancing of the permanent mortgage loan. This could mean either obtaining a new long-term loan large enough to repay the balance of the existing one, or extending or renewing the existing loan. To be most effective, refinancing should occur at a time when the original loan has been sufficiently amortized so there will be a cash surplus from the new loan for distribution to the partners. For example, if a $1,000,000 loan has been amortized to $950,000 and a new $1,000,000 loan is obtained, $50,000 would remain for distribution to the partners, after paying off the $950,000 balance. Furthermore, since the funds are derived from a loan rather than from income, the distribution should be non-taxable. This is one of the major benefits of refinancing. The other is that the partnership is still in the real estate business, generating cash flow.

Since the tax and economic consequences of sale or refinancing differ significantly for the limited partners, it is important that their consent be obtained before either action is taken. Often, the limited partners will have a priority with respect to distributions. However, since the general partners are responsible for initiating and controlling sale or refinancing efforts, it could aid these efforts if the general partners had some kind of financial incentive.

Ideally, a real estate project will progress as a successful business venture to a profitable sale or refinancing. Unfortunately, not all ventures are successful. When they fail, the adverse tax and economic consequences are usually triggered by a foreclosure.

Foreclosure

Many factors can plunge a venture into financial trouble: construction delays, rising material and utility costs, poor management, major repairs, changes in the rental market, etc. In theory, the general partners will be resourceful, experienced, and motivated enough to avert or correct any problems, without too much drain on the partnership's resources. Otherwise, lack of funds could force the partnership to default on its loan payments, thus causing the lender to foreclose on the mortgage. A mortgage is a written document which pledges the partnership's property as security for the loan. It generally provides that, in the event of default, the lender can go to court to claim possession of the property, which will then be sold to repay as much of the loan as possible. If the proceeds of the sale are insufficient for full repayment, the lender can then go after any guarantors to cover the balance. Fortunately, in the case of real estate ventures, the loans are usually non-recourse—which means the partners are not personally liable for any portion of repayment. Still, foreclosure means loss of investment, compounded by tax consequences, which as we shall see later, can be costly and severe.

"Used" Property

Much of the preceding discussion has focused on constructing new real estate projects from scratch. However, in times of high construction costs and/or high interest rates, new construction may not be economically feasible. It may make more sense to acquire an existing project if an attractive price and/or favorable financing terms can be worked out with the current owner.

Under prior law, ownership of a new project often produced much greater tax benefits in the early years than did ownership of used property. However, under the Economic Recovery Tax Act of 1981, not only are the basic tax benefits of owning a real estate project virtually the same whether the project is new or used, but there are also tax credits that are available only to certain used projects. These will be explored in detail in the next chapter. Suffice it for now to say that many of the concepts and cautions contained in this chapter apply also to used property.

We have covered the major elements, possibilities, and results of real estate ventures in general. We shall now go over the different kinds of real estate again, from an economic point of view, with an eye toward evaluating each as a potential investment.

CHAPTER VII
Types of Real Estate

Residential Real Estate

One of the objectives of government is to provide or encourage the development of adequate housing for all of its people. Therefore, real estate ventures, including tax shelters, involving multi-family apartment dwellings for rental purposes are generally afforded favorable treatment under the tax laws. Projects geared to the less privileged may also be eligible for government-sponsored economic benefits, such as favorable mortgage loan financing and rental subsidies, and, as in the case of low-to-middle income renovations, higher initial tax deductions.

On the basis of the different tax and economic consequences arising from government policy, we have divided residential real estate into three types of investment: conventional projects, or those without direct government assistance; federally financed or subsidized housing; and ventures involving the renovation of existing structures.

Conventional Residential Investments

Conventional projects must succeed on their own merits without federal aid. Therefore, it is especially important that they be thoroughly well-conceived, that is, well-located, well-designed, properly constructed, efficiently managed, and economically sound. These factors can and should be carefully analyzed before any investment is made. Here are some of the major points to cover:

Location: When building or purchasing an apartment property, location is key. A populated area, economically strong, with high occupancy levels and a need for more housing is a good place to start. This type of information is usually provided in the prospectus, or is readily available from the syndicator. Look for things like local industry, major stores and shopping centers, schools, churches, recreation facilities, and other indications of stability. Note the occupancy levels and rental rates of comparable projects in the area. Make sure there is sufficient and diverse commercial activity to ensure steady jobs and attract potential residents. If an area is dominated by one company or industry, there is always the danger of an economic slump that could send tenants packing in search of better employment opportunities.

Never rely solely on information that is handed to you. Seek out other, more objective sources, such as the independent appraisal of the property made for the permanent lender. This should provide an economic evaluation of the neighborhood, including population, occupancy rates, and neighborhood and area trends, which could be helpful in evaluating the potential of the venture. Remember, the building will be around for a long time, and neighborhoods can change. The one you are considering should be headed toward economic growth which, over the years, will increase property values and provide the opportunity for a profitable sale or refinancing.

Even the appraisal should be independently verified by the investor or his advisor. Cross checks are easily made through local chambers of commerce, realty boards, or by asking a personal bank to contact an affiliated bank in the area. Read the real estate pages of local newspapers; they can be surprisingly revealing about the rental market and leasing activity in the area. So can local real estate agents, brokers, and bankers. If possible, inspect the site, not only to get a firsthand look at the property and a feel for the neighborhood, but also to check out the competition and the local reputation of your contractor and manager. You should also be aware of any other new construction, either planned or under way, which could provide additional competition, or possibly oversaturate the market.

When evaluating an area, don't completely discount intuition and foresight. A case in point is a southwestern developer who decided to erect a garden apartment complex smack in the middle of a totally unpopulated but highly industrial area. He took a chance on his belief that people would rather live close to where they work. Despite the fact that he ignored many of the accepted criteria for selecting a residential site, 3 weeks after completion the entire complex was rented.

Design: Once you are satisfied with the location of the project, consider the design to determine whether it will fit into the community and be competitive. Architecturally and aesthetically, it should reflect the tastes and needs of the residents. It should also offer the amenities provided by comparable projects in the area. If they boast swimming pools, tennis courts, clubhouses, terraces, washers and dryers, etc., your project could go unrented without them.

Also important are the size and mix of units. Size refers to the number of square feet of rentable space, not the number of rooms. Naturally, if the apartments are small in comparison to the competition, they will be rentable only at lower rates. On the other hand, if they are too large, the high cost of building and maintaining them could necessitate rental charges that are not competitive. Incidentally, rent per square foot provides a valuable way of comparing the rental rates of similar ventures with variations in the size of apartments.

The mix of apartments, or the number and type of rooms within the units, can also be significant. One-bedroom units, attract different kinds of tenants than two-bedroom units, and two-bedroom units with two baths are generally more desirable than two-bedroom, one-bath arrangements. Again it becomes important to understand the needs and tastes of the neighborhood. Don't rely solely on overall occupancy levels which, alone, can be deceiving. Check the mix of units being rented by competitors; you may find the vacancy rates on certain types of apartments prohibitive.

The number of units can also be a factor in the performance of the venture. Too few can be inefficient, from both construction and management points of view, since there are certain fixed expenses, regardless of the number of units built or rented. On the other hand, too many units can oversaturate the area, inhibiting rent-up and draining the resources of the venture. If a large project is planned, it might be wise to construct it in phases, moving on only as each successive one is completed and rented.

One last design consideration has become increasingly significant in the past few years, as a result of the energy situation and ensuing hike in utility costs. Before that, it was not uncommon for building owners, especially in the southwest, to assume the cost of utilities. Now, however, the trend is clearly toward tenants paying their own utility bills. It is important to examine the market in your area. If other owners are assuming utility costs, you may have to also. Still, in the case of new construction, it would be wise to have the building designed for easy installation of separate or sub-metering. This would save considerable expense at a later time, if it is determined that the market could accept conversion to individual utility payments.

Construction: High-quality construction is crucial to the success of the venture. In this respect, you are largely dependent upon the ability, integrity, and possibly even the financial strength of the developer and contractor. Presumably, you have already checked them out through banks and local references. If the project is well-constructed, it will not only be more desirable, but less likely to run up future maintenance costs, which could greatly erode profits and increase operating deficits. Most managers will set aside a certain portion of each year's rental income as a reserve fund for repairs and replacements that arise naturally with time, wear, and tear. However, if poor construction results in premature expenses, the fund could be insufficient and the venture may find itself in trouble. To avoid this, many syndicators acquire commitments from the developer or contractor guaranteeing the quality of construction. Naturally, the degree of protection offered by these guarantees is only as great as the financial strength of the guarantors.

Operation: When evaluating a residential real estate project, construction costs, occupancy levels, and rental rates mean little without a realistic estimate of the day-to-day operating expenses of the venture. If you are acquiring an existing, operating property, the best indication of expenses is the prior year's financial statement and operating figures. If you are considering new property, planned or under construction, the costs projected by the developer should be verified by a comparative analysis of the actual experiences of similar ventures in the area.

Certain operating expenses are "fixed expenses" and thus can easily be ascertained or predicted. Others vary with local conditions and factors affecting the venture as well as certain broad economic trends. Fixed expenses include items such as real estate taxes, debt service (interest and amortization payments), and insurance. Real estate tax rates can be easily obtained from local taxing authorities. Insurance costs and debt service are generally set by contract, as are other fixed expenses such as trash removal, landscaping, furniture rental, and elevator maintenance. Variable expenses include telephone, postage, repairs, maintenance, supplies, cleaning, legal, accounting, advertising, rent, commissions, painting, utilities, etc. Again, when analyzing a new property, these can best be estimated by researching similar projects in the area. Also consider management fees, which are usually based upon a percentage of the gross rental income. Five percent (5%) is not uncommon in many areas. Sometimes, key management and maintenance employees are also given rent-free apartments or rate reductions, in lieu of higher salaries.

On the positive side, don't forget that, in addition to rental payments, you can expect income from sources such as parking, vending and washing machines, furniture rentals, forfeited security deposits, and pool and other recreational dues. These receivables can be quite significant and should not be overlooked.

Federally-Financed or Subsidized Housing

In an effort to stimulate the construction of adequate multifamily housing for low- and middle-income residents, Congress enacted legislation enabling the Department of Housing and Urban Development (HUD) to insure mortgage loans and, in some cases, provide rental subsidies for qualifying properties. Under one of the federal programs, lenders are authorized to grant loans of up to 90% of the cost of the property, with the government guaranteeing repayment. This is a far greater ratio of equity to borrowed capital than is generally available to conventional projects. These loans are further enhanced by favorable terms for repayment, often 40 years. The tax advantages and leverage afforded by this type of financing are obvious when you consider that, although the investors are putting up only 10% of the cost of the property (with the rest being supplied by a non-recourse loan), they are getting the benefit of an ACRS deduction based upon the full cost. This could mean initial deductions far greater than the funds actually invested.

The government may also subsidize low-income projects by providing financial assistance to tenants and owners in the form of rental subsidies. The direct subsidy program, called the Section 8 Program after a provision of the United States Housing Act, often involves state participation in the financing of the projects. A state housing authority may provide the construction and permanent loans, again in an amount up to 90% of the cost of the property. The funds provided by the state authority are often raised through the sale of tax-exempt housing bonds, with the interest received from the mortgage loans being used to pay interest to the bondholders. Usually, interest rates on these loans are quite competitive and, again, the term for repayment is often 40 years. Concurrently, HUD will enter into an agreement with the state authority to provide rental subsidies.

To qualify for rental assistance, the apartments must be rented to low-to-moderate-income famillies, so designated on the basis of the median income of the community in which the project is located. The maximum rent for each apartment is predetermined, with the tenants required to pay not more than 30% of their annual family income toward it. Very low-income families, or those with other serious financial problems, may have to pay only 15%. The rest is paid with funds supplied by HUD.

The price extracted for these benefits is generally a limitation on rental rates which has the effect of minimizing cash returns to the investors. Additionally, consent of the state authority or HUD is usually required to sell the property or refinance the mortgage loan.

The tax benefits available as a result of federal housing programs and the leverage afforded by large, federally-sponsored mortgage loans offer attractive incentives to investors. However, these projects are not only subject to all the construction and renting risks of conventionally-financed projects, but are also limited in their potential for annual returns and profits on sale or refinancing. Therefore, investments in federally-financed or subsidized housing are most attractive to those seeking immediate tax relief, rather than future gain.

Renovation of Existing Properties

When an existing apartment property is acquired, depending upon its age and physical condition, certain repairs and renovations are to be expected. If the property has been well-maintained, a face-lifting may be all that is necessary. Naturally, however, a well-maintained, successful property will be more costly to acquire than abandoned or rundown buildings in less than prime areas.

Since urban renewal is another goal of government, there are certain tax advantages connected with the renovation of low-to-middle-income residential projects. But first, let us consider the economics. The potential advantages of these types of projects are well-illustrated by the experience of a certain developer who acquired, and accomplished a major renovation on, 200 apartment units in a low-income area of a large southwestern city. The total cost of acquiring and renovating the property, including syndication costs, was $1,700,000, of which $1,000,000 was supplied by mortgage loan and $700,000 by investors. This amounts to a cost per apartment unit of $8,500 [$1,700,000 ÷ 200] which is less than half the amount it would have cost to erect 200 new units on the same site. This lower cost enabled the developer to establish rental rates well within the means of the low-income residents of the area and, as a result, to rent-up fast.

As for the tax benefits, the owners of residential property leased to qualified low-to-middle-income tenants are permitted (in lieu of the ACRS deduction) to deduct the costs of renovation over a 5-year period. This results in substantially greater tax benefits in the early years than if the costs were deducted via ACRS.

In addition, renovation of property which is at least 30 years old, and which will be used for commercial (as opposed to residential) purposes after the rehabilitation, can result in a tax *credit* equal to 15% of the cost of the rehabilitation. For buildings 40 (or more) years old, the credit is 20%. Rehabilitation of a building which is classified as "historic" can yield a tax credit of 25% of the cost of rehabilitation, whether the building is to be used for commercial or residential purposes. As you can imagine, initial tax benefits can soar as a result of any of these tax allowances. Furthermore, if the city in which the property is located is dedicated to rebuilding its urban areas, the project could be eligible for additional benefits, such as city tax abatements and other incentives.

If the renovation program is successful, property values in the area can be expected to rise, and those who purchased and renovated projects at relatively low costs will be in a position to reap substantial cash returns through sale or refinancing. On the other hand, there are certain risks associated with this type of property, as well as specialized management factors that should be considered. For example, if vandalism is a problem in the area, security, insurance, and maintenance costs could be significant, draining operating capital and profits. Or, if the economic recovery efforts of the area fail to gather momentum, property values could remain low or drop even further than before.

Commercial Real Estate

There are similarities between commercial and residential real estate ventures, but also significant differences with respect to construction, rent-up, operation, and tax treatment. Even then, within the broad category of commercial ventures there are different types of properties, including office buildings, shopping centers, hotels, motels, warehouses and factories, each with specific characteristics which we shall now explore.

Office Buildings

Once an office building is constructed and successfully rented, it will probably have fewer operating problems than a residential project since generally fewer services are provided and the tenant turnover rate is lower. To get to that point, however, the building must meet the same requirements as outlined for residential projects. To reiterate, it must be well-located, well-designed, properly constructed, and efficiently and effectively managed.

It is important for an office building to be placed where it will be convenient and desirable for potential tenants; ideally, in the heart of the business district of a community with high occupancy levels and rental rates. Once again, the developer and syndicator will provide information about the area, rental market, and competing properties, which should be verified in much the same manner as described before. The occupancy levels and rental rates of competing ventures should be scrutinized. The size of the business community and its ability to absorb additional office space should also be considered, as should any plans for new, possibly competing buildings in the area.

Naturally, many of the rent-up problems can be eliminated if all or a substantial portion of the building is "pre-leased," or rented prior to completion. Even then, unless the tenants are financially strong, it would be safer to locate the project in an area that could provide back-up tenants if necessary. In a recent situation, a substantial tenant of a small office building went into bankruptcy and vacated his office space. The rental market in the area was weak at the time and it took many months for the space to be re-rented. Fortunately, the venture had sufficient cash reserves to cover expenses during the lean period.

The design of the project again is of key importance in attracting tenants. Make sure it appeals to the needs and tastes of the business community and that there is adequate parking for tenants and their visitors.

Construction should be sound and fast. Generally, if the building is not of good quality, higher maintenance and repairs could result and quickly consume profits. In the case of office buildings, which are often pre-leased, construction must also meet the specifications of the tenants and be completed within the time limits specified in the leases. Failure to comply could mean the loss of tenants and possibly even monetary penalties or rental concessions in their favor.

As a general rule, when construction costs are estimated, provisions should be made for funds to cover operating expenses until sufficient rental income is generated. This includes items such as commissions for real estate brokers or rental agents employed to locate tenants. With office buildings, there is the added expense of alterations and improvements, such as partitions, painting, carpeting, etc., required by prospective tenants. If construction or rent-up is protracted, the funds reserved for these expenses could be quickly consumed by the fixed expenses, such as real estate taxes, interest, and insurance, which continue whether or not the building is rented. In a situation like that, you are dependent upon the ability and financial strength of the developer, as well as the foresight of the syndicator. A group of investors learned this several years ago, in a venture involving the construction of a moderate-sized office building in a successful office park. The syndicator of the deal was aware that with office buildings, like most real estate projects, there are certain critical financial periods that must be weathered. First, there is the construction period, when delays, price increases, and fixed expenses can drain resources. Then there is the rent-up, with the attendant costs and expenses of tenant alterations. With these in mind, the syndicator negotiated a package of agreements with the developer and others guaranteeing completion of construction, funding of the permanent loan, and successful rent-up. The developer, who was quite active in the area, also agreed not to start any competing buildings for a 2-year period, to give this venture a jump on the market. The price of the package was $600,000, to be paid in $200,000 installments; one upon completion of construction, one upon landing of the permanent mortgage loan; and the last upon achievement of 90% occupancy at projected rent levels. The $600,000 was obtained from investors, in payments timed to coincide with the payments due the developer.

The syndicator realized that by holding the investors' money in reserve, he would establish a fund to use in case the developer or builder was caught short of cash during the critical periods. It was fortunate that he did so, because construction was delayed by unusually poor weather. By the time the project was completed, the rental market had grown soft as a result of a financial slump in the area's major industry. The developer's plan to construct and rent-up quickly, with sufficient funds remaining from the construction loan to pay for rental commissions, tenant alterations, and operating expenses, fell apart. Fortunately, the permanent lender consented to fund the permanent loan upon completion of construction, waiving the occupancy requirement, and thus relieving some of the pressure by providing the funds to repay the construction loan. However, as rent-up continued to drag, under the weight of the fixed expenses, the venture was soon unable to meet its mortgage payments. That is when the final $200,000 held in reserve by the syndicator became important.

That $200,000 provided the money for debt service during the critical period, as well as for tenant alterations. It also helped induce the permanent lender to temporarily scale down the mortgage payments. Fortunately, the lender realized he had nothing to gain from foreclosure (especially since the loan was nonrecourse) and was willing to work with the venture. The project is now gradually struggling back to health, thanks to the commitment of the developer, the tolerance of the lender, and the $200,000 of the syndicator.

One last point: office buildings generally deal in relatively long-term leases, say 3 to 5 years, with options to renew. Since operating expenses such as taxes, utilities, labor, and insurance are likely to increase with time and inflation, it is essential that provisions be included in the leases for raising rents proportionately. Usually, these adjustments will be made on a yearly basis.

Once they are rented, well-run office buildings in economically stable or growing areas can be lucrative investments, with great potential for sale or refinancing.

Warehouses and Factories

Special-purpose buildings such as warehouses and factories are similar in many ways to office buildings, except that only one tenant is involved and the rental market for replacement tenants is limited by the nature of the building—unless, of course, the owner is willing and able to undertake substantial renovations. Shopping centers, on the other hand, are very different endeavors, as we shall now see.

Shopping Centers

Shopping centers thrive on shoppers and so, to be successful, they should be located near a populated, residential area. They should be easily accessible by car, which suggests placement adjacent to a major thoroughfare or, even better at or near the crossroads of a well-traveled intersection. Furthermore, since they require large areas of land to provide adequate parking for the Saturday multitudes, they must be located in sectors where land costs are reasonable.

While competition is a fear of most real estate ventures, shopping center owners often relish the thought of the increased traffic other centers can bring to an area, to the benefit of all merchants. Construction is also simpler, and thus less of a problem. In addition, many of the building services required by apartments and offices are not required in shopping centers and so, operating expenses are lower and management less complicated.

Usually, the developer will select an area or site, then seek, or be sought by, an "anchor" tenant. The anchor should be the type of store that will draw traffic into the area, such as a major department store, supermarket, or home improvement center. Adjacent space will become more desirable to merchants hoping to cash in on the overflow of customers. These tenants, sometimes referred to as "local" tenants, will usually rent smaller space, for shorter terms (2 to 3 years); at greater rental rates per square foot. Often, they will provide the developer with his margin of profit.

The anchor tenant will rent a larger area, for a longer term (15 to 20 years), at a lower per-square-foot rate. However, it is not unusual for the lease to provide for additional rental payments, called overage rent, if a specified volume of sales are made by the tenant during the year. The lease may also require that the anchor assume a certain portion of the maintenance charges, as well as increases in real estate taxes and insurance.

Most shopping centers are designed either as "strip centers," which are the familiar rows of stores that line so many thoroughfares, or shopping "malls." Usually, the design is uncomplicated, as is the construction. Still, it is crucial that the time limits for completion of the project required by the tenant leases and mortgage loan commitment be met, and that the center be built according to the specifications of the tenants and lender. One of the most serious problems a center can face is the loss of its anchor tenant. Many owners discovered this recently when a major chain went into Chapter 11 (bankruptcy) and was forced to abandon most of its locations. As a general rule, anchor tenants should have the best credit rating possible; "AAA rating" is what to look for in a prospectus.

In spite of the risks, shopping centers leased to financially sound tenants can be stable, easily-managed investments, which can appreciate significantly in value with time.

Hotels and Motels

With the vast array of amenities and services included in their operations, hotels and, to a lesser extent, motels differ significantly from other types of real estate ventures. In addition to the usual maintenance and management services, they must provide dining facilities, linen and maid service, beauty shops, snack bars, and a full range of leisure activities, such as swimming, tennis, golf, boating, and nightclub entertainment. As a result, construction is often more complicated and expensive; management is more demanding; and labor, equipment, maintenance, and other operating expenses are higher.

When considering a hotel or motel property, location is of key importance. Since you are seeking to attract lodgers who are primarily vacationers, tourists, and business travelers, it would be best if the venture were set either on a well-traveled route, near an airport or train station, in a resort area, or perhaps near a business center. Such areas are usually prime, which means land costs are likely to be high.

Construction can range from relatively simple and inexpensive, as in the case of a small motel, to vast, complex, and costly, as with a luxury resort hotel. Construction and pre-operation costs now will include items such as furniture, carpeting, linens, TV's, restaurant equipment, and accessories for the activities offered. The developer will also have to allow for greater advertising, operating, and labor costs, as well as unforeseen contingencies that may arise during the period immediately following construction, when vacancy rates are likely to be high and operations not yet perfected.

A market study will usually be available from the developer, indicating the occupancy levels, room rates, and operating costs of comparable ventures in the area, as well as any seasonal fluctuations to be encountered. Monies earned in the high seasons will have to be set aside to meet expenses during the low.

Because of the complexity of the operations, the skill and experience of the manager become all the more important in a hotel or motel deal. Not only must he efficiently and effectively administer the staff and all the activities of the venture, but he must direct the advertising and other programs aimed at attracting customers. You want a manager with a strong reputation and a record of past successes in similar types of ventures, backed by an equally reliable developer and syndicator.

Once the hotel or motel is established, or if it is part of a well-known chain, word-of-mouth and referrals should keep its occupancy level high. Over the years, if construction is of high quality and management the same, the property should yield lucrative returns while it steadily appreciates in value.

Ground Leases

An additional financing possibility with all types of real estate ventures is for the developer and/or partnership not to purchase the land outright, but to lease it on a long-term basis. Under these "ground leases," the developer has the right to build and operate a venture on the property. In return, the landowner receives fixed rental payments, and in most cases, bonus payments or "overage" rent if yearly earnings exceed a specified level. Sometimes, the developer will first buy the property, then sell it and simultaneously lease it back, in what is called a "sale-leaseback" arrangement. In any case, if the term of the lease is long enough (many exceed 50 years), the venture should be able to recoup its investment from annual returns and, eventually, from the sale of the leasehold interest, or refinancing of the mortgage loan. Naturally, the longer the term of the lease, the better the possibility for sale, since a purchaser would be buying the right to use the property for the duration of the lease, and thus would be interested only if enough time remained for him to recoup his investment.

From a developer's point of view, a ground lease or sale-leaseback can be viewed as a type of financing, since it spares him the cash drain that would result from the purchase of the land. This leaves virtually all of the proceeds of the mortgage loan to be devoted to actual construction and pre-operation costs. Occasionally, the owner of the land will also be the permanent mortgage lender. This gives the lender the two-fold benefit of a greater return on his money than could be obtained at prevailing interest rates (especially if there is an overage rent provision) and ownership of the project when the lease expires.

When evaluating a ground lease, look for any restrictions on the use of the land and at the rights of the lessor in the event of default. Also be sure that any overage rent provisions do not preclude the possibility of greater profits, or any profits at all. In a recent situation, the ground lease provided for additional rent payments to be made when the venture's gross receipts topped a certain level. Eventually they did, but operating expenses also increased significantly. As a result, it took all the venture's cash flow just to meet costs and overage rent charges, leaving no return for the investors.

Now, on to taxes . . .

CHAPTER VIII
Real Estate: The Tax Aspects

You know now that tax shelters are essentially business ventures structured to combine and maximize the tax incentives and allowances permitted by the Code. You also know that the benefits of these ventures can be passed on to you, the investor, given the proper organization. And you know that real estate offers certain advantages as a tax shelter activity which are not available to other types of enterprises.

Given a variety of real estate investments—all solid and economically promising—your tax needs might well determine the type of property you choose. For just as the different kinds of projects differ economically, they also have different tax results. In the following section, we will explain how the provisions of the Code apply to each kind of real property. You will see that there are "rules within the rules," affecting the magnitude and timing of the benefits.

The tax benefits offered by well-structured real estate ventures generally take two forms: cash returns on investment, which can be tax-free for many years; and substantial excess deductions and credits, which can offset an investor's income from other sources and reduce or even eliminate his income tax bill. These benefits are the result of a combination of allowances, the most significant of which are: the ACRS deduction; the investment tax credit; and the so-called soft costs.

"Soft" costs are those expenses which generally are deductible when paid, such as "ordinary and necessary" business expenses, taxes, and, most significantly with respect to real estate, interest on mortgage loans. "Hard" costs are usually related to the cost of acquiring an asset, such as material and labor, and are deductible over a period of years as part of the ACRS deduction.

Accelerated Cost Recovery in Real Estate

One of the great advantages of real estate shelters is the ability to leverage relatively small amounts of invested capital into large ACRS deductions. As you recall, these deductions are permitted by the Code to enable investors to recover the cost of business or investment-related property, regardless of whether there has been an actual decline in value as a result of wear and tear or obsolescence.

In real estate, the building and its components (i.e., heating, plumbing, electrical wiring, etc.), as well as any personal property used in connection with the venture (i.e., business machines, furniture, fixtures, etc.), are considered cost recovery assets. The cost of land, which is not subject to wear and tear or obsolescence, may not be recovered under ACRS. In analyzing a project, particularly a used property, be sure there has been a reasonable allocation of costs between land and buildings. Sometimes a very small amount of the cost of a project will be allocated to land, although the land is quite valuable. In such a case, the IRS may reallocate a much greater portion of the project's cost to the land, substantially reducing ACRS deductions for the buildings.

The ACRS deduction for an asset is computed on the basis of its cost. For purposes of ACRS, cost means only "hard" costs attributable to construction or purchase, such as labor or material, rather than the "soft" costs, such as interest or taxes. Cost is in no way limited by the amount of money actually invested; it includes borrowed funds—loans, non-recourse or otherwise—which generally account for a major portion of the cost.

As noted earlier, the Accelerated Cost Recovery System eliminates the requirement that the useful life of an asset be estimated in order to compute the annual depreciation allowance. The bias in favor of new buildings—they could be depreciated faster than used buildings under the old rules—has also been eliminated. Instead, all real estate—new or used, commercial or residential—is assigned a 15-year cost recovery period. The percentage of the cost that is deductible each year is determined simply by glancing at a table prepared by the IRS. These tables, one for low-income housing and one for all other real property, appear on pp. 93 and 94. As you can see, the deductible percentage for low-income housing is slightly higher for about the first six years.

Here is an example of how the ACRS allowance is computed. Refer to Chart A. If construction on a new office building is completed and it is ready to be rented in June of 1982, 7% of the cost of the building may be deducted that year. This is determined by referring to the sixth vertical column, which corresponds to June, the month the property was placed in service, and the first horizontal column, indicating the first recovery year. Continuing down to the second recovery year, 1983, 11% of the cost may be deducted. Allowable cost recovery deductions for later years are computed simply by continuing down the same column on the table, which corresponds to the month the property was originally placed in service.

One further note: instead of using the percentages listed in these tables, a taxpayer may elect to use straight-line cost recovery, over a period of either 15, 35, or 45 years. Ultimately, if the property is owned for a long period of time, the total of the ACRS deductions will be the same no matter what method is used. The difference is that under the straight-line method the cost will be recovered in equal annual amounts over the period chosen, whereas with the 15-year tables, which are based on "accelerated methods," greater deductions will be available in the early years of use, and lesser deductions in the later years.

CHART A
ACRS Cost Recovery Tables for Real Estate
All Real Estate (Except Low-Income Housing)

If the Recovery Year Is:	The applicable percentage is: (Use the Column for the Month in the First Year the Property Is Placed in Service)											
	1	2	3	4	5	6	7	8	9	10	11	12
1	12	11	10	9	8	7	6	5	4	3	2	1
2	10	10	11	11	11	11	11	11	11	11	11	12
3	9	9	9	9	10	10	10	10	10	10	10	10
4	8	8	8	8	8	8	9	9	9	9	9	9
5	7	7	7	7	7	7	8	8	8	8	8	8
6	6	6	6	6	7	7	7	7	7	7	7	7
7	6	6	6	6	6	6	6	6	6	6	6	6
8	6	6	6	6	6	6	5	6	6	6	6	6
9	6	6	6	6	5	6	5	5	5	6	6	6
10	5	6	5	6	5	5	5	5	5	5	6	5
11	5	5	5	5	5	5	5	5	5	5	5	5
12	5	5	5	5	5	5	5	5	5	5	5	5
13	5	5	5	5	5	5	5	5	5	5	5	5
14	5	5	5	5	5	5	5	5	5	5	5	5
15	5	5	5	5	5	5	5	5	5	5	5	5
16	—	—	1	1	2	2	3	3	4	4	4	5

CHART B
ACRS Cost Recovery Tables for Real Estate
Low-Income Housing

If the Recovery Year Is:	The applicable percentage is: (Use the Column for the Month in the First Year the Property Is Placed in Service) 1	2	3	4	5	6	7	8	9	10	11	12
1	13	12	11	10	9	8	7	6	4	3	2	1
2	12	12	12	12	12	12	12	13	13	13	13	13
3	10	10	10	10	11	11	11	11	11	11	11	11
4	9	9	9	9	9	9	9	9	10	10	10	10
5	8	8	8	8	8	8	8	8	8	8	8	9
6	7	7	7	7	7	7	7	7	7	7	7	7
7	6	6	6	6	6	6	6	6	6	6	6	6
8	5	5	5	5	5	5	5	5	5	5	6	6
9	5	5	5	5	5	5	5	5	5	5	5	5
10	5	5	5	5	5	5	5	5	5	5	5	5
11	4	5	5	5	5	5	5	5	5	5	5	5
12	4	4	4	5	4	5	5	5	5	5	5	5
13	4	4	4	4	4	4	5	4	5	5	5	5
14	4	4	4	4	4	4	4	4	4	5	4	4
15	4	4	4	4	4	4	4	4	4	4	4	4
16	—	—	1	1	2	2	2	3	3	3	4	4

Under the straight-line method, the cost of an asset is divided by the recovery period chosen (15, 35, or 45 years). The result is the annual ACRS deduction. The annual rate of cost recovery under the straight-line method is determined by dividing 100 (which represents 100% cost recovery) by the number of years in the recovery period. For example, if a building has a recovery period of 35 years, its annual rate of cost recovery under the straight-line method is 100 divided by 35, or 2.86%.

When accelerated methods of computing ACRS are used, the annual rate can be much higher, in some cases 200% of the rate allowed under the straight-line method. Naturally, the higher the rate, the greater the deductions in the early years of the venture. The 15-year cost recovery tables are based upon the 175% declining-balance method (200% declining balance in the case of low-income housing).

Personal property used in connection with a real estate venture (such as furniture in a hotel or motel) will also be subject to ACRS. Depending upon the type of property involved, it will have a cost recovery period of either 3 or 5 years, with the percentage deductible each year contained in a schedule similar to the schedules used for real estate. For personal property placed in service before 1985, the annual ACRS deduction contained in the schedule is based on the 150% declining-balance method. In 1985 the schedule will be based on the 175% declining-balance method, and from 1986 on the 200% declining-balance method will be used.

Rapid Amortization for Low-Income Housing Renovations

Certain ventures involving the renovation of existing low-income housing are eligible for even more rapid deductions than are available through ACRS. In lieu of the ACRS deduction for the property involved, the owners of such projects are permitted to fully deduct their renovation costs over the 5-year period immediately following completion. This advantage is open to ventures satisfying the following criteria: (1) renovation costs must exceed $3,000 per apartment unit; (2) the useful life of the improvements must exceed 5 years; (3) the apartments must be rented to "low-income" tenants, as defined by the Treasury Department on the basis of income levels in the area; and (4) more than 50% of the units must not be rented on a transient basis. Only the cost of the rehabilitation qualifies for this rapid write-off. The cost of the building still must be recovered under ACRS.

Rehabilitation of Older or Historic Properties

The Code provides very substantial tax benefits to ventures that rehabilitate buildings. For commercial properties at least 30 years old, an investment tax *credit* equal to 15% of the rehabilitation expenses may be claimed. The way the property is used *after* the rehabilitation determines whether it qualifies. Thus, an old residential building which is renovated and converted into office space may be eligible.

If the structure is at least 40 years old and used for commercial purposes after the rehabilitation, a 20% tax credit may be claimed. If the credit is claimed, the amount must be subtracted from the owner's basis and the balance of the costs of the rehabilitation must be recovered using the straight-line method, over not less than 15 years. For example, if a 40-year-old building is rehabilitated at a cost of $1,000,000, a credit of $200,000 may be claimed. The remaining basis of $800,000 [$1,000,000 cost minus $200,000 credit] may be recovered over a 15-year period, using the straight-line method.

Even larger tax breaks are available to ventures which rehabilitate historic structures. The credit allowed is equal to 25% of the cost of the rehabilitation work. In addition, the basis of the building does not have to be reduced by the credit claimed. Instead, the entire amount can be written off over 15 years using the straight-line method. Historic structures can be used for either commercial or residential purposes after the work is completed and still qualify for the credit.

To qualify for any of these tax credits, the costs of the rehabilitation over a 24-month period must at least equal the adjusted basis of the building being renovated. This is something to watch for since some buildings, particularly historic structures, may have a high initial cost. If the rehabilitation costs don't exceed the costs of acquiring the building (excluding the cost attributable to the land), the credit will not be available.

Additionally, the 25% credit is available only for properties listed in the National Register of historic places or located in a historic district and certified as being significant to the character of the district. Historic rehabilitation projects must be approved by state historic preservation officials and the National Park Service. If you are considering an investment in such a venture, be sure the developer has taken care of the required paperwork and that these approvals have been obtained.

Recapture

As we said earlier, the tax benefits derived from tax shelter investments do not result in a permanent avoidance of tax liability, but rather a deferral, generally until such time as the property is sold or otherwise disposed of. However, whereas the sheltered income would probably have been taxed at ordinary income rates before, now all or part of it may be eligible for the more favorable capital gains rate. How much depends upon the type of property involved, the amount of ACRS deductions taken in connection with it, and the rules of "recapture" set forth in the Code.

When you sell or otherwise dispose of business or investment-related property, you are, naturally, taxed on the gain. Gain is the difference between the amount you receive (or are deemed to receive) for the property and the adjusted basis of your interest in it. Adjusted basis, you will remember, is the original cost of the property, less all ACRS deductions previously taken. The greater those deductions, the lower the adjusted basis, and the higher the taxable gain.

When *personal property* used for business or investment purposes is disposed of, all of the gain to the extent of any ACRS deductions taken will be taxed at ordinary income rates. For example, Larry G., a New York pizza baron, recently sold his ovens for a $5,000 profit. In prior years, he had taken $4,000 worth of ACRS deductions in connection with them. Therefore, of his $5,000 gain, $4,000 will be taxed at ordinary income rates and $1,000 at capital gains rates.

When *real property* is disposed of, the amount of gain subject to recapture (taxation at ordinary income rates by reason of prior ACRS deductions) varies according to the type of property, its use, the length of time owned prior to disposition, and the type of ACRS deductions previously claimed.

For *commercial* property, if the taxpayer elected to use the straight-line method of ACRS, over either a 15-, 35-, or 45-year life, all gain on the disposition of property held for more than one year will be capital gain. However, if the ACRS deductions claimed were based upon the percentages prescribed in the tables on pp. 93 and 94, *all* gain on disposition will be treated as ordinary income to the extent of any cost recovery allowances previously taken. This distinction can be very important for a commercial real estate venture that plans on holding a property for a relatively short time before attempting to sell it at a profit. Assume a venture purchases an office building for $1,000,000 cash on January 1, 1982. On January 1, 1987, the venture accepts an offer for $1,500,000 and sells the building. If cost recovery had been claimed under the accelerated method prescribed in the table, the venture would have claimed ACRS deductions of $460,000. Its adjusted basis would be $540,000 [$1,000,000 minus $460,000]. Its gain would be $960,000 [$1,500,000 minus $540,000], $460,000 of which would be taxed as ordinary income. The balance [$500,000] would be taxed as capital gain. Depending upon the tax bracket of the partners in the venture at the time the building is sold, the federal tax bill could be as high as $330,000.

If the venture had claimed cost recovery deductions based on a 15-year straight-line method, its ACRS deductions would have totaled $333,000. The basis upon disposition would be $667,000 and the gain would be $833,000, all of which would be capital gain. The maximum tax bill in this situation would be approximately $167,000. In general, using maximum accelerated cost recovery methods for commercial property makes sense only if the taxpayer plans on having other shelter available upon disposition.

For *residential* real property, gain is treated as ordinary income only to the extent the cost recovery allowed under the prescribed accelerated method exceeds the cost recovery that would have been allowed if the straight-line method had been used over a 15-year period. If the straight-line method is elected, all gain on property held for more than 1 year will be capital gain.

Once again, there is a favorable exception for residential property involved in any of the federal subsidy or assistance programs, or eligible for the 5-year write-off of renovation costs. For each month past the 100th month (8⅓ years) this type of property is owned, 1% of the additional depreciation will not be subject to recapture. That means that once the property has been held for 200 months (16⅔ years), any gain on sale or disposition will be taxed at capital gains rates.

This favorable recapture treatment, together with the high leverage afforded by government-sponsored loans, have made low-income projects most tempting to investors who seek tax benefits, as opposed to potential profit on investment. There is an additional incentive. If qualified low-income housing is sold to or on behalf of its tenants, taxes on the gain can be deferred to the extent the proceeds are reinvested in another similar project. Recapture does not even become an issue until the new property is also sold or relinquished.

Tax Effects of Sale, Foreclosure, or Refinancing

The sale of property and the foreclosure of a mortgage can result in similar tax consequences, primarily because of the Code's treatment of borrowed funds. If property is sold subject to a mortgage or the buyer assumes a mortgage liability in connection with the purchase, the amount realized by the seller will be deemed to include the liability. Therefore, it is possible for the taxable gain on a sale to exceed the actual cash received. Likewise, if property is lost because a mortgage is foreclosed, the borrower will be deemed to receive an amount equal to the unpaid balance of the loan from which he is relieved. This could give rise to taxable gain, even though the property is forfeited. Of course, if the selling price is high enough, a sale would still mean substantial profit. However, there is the danger, as with foreclosure, of serious tax problems, especially if all or part of the gain is subject to recapture. Here is an example of what could result from both possibilities:

On January 1, 1981, Martin R. and Dick B. each completed construction on office buildings which cost approximately $1,500,000 each, exclusive of land, interest, and other soft costs. From that time through December 31, 1985, each took maximum ACRS deductions totaling $690,000.

On December 31, 1985, the bank forecloses on Martin's property in satisfaction of the $1,500,000 mortgage loan that is still unpaid. On the same day, Dick sells his property for $100,000 in cash, with the buyer assuming his $1,500,000 liability. As a result of the foreclosure, Martin is deemed to receive $1,500,000, which is the amount of the liability from which he is released. As a result of sale, Dick is deemed to receive $1,600,000, which represents the cash payment plus the amount of the loan. Since each has an adjusted basis of $810,000 (the original cost of $1,500,000—$690,000 in ACRS deductions), Martin has a taxable gain of $690,000 ($1,500,000 - $810,000) and Dick has a taxable gain of $790,000 ($1,600,000 - $810,000). Actually, however, Martin has received no cash and Dick has received only $100,000. To make matters worse, since each claimed $690,000 in ACRS deductions at the maximum permitted rate, each will be taxed on that amount at ordinary income rates.

An alternative to sale or foreclosure is refinancing of the permanent mortgage loan. Refinancing offers a threefold benefit: first, the owner retains ownership of the property and the ability to earn future profits; second, tax-free cash distributions may become available; and third, the adverse tax consequences that could result from sale or foreclosure are avoided.

If the property has been well-maintained and profitable, the original mortgage loan will have been substantially reduced by the time refinancing is considered. The new loan, therefore, should be able to cover the remaining balance with enough left over for sizeable distributions to the owners. Because these funds represent loan proceeds rather than income, they are not taxable, except to the extent that the distributions exceed adjusted basis. Although the amount received through refinancing might be less than could be received through sale, when you consider the potential for future profits and refinancing, as well as the adverse tax possibilities of sale, the overall economic results of refinancing might well be better.

The Investment Tax Credit in Real Estate

The investment tax credit, as you recall, is a direct credit against tax due, rather than a deduction which reduces income upon which tax is computed. Investment credit is available upon the acquisition of certain business-related "tangible, personal property," which includes equipment, machinery, furniture, etc., but not land, buildings, or their components. On qualifying purchases, the credit may be as high as 10% of the cost of the property (see p. 29 for details of computation), including any portion of the cost financed by borrowed funds. Special credit for rehabilitation of certain types of buildings were discussed above.

The Code restricts the use of the investment tax credit on property purchased for residential projects, except for boilers, coin-operated vending machines, and coin-operated washers and dryers. Commercial projects, on the other hand, are eligible for the credit and derive substantial tax benefits from it. All the equipment, furniture, machinery, vehicles, etc., purchased in connection with hotels, motels, factories, shopping centers, etc., can qualify. However, like ACRS, investment tax credit is subject to recapture, and therefore could create tax problems in the event of early sale or foreclosure.

The "Soft Costs" in Real Estate

In addition to ACRS deductions and investment tax credits, real estate shelters depend upon the deductibility of many "soft" costs to provide tax benefits for investors. Some of these deductions are permitted under the general category of "ordinary and necessary" business expenses. Others, such as the interest deduction, are set apart and treated specifically by the Code.

The Interest Deduction in Real Estate

The Code specifically allows a deduction for interest paid or accrued during the year with respect to the debts of a taxpayer. This includes interest charges on personal and business loans. Prior to the Tax Reform Act of 1976, most interest was fully deductible when paid or accrued. Now, however, there are certain limitations on the deduction, especially with respect to interest charged during the construction period. Perhaps Congress felt that interest on a construction loan was part of the cost of a building and therefore should be deducted via depreciation, or perhaps they simply could not leave real estate, with all its obvious advantages, totally unscathed. Whatever the reason, a provision was included in the 1976 Reform Act that limits the immediate deductibility of interest charges (and real estate taxes) paid or incurred while a project is under construction. As a concession to the industry, the provision is being phased in over a period of years, with preferential treatment given to residential projects. Low-income housing is exempt from this provision.

Interest incurred during the construction of low-income housing will remain fully deductible when paid or accrued. For conventional residential properties, construction interest costs incurred in 1982 may be deducted over an 8-year period. Costs incurred in 1983 may be deducted over a 9-year period, and in 1984 and thereafter, such costs may be deducted over a 10-year period. This is still an advantage over commercial property, which began its phase-in with the passage of the Act of 1976 and must deduct construction interest costs at the rate of 10% a year beginning in 1982.

These limitations on the immediate deductibility of interest charges apply only until the construction period is over and the property is ready for rental. Then, however, certain other limitations on the amount of the interest deduction may apply. Generally, the Code limits the amount of interest that may be claimed each year in connection with a passive investment to $10,000, plus the amount of any income from such investment. This limitation does not apply to those ventures actively engaged in a trade or business. Usually, the operation of a rental real estate project will be considered a business and, therefore, will not be limited in its interest deductions. However, there is a possibility that it will be considered an investment, particularly in the case of shopping centers and office buildings, which often use "net leases." A "net lease" is one in which the tenants agree to pay not only a fixed rental charge, but also all or a major part of the operating expenses. This is not uncommon when large amounts of space are rented to one or a few tenants. The test for a net lease, and indirectly for an investment, is whether the landlord's "ordinary and necessary" business expenses exceed 15% of the rental income. If they do not, a net lease is considered to exist and the interest deductions will be subject to restriction. Unfortunately, two of the main expenses usually covered by the landlord—interest and real estate taxes—do not count for the purposes of the 15% test.

Since the interest deduction can be quite substantial, classification as an investment can seriously impair the tax benefits of a venture. Another kind of problem can also affect the interest deduction, as well as the allowances for such items as ACRS and taxes. That is the problem associated with "nominee" or "straw" corporations.

Tax Risks of Nominee Corporations

As we mentioned earlier, many states have enacted usury laws, which limit the rate of interest that may be charged for borrowed funds. The allowable rate is usually higher for corporations than for individuals or partnerships. Since the interest rates on construction loans generally fluctuate with the prime rate, construction lenders are naturally more reluctant to lend money to partnerships than corporations, if there is a chance the usury laws will be violated.

For many years, straw or nominee corporations were formed to front for partnerships and individuals for the sole purpose of executing construction loan agreements. The problem with this arrangement is that the corporation must give the lender a mortgage interest in the property and, to do so, must own the land and buildings. In many such situations, the IRS and courts have held that the corporation, as holder of the title to the property, is also entitled to the tax benefits arising from such items as interest, ACRS, and real estate taxes. Thus, the partnership and partners, although the true economic owners of the property, are deprived of a major portion of the anticipated tax benefits.

There are circumstances under which this result can be avoided. If the corporation is considered to be acting as an agent for the partnership, the tax benefits could be passed through to the partners. However, the distinction between an agent and a nominee (owner in name only) is subject to the ever-changing criteria of the IRS and courts. Essentially, it is a matter of form versus substance. Often, the courts will ignore the form, or manner in which a transaction is structured, and go straight to the substance, or heart of the matter, to determine the tax consequences. Unfortunately, in the case of nominee corporations, the courts seem to be placing more emphasis on form. Therefore, when dealing with a venture in which a corporation holds title, the opinion of tax counsel, or perhaps even an advance ruling from the IRS, should be sought.

"Ordinary and Necessary" Business Expenses in Real Estate

In addition to allowances for such specific items as ACRS, interest, and taxes, the Code permits the deduction of all "ordinary and necessary" business or investment expenses. To qualify, expenses must be "ordinary" in the sense that, although they may be unique to the taxpayer, they are not to the type of business involved. By "necessary," the Code seems to mean beneficial to the business and reasonable in amount.

In real estate ventures, ordinary and necessary expenses generally include utility charges, insurance, management fees and rental commissions, legal and accounting fees, salaries, minor repairs, supplies, etc. An expense generally will not fall into the category if it is considered part of the cost of an asset that is subject to ACRS. Certain ordinary and necessary expenses are deductible fully in the year they are paid. Others, if connected with an asset having value for more than one year, (i.e., legal fees for obtaining a permanent mortgage loan), must be deducted over the useful life of the asset (i.e., the term of the loan).

The deductibility of the fees of the developer and syndicator, who may play many roles in the venture (i.e., general partner, general contractor, manager, guarantor), depends upon the amount and type of service involved. Contractor's fees are generally considered part of the cost of construction and are therefore recoverable only through ACRS deductions. Syndicator's fees for selling or promoting the sale of partnership interests are not deductible. "Organizational expenses," or fees for organizing the partnership, must be deducted in equal amounts over a 5-year period.

One expense that has been a source of dispute and litigation is the fee for so-called "covenants not to compete," which are generally agreements by a developer not to build in the same area until a particular venture has had a chance to rent-up. Clearly, these agreements are beneficial, and so the courts have generally recognized the deductibility of their cost, if reasonable in amount. However, the IRS has continually tried to discourage taxpayers from claiming the deduction. Near the end of 1977, when many were immersed in last-minute tax planning, an IRS ruling was issued. It indicated that if a developer seems to have neither the desire nor ability to compete, or if competition in the area is not feasible, the fee for a covenant will be considered part of the cost of the building, deductible only along with the other capitalized costs of the building. The action seems to imply that a fairly bargained-for and valuable covenant will still be deductible over the term it is in effect. However, the IRS is obviously gunning for unreasonable or abusive claims.

An Illustration

We have tried thus far to give you a general understanding of the economics and tax aspects of investing in real estate. However, the "numbers" are what matter most in the long run. Therefore, let's plug some figures into a typical fact pattern to see the actual results of a tax-oriented real estate venture.

Late in 1981, Bert B., an active southwestern developer, decided to build a 125-unit garden apartment complex in a city in Texas. After examining the major indices of growth, Bert concluded that the city involved is one of America's most dynamic metropolitan areas, in terms of population, business activities, effective buying income, employment, and other standard measures of economic strength. Bert planned to place the project in an area of the city with high occupancy levels, on several acres of prime land which he had an option to purchase for $50,000.

Bert's architect designed the complex to conform with the surrounding community. It would feature such amenities as a swimming pool, 2 tennis courts, a clubhouse, and a laundry facility. On the basis of the plans, several experienced general contractors submitted estimates of what the project should cost to build. Bert selected one of them who guaranteed to complete construction for $2,970,000. The contractor anticipated the job would be completed approximately 12 months from the starting date, which was set for October 1, 1981.

Bert next contacted a mortgage broker to locate a permanent first mortgage loan as well as a construction loan. The broker was able to obtain a permanent loan commitment for $3,000,000 from an insurance company. The interest rate on the permanent loan is 14%. The yearly payments required are $433,500 ($36,125 per month) and the term for repayment is 25 years. At the end of that time, if all the payments are made, the loan will be fully amortized.

The broker was also able to obtain a commitment for a $3,000,000 construction loan from a local construction lender. The due date for repayment is January 1, 1983. The interest rate on the loan is 2 points above prime (for the purpose of our illustration, we will assume the prime rate to be 16%, and thus the interest rate on the construction loan is 18%). Bert calculated that his interest charges on the loan would be $15,000 for the last three months of 1981 and $250,000 in 1982. Since the loan is funded gradually in "draws" as construction progresses, interest is charged only on the amount funded.

The costs of obtaining the permanent loan included closing costs and legal fees of $15,000 and an additional fee to the lender equal to 1 "point," or $30,000. The costs related to the construction loan included a commitment fee of $30,000 and closing costs of $7,500. In addition, the mortgage broker must be paid $15,000 per loan for his part in obtaining them.

Next, Bert retained a management company to supervise rent-up and to manage the property. The manager agreed to work for an annual fee equal to 5% of the gross rental receipts. However, to cover the initial expenses of training personnel and setting up the bookkeeping and rent-up operations, he asked to receive, in addition to his 5% fee, $15,000 in 1981 and $15,000 in 1982. Based on his experience in similar ventures, the manager estimated that during rent-up, when occupancy levels and rental income are low, Bert would need an additional $100,000 to cover operating expenses.

At this point, Bert estimated the total funds he would need to complete construction and carry expenses until sufficient rental income is generated. The breakdown is as follows:

Land	$ 50,000
Construction costs	2,970,000
Interest 1981 (construction loan)	15,000
Interest 1982	250,000
Permanent loan, closing costs and attorney fees	15,000
Permanent loan points	30,000
Construction loan commitment fee	30,000
Construction loan closing costs	7,500
Mortgage broker fee construction loan	15,000
Mortgage broker fee permanent loan	15,000
Guaranteed management fee	30,000
Operating deficit	100,000
TOTAL CONSTRUCTION AND RENT-UP EXPENSES	$3,527,500

Obviously, there was a gap between the amount of the expenses and the amounts of the permanent and construction loans. Bert was $527,500 short. Rather than carry the burden and risk the loss, he contacted David T., a well-respected New York syndicator, who agreed to organize a limited partnership to purchase a major interest in the project and thus, supply the additional funds. David's conditions were that Bert personally guarantee completion of the project, serve as a general partner for at least 5 years, and consent to a covenant not to compete for a period of 15 months ending January 1, 1983. Bert agreed, but only in return for $30,000 for guaranteeing to complete and cover contingencies, $25,000 for acting as a general partner, and $15,000 for agreeing not to compete. Under this arrangement, if all goes well, Bert stands to make $70,000 on the deal.

David, meanwhile, calculates that it will cost him approximately $20,000 to organize the partnership, $20,000 to syndicate or sell the partnership interests, and $20,000 ($10,000 in 1981 and $10,000 in 1982) for legal and accounting advice related to tax issues. David also wanted to serve as a co-general partner for the first 5 years of the venture, as protection for the limited partners, for which he asked to receive $20,000.

Bert and David agreed to raise $680,000 from investors by selling 10 limited partnership interests at $68,000 each. (Half interests would also be available.) The $68,000 would be payable over a 4-year period and would entitle each investor to a 9% interest in the partnership. The general partners would each retain a 5% interest, for which they would each contribute $25,000. The $680,000 from the limited partners, plus Bert and David's $50,000, should cover: the $527,500 needed to complete construction and rent-up; Bert's fees of $70,000; the $80,000 needed for organization, syndication, legal, and accounting expenses; and David's fees; leaving $52,500 for contingencies.

Let us assume the limited partnership was formed on October 1, 1981, and construction is completed a few months after the projected date on December 31, 1982. On January 1, 1983, the permanent loan is funded and the construction loan repaid by its due date. Although expenses in the rent-up year exceed those anticipated by $40,000, the venture can absorb them. By January 1, 1984, 95% of the apartments are rented, and they remain so at profitable levels for the next 8 years. The income from the venture, commencing in 1984 when rent-up is achieved, equals $780,000, with $760,000 derived from rental receipts, and $20,000 from laundry and vending machines and miscellaneous items, such as forfeitures of rent security deposits and recreational dues. The operating expenses total $245,600, broken down as follows:

Management fee (5% of rents)	$ 38,000
Real estate taxes	52,000
Insurance	8,400
Maintenance, repairs, and cleaning	20,000
Salaries	31,700
Utilities	81,000
Telephone	2,000
Advertising	2,500
Supplies	6,000
Legal and accounting	4,000
TOTAL	$245,600

In addition, an annual reserve of $20,000 is set aside each year for anticipated repairs and replacements.

Now, let us consider the items that affect the tax results of the venture from the start of the construction period through the first 10 years of operation. The following is a schedule of interest and amortization payments, which begin when the permanent first mortgage loan is funded on January 1, 1983:

	Interest	Amortization	Total
1983	$419,109	$14,391	$433,500
1984	416,981	16,519	433,500
1985	414,536	18,964	433,500
1986	411,726	21,774	433,500
1987	408,496	25,004	433,500
1988	404,784	28,716	433,500

	Interest	Amortization	Total
1989	400,517	32,983	433,500
1990	395,613	37,887	433,500
1991	389,977	43,523	433,500
1992	383,499	50,001	433,500
		$289,762	

The ACRS deductions also begin on January 1, 1983, when construction is completed. They are based on a cost of $3,000,000, which represents $2,970,000 in actual building costs, plus the $30,000 paid to Bert to guarantee completion. The venture elects to use the most rapid form of cost recovery available under the statutory tables. On that basis, the ACRS deductions for the period from 1983 to 1992 would be as follows:

1983	$360,000
1984	300,000
1985	270,000
1986	240,000
1987	210,000
1988	180,000
1989	180,000
1990	180,000
1991	180,000
1992	150,000

The "soft" costs connected with the venture should receive the following tax treatment:

—Although the issue is not free from doubt, we shall assume that the commitment fee paid in connection with the construction loan is deductible over the 15-month term of the loan;

—Other loan expenses, such as the points on the permanent loan, attorney's fees and closing costs, brokerage commissions, etc., are deductible in equal portions over the terms of the loans. Costs connected with the construction loan we will assume are deductible over the 15-month period it is in effect; costs connected with the permanent loan are deductible over its 25-year term;

—The guaranteed management fee, we will assume, is an ordinary and necessary business expense, and thus deductible when paid or incurred, that is, $15,000 in 1981 and $15,000 in 1982;

—The $25,000 payable to Bert for acting as a general partner for

5 years is deductible in equal amounts ($5,000 per year) over the 5-year period;
—The $15,000 paid for the covenant not to compete should be deductible over the 15 months it is in effect;
—The $20,000 payable to David for acting as a general partner should be deductible over the 5-year period of service;
—The fees for tax advice and accounting are deductible in the years they are incurred, that is, $10,000 in 1981 and $10,000 in 1982;
—The expense for organizing the partnership is deductible over a 60-month period;
—The syndication expenses are non-deductible.

Putting it all together—income, expenses, deductions, etc.—the overall tax results of the venture should be as follows on Chart I on page 111.

Footnotes to Chart I

[1] In 1981 and 1982, during construction, we have assumed there will be no rental income. In 1983, during the rent-up period, only part of the potential rent roll has been achieved. Thereafter, we have assumed a constant rental income level, although in actual practice the level would probably rise with inflation, or fall in a poor rental market.

[2] Operating expenses are assumed to follow the same pattern as rental income.

[3] In accordance with the Tax Reform Act of 1976, the $15,000 construction interest charged in 1981 must be deducted over a 7-year period (i.e., $2,143 per year) and the $250,000 of construction interest charged in 1982 must be deducted over an 8-year period (i.e., $31,250 per year).

[4] Only the interest portion of the annual payments on the permanent mortgage loan is deductible. The amortization portion, or repayment of principal, is not.

[5] The commitment fee of $30,000 paid with respect to the construction loan we will assume to be deductible over the 15-month term of the loan.

[6] Bert and David's general partner fees are deductible in equal amounts over the 5-year period of service.

[7] The $15,000 fee for the covenant not to compete is deductible over the 15-month period the covenant is in effect (3 months, or $3,000, in 1981 and 12 months, or $12,000, in 1982).

[8] The $30,000 guaranteed management fee is deductible $15,000

in 1981 and $15,000 in 1982, which are the years in which the fee is earned.

[9] The $20,000 in partnership organizational fees is deductible in equal portions over a 60-month period ($1,000 every 3 months).

[10] The ACRS deductions begin in 1983 when construction is completed.

[11] The fees for tax advice are deductible when paid in 1981 and 1982.

[12] The construction loan costs are deductible equally over the 15-month term of the loan.

[13] The permanent loan costs are deductible equally over the 25-year term of the loan.

[14] The total tax losses or taxable income for a given year is determined by adding up the deductions. If they exceed the income, the excess is available to the partners in accordance with their interest in the partnership and may be used to offset income from other sources. If income exceeds deductions, as it will do from 1993 on, each partner must report his share of the excess as additional income on his personal tax return.

Chart I reflects only those items with tax consequences. In order to determine whether the operations will generate excess cash for distribution to the investors, we must also include under expenses such non-deductible costs as the amortization of the permanent mortgage loan and the $20,000 set aside each year for repairs and replacements. In addition, we must subtract the ACRS deductions (since it does not involve a cash expenditure), as well as those items which are paid for out of loan proceeds and partners' capital contributions rather than out of income, such as construction loan interest, commitment fees, general partners' fees, fees for covenants not to compete, guaranteed management fees, organizational expenses, fees for tax advice, and construction and permanent loan costs. With these adjustments, the chart for cash flow purposes, beginning in 1983 when full rental is achieved, appears on Chart II on page 113.

Bert and David are each entitled to 5% of the $80,900 cash flow, or $4,045 each per year. As a group, the 10 limited partners are entitled to the remaining 90% of the cash flow, or

CHART I
Tax Consequences

	1981	1982	1983	1984	1985	1986	1987	1988	1989	1990	1991	1992
Rental Income [1]	-0-	-0-	485,000	760,000	760,000	760,000	760,000	760,000	760,000	760,000	760,000	760,000
Laundry, vending machines and miscellaneous income			4,000	20,000	20,000	20,000	20,000	20,000	20,000	20,000	20,000	20,000
TOTAL INCOME			489,000	780,000	780,000	780,000	780,000	780,000	780,000	780,000	780,000	780,000
Deductions												
Operating Expenses [2]			196,000	245,600	245,600	245,600	245,600	245,600	245,600	245,600	245,600	245,600
Interest Construction Loan [3]	2,143	33,393	33,393	33,393	33,393	33,393	33,393	31,250	31,250			
Interest Permanent Loan [4]			419,109	416,981	414,536	411,726	408,496	404,784	400,517	395,613	389,977	383,499
Commitment Fee on Construction Loan [5]	6,000	24,000										
Bert, General Partner Fee [6]	5,000	5,000	5,000	5,000	5,000							
David, General Partner Fee [6]	4,000	4,000	4,000	4,000	4,000							
Bert, covenant not to compete [7]	3,000	12,000										
Guaranteed management fee [8]	15,000	15,000										
Partnership organizational expenses [9]	1,000	4,000	4,000	4,000	4,000	3,000						
ACRS [10]			360,000	300,000	270,000	240,000	210,000	180,000	180,000	180,000	180,000	150,000
Tax Advice [11]	10,000	10,000										
Construction loan costs [12]	4,500	18,000										
Permanent loan costs [13]			2,400	2,400	2,400	2,400	2,400	2,400	2,400	2,400	2,400	2,400
TOTAL DEDUCTIONS	50,643	125,393	1,023,902	1,011,374	978,929	936,119	899,889	864,034	859,767	823,613	817,977	781,499
TAXABLE INCOME OR (LOSS) [11]	(50,643)	(125,393)	(534,902)	(231,374)	(198,929)	(156,119)	(119,889)	(84,034)	(79,767)	(43,613)	(37,977)	(1,499)

$72,810 per year, which breaks down to $7,281 for each limited partner. In accordance with the rules of partnership taxation, these distributions are tax-free, so long as they do not exceed the adjusted basis of the partner's interest in the partnership. Adjusted basis, you will recall, is equal to a partner's cash contribution, plus his share of partnership liabilities and taxable income, minus his share of tax losses and cash distributions. In this venture, the limited partners have each contributed $68,000 and, for the purposes of increasing basis, are entitled to a 9% share of the $3,000,000 non-recourse mortgage loan, or $270,000. Therefore, the starting adjusted basis for each limited partner is $338,000 ($68,000 + $270,000). Each partner's share of losses and distributions must exceed that amount before the distributions will become taxable. Here is how the overall tax losses and distributions from the venture appear through 1987:

	Tax Losses	Distributions
1981	$ 50,643	$ -0-
1982	125,393	-0-
1983	534,902	-0-
1984	231,374	80,900
1985	198,929	80,900
1986	156,119	80,900
1987	119,889	80,900
1988	84,034	80,900
1989	79,767	80,900
1990	43,613	80,900
1991	37,977	80,900
1992	1,499	80,900
	$1,664,139	$728,100

The combined total of the losses and distributions for the period is $2,392,239, of which each limited partner's share is $215,302. Since adjusted basis is $338,000, none of the distributions would be taxable and, in fact, at the end of the period each limited partner would still have a basis of $122,698 ($338,000 - $215,302). Thus, each could receive distributions, losses, or a combination of both, equal to that amount before the distributions would be taxed. In 1993, when income starts to exceed losses, the partners will be taxed on a share, but will also be able to increase their basis by that amount.

An examination of Chart I reveals that partnership tax losses

CHART II
Cash Flow

	1984	1985	1986	1987	1988	1989	1990	1991	1992
TOTAL INCOME	780,000	780,000	780,000	780,000	780,000	780,000	780,000	780,000	780,000
EXPENDITURES:									
Operating Expenses	245,600	245,600	245,600	245,600	245,600	245,600	245,600	245,600	245,600
Permanent Mortgage Loan Interest	416,981	414,536	411,726	408,496	404,784	400,517	395,613	389,977	383,499
Permanent Mortgage Loan Amortization	16,519	18,964	21,774	25,004	28,716	32,983	37,887	43,523	50,001
Reserves for Replacements	20,000	20,000	20,000	20,000	20,000	20,000	20,000	20,000	20,000
TOTAL EXPENDITURES	699,100	699,100	699,100	699,100	699,100	699,100	699,100	699,100	699,100
CASH AVAILABLE FOR DISTRIBUTION	80,900	80,900	80,900	80,900	80,900	80,900	80,900	80,900	80,900

gradually diminish through the years before ending in 1992. Thereafter, partnership operations result in a gradually increasing amount of taxable income. Cash flow remains constant, however, so that eventually, as interest and ACRS deductions continue to decline and payments of mortgage principal (which are not deductible) increase, the partners will be taxed on more money than they receive. This is one of the reasons tax shelters do not result in a permanent avoidance of tax, but rather a deferral.

The eventuality of taxes can be further deferred by refinancing the permanent mortgage loan. Assume that on January 1, 1992, the partnership obtains a new $3,000,000 mortgage loan on the same terms as the old, and uses the proceeds to repay the balance remaining on the original loan. Thereafter, the interest deductions would be the same as those beginning in 1983. Thus, in 1992 the interest deduction would be $419,109 rather than $383,499, a difference of $35,610. That would increase the partnership's taxable loss from $1,499 to $37,109 [($1,499) + $35,610], with similar results for the next several years, until the interest payments are again substantially reduced.

Another favorable result of refinancing is the excess cash it produces for distribution to the partners. Here is why that excess exists: if we examine Chart II, we find the total of the amortization payments through 1991 to be $239,761 (including the 1983 amortization payment of $14,391, which does not appear on the chart). That means, during the period, the original $3,000,000 mortgage loan has been reduced to $2,760,239. Thus, when the new $3,000,000 loan is obtained and used to repay the original, $239,761 will be left over. If we assume that fees and other costs in connection with the new loan equal $60,000, that still leaves $179,761 for repairs to the property and distribution to the partners. Naturally, to the extent the distributions do not exceed adjusted basis, they will be tax-free.

Let us now, for the purposes of illustration, shelve the possibility of refinancing and analyze the effects of this venture on one investor. Our investor is Brad B., a successful publisher in the 50% bracket who, like the other 9 limited partners, paid $68,000 for his partnership interest. Payment was required over a 5-year period: $10,000 in 1981, $15,000 in 1982, $20,000 in 1983, $15,000 in 1984, and $8,000 in 1985. During that period through 1992, the results to Brad were as follows on Chart III on the next page.

In 1981 Brad paid $10,000 for his interest in the partnership.

CHART III

Limited Partners Investment Analysis Per Unit

	[a]	[b]	[c]	[d]	[e]	[f]
	Capital Contributions	Taxable Income or (Losses)	Tax Savings or (Tax Costs)	Cash Distributed	Annual Benefit (Cost)	Cumulative Benefit (Cost)
1981	$10,000	$(4,558)	$ 2,279	$ -0-	$(7,721)	$(7,721)
1982	15,000	(11,285)	5,643	-0-	(9,357)	(17,078)
1983	20,000	(48,141)	24,071	-0-	4,071	(13,007)
1984	15,000	(20,824)	10,412	7,281	2,693	(10,314)
1985	8,000	(17,904)	8,952	7,281	8,233	(2,081)
1986		(14,051)	7,026	7,281	14,307	12,226
1987		(10,790)	5,395	7,281	12,676	24,902
1988		(7,563)	3,782	7,281	11,063	35,965
1989		(7,179)	3,590	7,281	10,871	46,836
1990		(3,925)	1,963	7,281	9,244	56,080
1991		(3,418)	1,709	7,281	8,990	65,070
1992		(135)	68	7,281	7,349	72,419
TOTAL	$68,000	$(149,773)	$74,890	$65,529		$72,419

His share of tax losses [column b] was $4,558. In other words, if he had not invested, his taxable income would have been $4,558 higher, and since he is in the 50% bracket, he would have paid taxes on that amount equal to $2,279. He has thus saved that much, simply by investing. If we subtract $2,279 from the $10,000 he paid for his interest [column a minus column c], his investment really cost him only $7,721 [column c] at the end of 1981.

At the end of 1982, the cost of the investment is $9,357, which, when added to the 1981 figure, represents a cumulative real cost [column f] of $17,078. In 1984 he will begin to receive cash distributions in addition to the tax benefits, and by 1985 his actual cost for the interest will be $2,081, even though he has paid $68,000 by that time. The cumulative effect by the end of 1992 is that Brad will have saved a total of $74,890 in taxes and received $65,529 in cash distributions, for a net benefit of $140,419. Since he invested only $68,000, he is $72,419 ahead of the game.

As the years pass, if the loan is not refinanced, more and more of the partnership income will be taxable, so that eventually Brad will be paying more than he receives, thus reducing his net benefit. Theoretically, by the time the loan is fully amortized, his benefit (exclusive of cash distributions) will be zero. At that point, he should begin receiving greater distributions, since loan payments will no longer be draining cash flow. However, since the ACRS deductions will also be exhausted, the entire cash flow should be taxable. Again we see why shelters are merely a deferral of taxes. Ideally, in the later years, when Brad begins paying tax on his share of partnership income, his bracket will be lower. However, there is the possibility it will be higher. With this in mind, does it still seem that shelters are as grossly unfair as their critics claim? Not really, since the piper is eventually paid. In some cases, he is paid even sooner than in others, as a result of sale of a partnership interest, sale of the property, or foreclosure of the mortgage.

Let us first consider the tax consequences of selling a partnership interest. Assume Brad sells his on January 1, 1993, for $35,000. His taxable gain, you will recall, is measured by the difference between his adjusted basis and the amount he is deemed to realize from the sale. The starting point for determining Brad's basis is his $68,000 contribution. To this we add his share of the $3,000,000 mortgage liability, which by 1993 has been reduced by amortization payments to $2,710,238. Brad's share is $243,921. Added to the $68,000 contribution, this equals $311,921. If we subtract from that the cash distributions Brad received through 1982 of $65,529, and the net tax losses of $149,773, his adjusted basis as of January 1, 1993 is $96,616.

The amount he is deemed to realize from the sale of his partnership interest is $278,921 ($35,000 in cash, plus his $243,921 share of the partnership liability). If we subtract his adjusted basis of $96,616 from that amount, his taxable gain on the transaction is $182,305, even though he received only $35,000 in cash. Don't forget, part of that gain will be taxed at ordinary income rates.

Suppose, instead of a sale by Brad, on January 1, 1993, the partnership itself sells the building and other depreciable property for $600,000, and the land for its original cost of $50,000. As part of the deal, the buyer assumes the mortgage liability, which has a balance remaining of $2,710,238. There is no gain or loss with respect to the land, since it was sold for an amount equal to its basis of $50,000. As for the gain on the sale of the depreciable property, we must first determine the partnership's basis at the time it is sold. The original cost was $3,000,000. From that we subtract all the ACRS deductions taken with respect to the property as of January 1, 1993. They total $2,250,000. Thus, the adjusted basis at the time of the sale is $750,000. The amount realized from the sale is $3,310,238, which is the $600,000 in cash, plus the $2,710,238 liability assumed by the buyer. If we subtract the adjusted basis, we are left with a taxable gain of $2,560,238. Brad's 9% share of the gain is $230,421, whereas his share of the cash received is only $54,000 for the depreciable property, and $4,500 for the land. Fortunately for Brad, only $250,000 of the total gain is subject to recapture. Of Brad's share of the gain, $22,500 (9% of $250,000) will be taxable as ordinary income as a result of recapture, and the balance will be taxed as capital gain. At a 50% tax bracket, Brad should be left with approximately $6,000 after taxes.

Finally, let us assume that on January 1, 1993, the partnership fails to meet the payments on the permanent loan and the mortgage is foreclosed. The partnership's basis is $750,000 in the depreciable property, plus $50,000 for the land, for a total of $800,000. The partnership is deemed to realize an amount equal to the $2,710,238 unpaid balance of the mortgage loan. The taxable gain is the difference between the two amounts, or $1,910,238, of which Brad's share is $171,921. Unfortunately, in the case of foreclosure, there is no cash distribution to lighten the load. Brad will pay approximately $41,000 in taxes as a result of recapture and capital gains. As we indicated earlier, at the end of 1992 he was more than $72,000 ahead on his investment. Now, as a result of foreclosure, his net benefits as a result of the investment are reduced to approximately $31,000, where they will forever remain. Thirty-one thousand dollars is not that impressive a net yield on an investment undertaken almost 12 years earlier. However, it is better than what would have happened had the foreclosure occurred earlier, say in 1987, before Brad had received substantial cash distributions and while a significant part of the ACRS deductions were still subject to recapture. Then Brad could have suffered a severe net economic loss.

With the effects of foreclosure clearly before you, you can see why it is important to analyze the economics of a venture before investing.

PART III
Oil, Gas and Other Mineral Shelters

CHAPTER IX
Oil and Gas

From the moment oil began to flow from the first producing well in Pennsylvania in the mid-1800s, the days of coal's pre-eminence in the energy field were numbered. Today, however, although oil and natural gas still supply more than 75% of our annual energy needs, we may again be in the twilight of an era. For the Earth contains only a finite amount of these minerals, and reserves are dwindling fast. United States oil imports have averaged between 6 and 9 million barrels per day in the past five years. Soon, even foreign sources will be unable to meet our voracious needs (Americans alone consume approximately 16 million barrels of oil a day!) and those of other industrial nations. According to the experts, barring some dramatic breakthrough in the industry's technology, the world will be demanding more oil than it can produce before the year 2000.

In the meantime, an all-out effort to delay the inevitable is in progress, especially in America, the most drilled nation in the world, where oil and gas companies are working feverishly to find and extract whatever supplies remain. Spurred on by high prices set by the OPEC nations and relaxed government price controls (especially with respect to newly discovered reserves), exploration and development are on the rise. Old fields are being revived; rigs are drilling deeper and deeper; companies are involved in major offshore drives. There is renewed opportunity for investment and profit, both in developed properties already producing oil and natural gas, and in ventures, undertaken to explore for new reserves.

For the purposes of tax shelter, ventures involving the acquisition of producing wells are not effective, since although they can provide some tax benefits by virtue of the depletion allowance, they generally do not offer excess deductions to offset income from other sources. Excess deductions are available, however, from ventures engaged in exploratory and development drilling which, therefore, will be the focus of our discussion. Two preliminary points: first, unlike real estate ventures, oil and gas shelters generally offer excess losses only in the first year of operation; second, in order to achieve the other main benefit of tax shelter—namely, partially tax-free returns to investors—the exploratory and development activities of the venture must be successful.

Exploratory and development activities generally involve either drilling to determine the limits of partially developed fields; drilling wells in areas of proven reserves; or drilling wells in areas where no oil or gas has yet been found. The chances of hitting in a purely exploratory situation ("wildcatting") are not great. According to some sources, the odds are 10 to 1 against the driller of an exploratory well finding oil or natural gas, and 50 to 1 against his finding a commercially exploitable reservoir. The odds are substantially better for development wells in areas of proven reserves, but, naturally, the cost of acquiring the rights to such property is higher and the potential for returns more moderate.

The economic activities of oil and gas ventures can be broken down into three phases: the search; the drilling; and the production and sale.

The Search

Contrary to popular belief, oil and gas are not located in vast underground rivers or pools. Instead, they are found in porous, usually sedimentary rock, similar to water collected in a sponge. Oil and gas are believed to have migrated upwards from where they were formed—in prehistoric times from the remains of plants and animals—until they met with layers of non-porous or "impervious" rock that halted their flow. There they collected, usually in combination with water, the lighter gas seeping to the top, the oil next, and the water below. In some cases, the deposits formed only a few hundred feet beneath the surface. More often they are located several thousand feet underground.

The search for a commercially exploitable field begins with the location of an area, or "prospect," that seems to be geologically compatible with the presence of oil and gas. This operation is directed by a geologist and later a geophysicist who use data and specialized tools to analyze the surface and subsurface conditions of the area. Tests might involve core drilling and the use of gravimeters, magnetometers, and seismographs. Even with favorable results, however, the tests are far from conclusive, since they only indicate whether or not the geology is compatible with the existence of the mineral. The only way to positively verify the presence of commercially exploitable oil and gas reserves is to drill.

Sometimes, to minimize the risk of total loss, oil and gas ventures are structured so that a certain portion of the funds invested will be used for exploration, and the balance to drill development wells, or, if the exploration proves unsuccessful, to purchase producing properties. In most cases, however, to increase the chances of a successful hit, ventures will spread the investors' capital over a number of different exploratory wells. Either way, because of the high cost of drilling—from under one hundred thousand dollars for shallow and uncomplicated wells to several million dollars for deeper and more difficult ones—the limited partnership form will usually be used in participation with other ventures to raise the necessary capital. Although the partnership now owns a smaller piece of each well, its chances of a successful find are greater.

When several prospects are involved, the tax shelter offering memorandum may either specifically designate the properties to be drilled, including supporting geological data, or it may be a "blind pool offering," in which none are identified until after the investors have entered the partnership. In either case, you have little control over your investment and are totally dependent upon the competence of the partnership's geologist, operator, and drilling contractor. We have identified the geologist. The operator is the person who supervises the operation, making all decisions and directing the accounting and administrative functions on behalf of the participants. When a partnership owns 100% of a drilling operation, the operator will frequently be the general partner. When it is a participant with others, the party with the greatest interest or experience usually will serve as operator.

It is imperative that you review the background material on the geologist, operator, and drilling contractor, since their skill, experience, and financial strength may well determine the success or failure of the venture. Check their track records in finding commercially exploitable reserves for other ventures, paying particular attention to ventures they have drilled in the same vicinity as yours. Look not only at the percentage of wells they hit, but also at how much was invested and what returns were actually realized by the investors and when. The mere fact that the track record indicates a high percentage of completed and producing wells does not mean that their investors have been successful. The real indicators are how much money has been returned to the investors, over what period of time, and the magnitude of the reserves found. Compare the amount of overall distributions to the distributions made in the last few months. Such comparisons may indicate whether production is remaining steady or decreasing.

It should be noted that when a partnership participates with others in a drilling operation, each will be required to bear its proportionate share of the costs and expenses. If oil or gas is discovered in commercially exploitable amounts, there will be considerable completion and production costs and perhaps the costs of drilling other development wells in the area. No participant, including your own venture, should leave the operation short of funds. Ascertain how your capital is to be used. If all invested funds are earmarked for exploration, how will the costs of completing a potentially profitable well be met? In some cases, the general partner (if he has the financial resources) will bear the costs. In others, bank borrowings may be anticipated, or the general partners may have the right to call upon the limited partners for additional contributions, at the risk of forfeiting all or part of their investments. At worst, the venture may be forced to sell out its interest for lack of funds.

By the time the exploratory or development drilling prospects have been chosen, the right to enter the property, drill, and extract any oil or gas discovered has probably been secured. This is usually accomplished by lease, in return for an initial "bonus payment" to the landlord, as well as royalty payments based upon the amount of oil and gas extracted once production begins. The lease may also provide for certain minimum rental payments, called "delay rental", until such time as production begins or the lease is terminated because of unsuccessful drilling, as well as "production payments" based upon the production from the property. The costs of acquiring a leasehold interest will vary significantly with the type of property involved. Naturally, if the area contains proven reserves and a development well is planned, the costs will be much greater than for a purely exploratory operation. You should ascertain whether the leasehold interest covers enough property to enable you to drill additional development wells in the event that exploratory drilling proves successful. Many states will require minimum spacing (e.g., forty acres for each oil well drilled) for drilling operations. In any case, once a leasehold, or "working interest," has been obtained by the venture, the drilling can begin.

Drilling

At this point, a drilling contractor takes over. He may be the operator or an independent party hired by him. The drilling contractor will usually supply the labor, drilling rig, tools, and machinery. In addition, he may function much like the general contractor in a real estate deal, supervising the services required for the drilling operation, including site preparation, road building, installation of power and water sources, etc. He may also hire the necessary subcontractors, such as drilling mud and chemical specialists, and fishing tool companies whose functions will be explained later.

Arrangements may be made to pay the drilling contractor on a footage basis according to his drilling progress; on a per diem basis; or he may agree to drill the well for a fixed price, which is referred to as a "turnkey" contract. It would seem that footage or turnkey arrangements would offer greater incentive to get the job done expeditiously, since additional time spent would not mean additional pay. Many drilling ventures utilize turnkey contracts, since theoretically they offer protection against extraordinary costs that might arise if problems occur during the drilling operations. But the turnkey contract does not offer any protection if the drilling contractor lacks the net worth to meet its obligations. Furthermore, you can assume that you will be paying top dollar for a turnkey contract.

If your venture is drilling in an area which is not particularly hazardous or difficult, it may be more economical not to use a turnkey contract. If a turnkey contract is not involved it is important to evaluate the operator's estimated drilling costs and to investigate whether the area has a history of difficult and costly drilling, as well as whether the operator has been accurate in estimating costs for other ventures in the area. It is also important for the venture to set aside a reserve fund to meet any extraordinary expenses that could arise. If the drilling is in an area where there is potential for a "blow-out" (a "gusher" caused by extreme pressure), you should ascertain whether blow-out insurance is available. Either a blow-out or a fire could be extremely costly, and if uninsured, your venture could find itself spending much, if not all, of its funds controlling the well and restoring the land.

The drilling itself is quite simple in theory. A drill bit is attached to the lower end of a string of "drill pipe," with additional lengths of pipe being added as the hole gets deeper. The diameter of the bit is greater than the drill pipe, leaving a space between the pipe and the wall of the hole. The bit and pipe are hollow so that a mixture of water, clay, and chemical additives called "drilling mud" can be pumped down through them. The mud is forced back up to the surface in the space between the pipe and the wall carrying with it, and thus removing, the rock and dirt displaced by the bit. When the mud reaches the surface, it flows into pits to be cleaned and used again.

The drilling mud, which is carefully prepared by mud and chemical specialists who monitor its viscosity, performs several vital functions. In addition to cooling and cleaning the drill bit and well, it coats the side of the hole, preventing cave-ins, infiltration from or contamination of underground water supplies, friction build-ups, fires, and blow-outs. When the well reaches a certain depth, it is also reinforced by lengths of heavy steel pipe called "casing," which are cemented to the walls of the hole.

If drilling sounds like a simple proposition, remember that several thousands of feet of pipe are rotating a bit located that far beneath the surface of the Earth—a bit, by the way, that periodically wears down and must be raised and changed. Changing the bit involves removing and disconnecting the entire string of pipe then replacing it—length by length—in the well. Imagine if, in the process, a length of pipe or tool should go plummeting down to the bottom of the hole. Costly "fishing" expeditions, conducted by aptly-named fishing tool companies, could result or you might be forced to drill around the obstruction or abandon your efforts.

One of the more serious risks is that the side of the hole may cave-in or the well may become blocked, causing you to "lose your hole." Considering the high costs of drilling, you may not have enough money to start again from that spot. To make matters worse, you still don't really know what lies beneath your prospect. In situations like this, rather than face total loss, a venture might "farm out" its working interest to another drilling group in return for an "overriding royalty," which means a share of the production if the well is successful.

Let us hope, however, that drilling will progress smoothly, and, at some point, an analysis of the mud coming up will indicate the presence of oil and gas. It then becomes necessary to determine whether the reservoir can be exploited in a commercially feasible manner. This, of course, depends upon the quantity of the minerals, and also on such factors as how fast they can be recovered, at what cost, and at what price they can be sold. The recovery rate of reserves can be estimated by determining the size of the reservoir, measuring the pressure which the mineral is under, and establishing the permeability of the rock, (which determines how fast the minerals will migrate through it).

The geologist and petroleum engineers utilize certain tests to determine whether a well should be completed as a producer. One of the first indications is a "drilling break," which is an increase in the rate of penetration of the drill bit in a formation. The drill bit will progress more rapidly in a porous formation than a non-porous one. When a drilling break occurs, the drilling mud that is circulated up from that particular zone is carefully analyzed to determine whether any hydrocarbons are present. As the drilling progresses, if a particular zone looks promising the geologist may call for a "drill stem test," particularly in wildcat situations. A drill stem test can indicate the presence of oil, gas, or water, as well as the porosity of the formation. Although it is a fairly good measure of commerciability, depending upon the area, it is not always conclusive. When the well has reached its total depth, "logs" will be run to further measure porosity, hydrocarbons, and water saturation, and to help determine where to complete the well in a particular zone.

If indications are that the reserves can be profitably exploited, the well must then be "completed" as a producer. The drill pipe and bit are removed. Complicated processes are used to open passages in the rock formation through which oil and gas can flow into the well. Tubing is installed in the casing and may, in the case of gas wells, be topped off by a branch-like group of valves, called a "Christmas Tree," designed to control and regulate the flow once production begins. With the tubing and regulatory valves in place, the rig is removed and the well is ready for production.

Production and Sale

Once found, the oil and gas must be brought to the surface. Often, in the initial phase of production, the oil will migrate and rise naturally, as a result of the pressure provided by the accompanying gas and water. Some wells never flow naturally and must be immediately put on pumps. Others require pumping only when the natural pressure dissipates or to remove fluids that may be inhibiting the flow of the minerals.

Whether a well flows naturally or requires pumping, it is essential to maintain an even rate of flow geared to the actual rate at which the mineral migrates to the well bore. By controlling the rate of production, recovery can be maximized. Furthermore, too rapid a flow may pull water, which moves more easily through the rock, rather than oil, to the well. Once this happens, it may be impossible to reverse. Many a potentially profitable well has been prematurely "watered out" of production.

As the well matures, natural pressure will eventually diminish and, at some point, pumping will be indicated. When pumping is no longer adequate, if the economics and geological conditions justify it, "secondary recovery methods" may be employed. Basically, these involve re-pressurizing the deposits by injecting water or gaseous matter into them through adjacent "service wells." In some cases, a third harvest of minerals may also be coaxed from the well by means of "tertiary recovery methods." These involve the injection of steam into the reserves to allow the oil to flow more freely. Secondary and tertiary operations are used only when the price of oil merits them, since they can be quite expensive.

While a producing well does not require the same kind of attention as a drilling operation, the well completion and production skills of the operator are key to the success of the venture. Pressure and production flow must be carefully monitored and equipment must be maintained to ensure maximum life and performance. In addition, the transportation of the minerals must be supervised.

Since gas does not store as easily as oil, it is usually sold at the wellhead to pipeline companies, who will run pipelines to the well into which the gas can flow and be transported to consumers. If the gas contains impurities or by-products such as condensate or natural gas liquids, it might first be piped to plants for purification, or separation. Oil, when it comes from the well, is usually collected in nearby tanks where the heavier water is allowed to settle to the bottom and is subsequently drained out. The oil is then transported to refineries—its major purchasers—via pipeline, tanker, train, or truck. The location of the mineral property is an important factor to consider in light of the availability and cost of bringing in pipelines or other means of transportation, which may ultimately affect the profitability of the find or its commercial feasibility. This is especially important in the case of gas wells, which usually do require pipelines. If a prospect is not near a gas pipeline it could be non-productive for a substantial period of time, until gas lines are installed in the area.

The price a venture receives for its minerals depends upon many factors, not the least of which is the supply and demand of the market. The destination of the minerals is also relevant, since it can determine the applicability of government price controls. However, government pricing policy is in a state of transition. Recent Congressional action seems to indicate that we are moving toward deregulation of natural gas prices. The newspapers may be your best indicator of trends to come.

Once a well is successfully producing, it can supply its investors with a steady stream of income until it is naturally depleted. The life-span of a well varies greatly from field to field, depending upon the size of the reserves and the rate of recovery. Many state oil and gas boards will limit the number of barrels that can be removed each day, to maximize the yield from the well. In its later years, the well will reach a point when it can be operated only intermittently, in order to allow the oil to flow to, and accumulate in, the well bore. These so-called "stripper wells" account for a slow but steady percentage of our national production. Depending upon the price of oil, they can still operate at profitable levels.

A Word from the Securities and Exchange Commission

The Securities and Exchange Commission (S.E.C.), a federal regulatory agency, was established to monitor the sale of securities to the public. Partnership interests in oil, gas, and other ventures are considered securities, and thus may be under the jurisdiction of the S.E.C. In April, 1978, the Commission published a pamphlet entitled "Investing in Oil, Gas, and Coal." It contained, in part, the following advice and warnings for investors:

Exercise Caution in Selecting Your Investment

Most oil, gas, and coal investment opportunities, while involving varying degrees of risks to the investor, are legitimate in their conception, businesslike in their marketing, and prudent in their operations. However, as in many other investment opportunities, it is not unusual for unscrupulous promoters to attempt to take advantage of increased investor interest by engaging in fraudulent practices . . .

In one case investigated by the Commission, promoters solicited funds from the public for the purchase of interests in oil and gas wells that had been capped and abandoned. . . . Other investigations have revealed instances in which:

* "Producing wells" indicated on the map which was shown to investors for the purpose of inducing them to invest had not been drilled.

* Prospective limited partners were told that "scientific equipment" designed and built by the promoter would improve "risk-reward ratio 400% in wildcat prospecting for oil and gas." No such equipment existed.

* Prospective investors were not told that the amount being charged by the promoter for drilling and completion of the wells was substantially higher than rates for such services generally prevailing in the area.

Watch for "Boiler Room" Techniques

In order to attract the interest of individual investors, unprincipled promoters have revived what became known as "boiler-room" techniques when they were employed in the 1920's and again in the 1950's. . . . Typically, they make claims that are without foundation and predict potentially spectacular profits . . .

In a typical "boiler-room" sales pitch relating to oil, gas, and coal investments, potential investors may be told:

* they will be sold an interest in a well that cannot miss;

* the risks are minimal—that the exploration efforts "can't fail"—"are a lead-pipe cinch" etc.;

* a geologist in the company has given the salesperson a tip;

* the salesperson has personally invested in the venture;

* the Securities and Exchange Commission has approved the offering, an action which the Commission never takes;
* the promoter has "hit" on every well drilled so far;
* there has been a tremendous "discovery" in an adjacent field;
* a large, reputable energy company is operating or planning to operate in the area; and,
* only a few interests remain to be sold and the investor should immediately send in his money to assure the purchase of an interest.

Be Certain You Know

* the amount of commission paid to the promoters and salespersons, including compensation in the form of interests in the venture for which the promoters or salespersons will contribute no money;
* how the funds you invest will be held. If separate accounts are not maintained for money contributed by the public investors, the investors' money may be subject to the claims of the promoters' other creditors from other projects;
* the level of experience in oil and gas drilling on the part of all persons responsible for the venture. If a company is involved, you should know the experience of its principal officers and directors and the length of time that the company has been in existence;
* the existence of any conflicts of interest arising out of undisclosed interests in the venture or its properties which are held by the promoters.

What To Do

* Resist pressures to make hurried uninformed investment decisions.
* Insist that all representations be made in writing.
* Be skeptical of suggestions or promises of spectacular profits.
* Read carefully all prospectuses, offering circulars, or sales literature. Obtain explanations of any matters you do not fully understand. Don't invest until all answers and explanations are fully understood.
* Request and obtain written information about the background of all persons responsible for the venture, and if a corporation is involved, request such information about the company and its principal officers and directors.
* Consider the risks in relation to your own financial position and needs. Understand fully the difficulties that may be encountered in an attempt to resell the investment should you find at some

future date that you need the funds which you invested. Ask yourself if you can afford the potential loss, which in some instances could exceed the amount of your investment.

What To Ask

* Ask for a copy of any geological report that may have been prepared, especially if the offering is a private offering. Bear in mind, however, that such reports are not assurances of the presence of oil, gas, or coal. They often contain references to "[proven] reserves" or "probable reserves," which are only estimates and do not assure that total production will be substantial or that production will be at a rate that will be profitable.

* Review the geological report with a geologist, petroleum engineer or other person who is knowledgeable and unaffiliated with the company and who can evaluate this type of investment.

[Excerpted from "Investing In Oil, Gas, and Coal."]

Before we move on to the tax aspects of oil and gas, there is one further element to consider in oil and gas ventures. Sometimes, a partnership agreement will grant an option to the general partners or operator to repurchase the limited partnership interests at some point in the future. Obviously, if the option exists, you can expect it to be exercised only if it will prove profitable to the general partners, which means only if the venture is successful. If you are entering a deal with this type of provision, make sure you are aware of it and that you will be fairly compensated for your interest, not only in terms of current oil and gas prices, but future prices—which are sure to head upwards.

Tax Aspects of Oil and Gas Investments

As you know, oil and gas ventures have the ability to provide substantial first-year tax deductions, which can be used to offset income from other sources. These benefits are available primarily because of the deductibility of certain costs incurred in connection with a drilling operation, known as "intangible drilling and development costs."

Intangible Drilling and Development Costs

For tax purposes, the costs of developing oil and gas properties are generally divided into two categories: the costs of acquiring tangible property or equipment, such as tools, pipe, casing, machinery, etc.; and the intangible drilling and development costs. Equipment costs are considered capital expenditures and must be recovered through the ACRS deduction. Intangible costs, which frequently account for a major portion of the total cost of the drilling operation, may be deducted in the year paid or incurred, if the owner of the operating rights to the property so elects.

According to the Treasury Regulations, intangible costs include "wages, fuel, repairs, hauling, supplies, etc." used in [1] clearing ground, draining, road making, surveying, and geological work necessary to prepare for drilling; [2] construction of derricks, tanks, pipelines, and other physical structures; and [3] drilling, shooting (opening passages), and cleaning the wells. In addition, the amounts paid to drilling contractors, including those paid pursuant to turnkey contracts, are considered intangible costs.

The percentage of drilling costs deductible as intangibles may be as high as 75% of the total cost of drilling, with the rest deductible mainly through ACRS. If the drilling activities result in a dry hole, generally all the costs will be deductible, except those related to property that can be used again or re-sold. The drilling phase usually produces no income and therefore the operations in the first year should result in substantial deductions to offset unrelated income. These deductions can be further enhanced by effective structuring of the deal. For example, since intangible costs include payments on turnkey contracts, many ventures organized toward the end of the year will provide for pre-payment of the contractor's fee, in advance of drilling, before the year ends. Investors will therefore get the benefit of the deduction in the current year. Of course, the Internal Revenue Service might argue that the deduction must be taken in the year the drilling actually occurs, unless the venture can establish a valid economic purpose for the pre-payment aside from providing year-end tax benefits. To establish a valid purpose, the turnkey contract should clearly require the pre-payment and specify the well to be drilled. The payment should preferably be made to an independent contractor (not the general partner), within a reasonably short time before the drilling begins, and all of the participants in the well should be required to pre-pay the drilling costs. In addition, it should trigger some concrete benefit to the venture, such as a better price or guarantee of obtaining the drilling rig.

Another way of maximizing the investors' initial deductions is through the use of special allocations, i.e., assigning all the intangible drilling and development costs to the limited partners, and the completion and other costs to the general partner. The viability of this structure has been established. In a situation in which the investors' funds were earmarked and used to meet intangible costs, the IRS ruled that the investors could be allocated the resulting deductions. However, as you recall from our discussion of partnerships, special allocations run the risk of being disregarded for tax purposes, if it is determined that the allocation does not have substantial economic effect aside from tax benefits. It is therefore essential that special allocations be consistently applied. If a general partner is to bear the cost of completing the well, he should be allocated the resulting deductions and the proceeds from the sale of any property involved.

In addition to raising legal and economic questions, special allocations can place a general partner in a potential conflict of interest situation. Often it is the general partner, serving as the operator, who determines whether a well is commercially exploitable. If, after drilling, he feels the well will only be marginally profitable to him in light of the completion costs he must bear, he may decide to abandon it as a dry hole. Obviously, this would not be in the best interests of the limited partners, whose money has already been spent on drilling.

To the detriment of oil and gas investors, the Tax Reform Act of 1976 included a provision requiring all or a portion of previously deducted intangible drilling and development costs to be recaptured upon sale of the property, or sale of a partnership interest, or subchapter S corporation stock. In essence, the new rule provides that the gain on disposition will be taxed at ordinary income rates, rather than capital gains rates, to the extent the intangible deductions claimed exceed those that would have been available had the venture elected to deduct the intangible costs through depletion. The similarity to recapture of ACRS deductions is obvious.

Depletion

Whereas intangible drilling and development costs are the major source of excess deductions in the first year of a drilling operation, the depletion deduction is largely responsible for sheltering a portion of the income from the venture during the producing years. Theoretically, depletion is a way for the owner of an "economic interest" in mineral deposits to recover the cost of the deposits as they are being diminished in value through extraction. Generally, a lessee, or the holder of either a working or royalty interest in mineral property, will be considered to have an economic interest and the right to claim depletion deductions.

The two methods of computing depletion—cost depletion and percentage depletion—are discussed in detail in Chapter III. Here is a quick review, with a look at the special provisions that apply to oil and gas:

Under cost depletion, the owner of mineral property is permitted to deduct his cost per unit for the mineral (i.e., per barrel of oil or per cubic foot of gas) for every unit he sells. Cost per unit is determined by dividing the cost of the mineral property by the estimated quantity of reserves. For example, if it costs $250,000 to obtain the rights to an estimated 25,000 barrels of oil, the cost per barrel is $10.00. Therefore, the owner can deduct $10.00 for every barrel of oil he extracts and sells. If he sells 10,000 barrels in a year, his cost depletion deduction will be $100,000.

Each year, the depletion allowance must be computed using both methods, for the Code generally provides that the one yielding the greater allowance must be applied. Usually, that will be percentage depletion, which was created in 1926 expressly for the purpose of encouraging exploration for new mineral reserves. Percentage depletion is computed by applying a statutory fixed percentage against the gross income from the property, with the result not to exceed 50% of the taxable income. Gross income is basically the total income derived from the mining processes, less rents and royalties. Taxable income is the gross income, minus the deductible items incurred in producing the income, such as intangible drilling and development costs, operating expenses, transportation costs, administrative costs, and interest charges.

The fixed percentage for oil and gas currently is 18%. However, Congress in the Tax Reduction Act of 1975 has repealed the availability of percentage depletion for many oil and gas operators. Fortunately for tax shelter investors, small producers are exempt from the restriction, although more of them will be affected in the next few years. In 1978, taxpayers were eligible for percentage depletion on production up to an average of 1,400 barrels of oil a day; in 1979, only production up to 1,200 barrels was eligible; and from 1980 on, the limit is now 1,000 barrels a day. For natural gas producers, the limits are 8,400,000 cubic feet in 1978; 7,200,000 cubic feet in 1979; and 6,000,000 cubic feet from 1980 on. For those involved in both activities, total production will be taken into account, with the producer being allowed to claim percentage depletion on 6,000 cubic feet of gas for every barrel of oil that his production falls below the allowable maximum.

In addition to these limitations, the fixed depletion percentage for oil and gas will drop to 16% in 1983, and 15% from 1984 on. Only oil and gas produced through secondary or tertiary recovery methods will retain a 22% rate through 1983. Percentage depletion is not available at all to those who purchase property with proven oil or gas reserves, unless, again, secondary or tertiary methods are used. It is also not applicable to those engaged in the retail sale of oil and gas in excess of $5,000,000 per year, or in the refining of more than 50,000 barrels of oil on any given day during the year.

Significantly, in the case of partnerships, the depletion allowance and the limitations on the amount of oil or gas produced are computed separately for each partner. (Generally, each is required to keep his own records on depletion for tax purposes, with information usually furnished by the partnership.) Therefore, depending upon their other oil and gas investments, certain partners may qualify for percentage depletion, while others may not.

One final restriction: in addition to being limited to 50% of the taxable income from the property, the percentage depletion allowance may not exceed 65% of a taxpayer's taxable income from all sources for the year. However, any amount not allowed as a deduction because of the 65% limitation my be carried over for use the next year.

Here is how percentage depletion works:

Assume that in 1982 an oil venture, as a result of successful exploratory drilling, has a producing well that generates gross income of $1,000,000, and taxable income of $800,000. If there are 10 limited partners, each owning a 10% interest in the venture, each would be entitled to a percentage depletion allowance of $18,000 that year, computed as follows:

18% (fixed percentage) x $1,000,000 (gross income) x 10% (each partner's interest) = $18,000.

That does not exceed 50% of the taxable income from the venture, of which each partner's share is $40,000 [$800,000 (taxable income) x 10% (each partner's interest) x 50%]. Therefore, each could claim the $18,000 depletion allowance, assuming it does not exceed 65% of his taxable income from all sources for the year.

Mineral Acquisition Costs

Generally, the costs incurred by a venture in connection with the acquisition of a leasehold interest in oil and gas properties are not currently deductible, but must be added to the basis for cost depletion, or depreciation, if tangible assets are acquired along with the mineral rights. Usually, acquisition costs will include bonus payments, commissions, geological and geophysical costs, and production payments made to the lessor.

Bonus payments, which are sums paid to the lessor upon acquisition of the lease, together with commissions paid to brokers for services performed in connection with the lease, are added to the cost of the minerals when computing cost depletion. Geological and geophysical costs, which include surveys, maps, and testing, and production payments, which entitle the lessor to a share of the production or proceeds from the mineral property, also are considered part of the costs of the mineral. Production payments are similar to royalties, except that they run for a shorter period of time than the estimated economic life of the reserves. They may be geared either to time, e.g., 50% of the proceeds for the first 3 years; quantity of mineral, e.g., 50% of the proceeds from the first 3,000 barrels of oil produced; or dollars, e.g., $300,000 payable from 50% of the oil produced. In any case, they are not currently deductible and, in fact, may be deducted only if cost depletion is used.

If tangible assets are acquired along with the leasehold interest, the cost of these assets must be recovered through the ACRS allowance and tax credits. In this event, the total leasehold costs must be allocated between the minerals and the depreciable assets, based upon their relative fair market values.

Deductions Arising from Unsuccessful Ventures

If only intangible drilling and development costs are deductible currently during the drilling phase, what happens tax-wise to the mineral acquisition costs if the drilling comes up dry? Considering the odds against a successful find, this is an important consideration.

Fortunately, the Code allows a deduction for losses incurred in a trade, business, or other transaction engaged in for profit, including losses (i.e., all costs not previously deducted) sustained when business or investment properties, such as oil and gas mineral rights, are proven worthless. The loss deduction may be claimed at the time the worthlessness of the property is fixed by an identifiable event, such as the loss of mineral rights, abandonment of the mineral lease (unless the property was proven worthless prior to that time), or the drilling of a dry hole. The cost of tangible property abandoned in an unsuccessful venture should also be deductible, to the extent it cannot be salvaged or sold.

Ordinary and Necessary Business Expenses and Other Operating Costs

Let us assume the drilling is successful and results in an operating, producing well. As in all types of business ventures, the ordinary and necessary business expenses will be deductible. These include wages, equipment rentals and maintenance, supplies, management fees, taxes, transportation costs, administrative costs, sales commissions, delay rentals, and royalties. The last 2 items, which are unique to mineral ventures, bear explanation.

Delay rentals are paid to the landlord essentially to buy more time to develop the property. They cease when production commences, or when the property is abandoned. According to the Regulations, they may be deducted by the venture when paid or accrued.

Royalty payments, in the context of mineral ventures, are based upon production from the well. The holder of a royalty interest is deemed to have an economic interest in the oil and gas and thus, is entitled to a share of the mineral, or the proceeds derived from its sale. A royalty interest retained by the lessor of the land in connection with the granting of mineral rights is referred to as an "underlying royalty." A royalty interest retained by the lessee, who in turn farms out his right to exploit the minerals, is called an "overriding royalty." In either case, the party that pays the royalties may exclude or deduct an equivalent amount from his gross income when computing his taxable income for the year. However, he must also exclude the amount of royalties and rents from his gross income when determining the percentage depletion allowance. This is because the recipient of the royalties is permitted to use the depletion allowance to offset the royalty income he receives.

Unlike production payments, royalties extend to all the minerals produced, unlimited by time, money, or quantity. Since royalty payments are deductible from gross receipts, whereas production payments are not, the proper classification can be significant to the venture for tax purposes. Check this point with tax counsel.

ACRS and Investment Tax Credit

If the venture acquires tangible property in connection with its drilling operations, such as oil rigs, pumps, well equipment, pipelines, and oil storage facilities, the cost of the equipment will be subject to ACRS deductions and the investment tax credit. However, in the case of premature disposition of the property, the gain, to the extent of ACRS, will be subject to recapture, as will the investment tax credit.

The Crude Oil Windfall Profit Tax Act of 1980

In April 1979 the Carter Administration announced that it would phase out its price controls on domestically produced crude oil. As a result, Congress enacted the Crude Oil Windfall Profit Tax Act of 1980, imposing a tax on the increased profits expected to result from the higher selling price of oil.

The Windfall Profit Tax applies to all domestically produced crude oil, unless, for some reason, it is exempt. The amount of the tax depends upon the classification of the oil into one of three "tiers."

"Tier I" oil is generally oil produced from a property which was in production prior to 1979. A tax rate of 70% is levied on the difference between the selling price of the oil and $12.81

per barrel (adjusted quarterly for inflation and state severance taxes).

"Tier II" oil is generally oil produced from "stripper wells" (wells that have historically produced at an average daily rate of 10 barrels or less). A tax rate of 60% is levied upon the difference between the selling price and $15.20 per barrel (adjusted also for inflation and state severance taxes).

"Tier III" oil is generally newly discovered oil (oil produced from properties beginning after 1978); heavy oil (oil with a specific gravity of 16 degrees "API" or less); and oil produced by qualified tertiary methods. A tax rate of 30% is levied on the difference between the selling price of the oil and $16.55 per barrel (also adjusted quarterly for inflation plus 2% and state severance taxes).

Independent producers (1,000 barrels per day or less) are eligible for a 50% tax rate on Tier I oil and a 30% rate on Tier II oil. In the case of partnerships, independent-producer status is determined separately for each partner, as is the windfall profit calculation.

The Windfall Profit Tax is limited to 90% of the net income attributable to the oil.

The Economic Recovery Tax Act of 1981 modified the Windfall Profit Tax by implementing a gradual reduction of the tax rate on newly discovered Tier III oil from 27.5% in 1982, to 15% in 1986 and thereafter; and by exempting Tier II stripper oil from the tax under certain conditions. To qualify, the stripper oil must be recovered after 1982, by an independent producer, as a result of his working interest in the property. Furthermore, the property must not have been transferred by a non-independent producer on or after July 23, 1981.

The Windfall Profit Tax is scheduled to be phased out over a 33-month period, starting in January 1988, or the month after the aggregate revenues from the tax exceed $277.3 billion (but not later than January 1991).

As we mentioned above, state severance taxes are taken into account when computing the Windfall Profit Tax (to the extent the severance tax rate does not exceed 15%). The IRS has recently ruled that certain state taxes do not qualify as severance taxes, and thus will not be considered for purposes of reducing potential Windfall Profit Tax payable. The states adversely affected with respect to their taxes as of this writing are Alaska, Arkansas, California, Colorado, Louisiana, Nevada, Ohio, Texas, and West Virginia.

Sale or Disposition of Oil and Gas Property

If a venture sells its interest in the oil and gas property and equipment, subject to the rules of recapture, the gain will generally be taxed at long-term capital gains rates, provided the property has been held for at least 12 months.

In recent years oil and gas syndicators have come up with some innovative techniques to enable investors to transfer or dispose of their investments without adverse tax consequences. The "exchange offer" is one of the most popular of the new formats being utilized. Generally speaking, in an exchange offer, investors in an oil and gas partnership are offered stock in a newly formed public corporation. This gives the investor the ability to sell his interest at any time, rather than wait for the long term pay-out from the producing wells. If the corporation is newly formed, according to the Code, the exchange will generally be tax-free. The investor will, however, be taxed on the gain when he disposes of the stock. The gain is the difference between the selling price and the investor's basis for his stock (which is the same as the basis for his partnership interest).

There are certain negative aspects of the exchange offer which should be considered. For example, the promoters will, when valuing the partnership interest to be exchanged, discount the value of the proven reserves, which are usually conservatively estimated in the first place. Furthermore, there is no guarantee that the stock you acquire will be saleable at the price indicated in the offer. Examine the offer carefully. Remember, you are giving up a partially tax-free stream of income for the stock.

Another disposition technique which is frequently being utilized involves the transfer of an oil and gas interest to a "Clifford Trust." A Clifford Trust is a trust which is set up to last for more than 10 years, after which time the property is returned to the grantor (in our situation, the investor). In this manner the investor can utilize the tax deductions in the initial years of the venture and then, when it turns profitable, transfer the property to a trust for the benefit of his children or others who are in a lower tax bracket. They will receive the income from the venture during this period and also will be taxed on the gain (hopefully at rates lower than the investor). If the trust is set up properly, it may even be possible for the investor to retain the portion of the income from the venture that is sheltered by depletion.

Oil and Gas and At-Risk

Exploring for, and exploiting, oil and gas reserves is affected by the at-risk provision of the 1976 Tax Reform Act. Investors in these activities may not claim tax losses generated by the ventures beyond the amount they are considered at-risk. As you recall from Chapter V, an investor will be considered at-risk to the extent of his contribution to the venture, plus the amount of any loans for which he is personally liable, or for which he has pledged property (other than his interest in the venture) as security.

This, however, does not eliminate the possibility of using leverage. Many oil and gas shelters are structured to give investors tax benefits in the initial year that exceed the cash invested, while still complying with the at-risk provision. This involves the use of invested capital, together with borrowed funds, to meet the intangible drilling and development costs of the venture. Although the investors must assume personal liability or pledge security for a portion of the loan, they will get the benefit of a substantially greater current deduction, without expending any additional money, until later years when the loan must be repaid.

It should be noted that an investor will not be considered at-risk to the extent he is protected from loss by guarantees or other such arrangements. Sometimes, the general partner or operator of an oil and gas deal will agree to buy back an investor's interest at a specified future date. If the repurchase obligation is not contingent upon the success of the venture, it might be considered a form of guarantee that could reduce or eliminate the amount the investor is at-risk.

An Illustration

On July 1, 1982, two identical drilling ventures are organized, each to drill a single well in search of oil and gas. The participants in each venture invest a total of $200,000, which is earmarked for drilling expenses and entitles them to 60% of the venture and 100% of the intangible drilling and development costs. The remaining 40% of the ventures, as well as the completion costs, are allocated to the respective operators.

Drilling Fund #1 is a purely exploratory operation, acquiring by lease the rights to 500 acres of previously undeveloped land. Drilling Fund #2 also leases the rights to 500 acres of land, but in an area of proven reserves. In both cases, the landowners receive a $25,000 bonus payment upon signing of the lease and retain a royalty interest equal to ⅛ of the production from the property. However, because the property leased to Fund #2 is obviously more valuable, its owner also demands a production payment worth $600,000, payable from 25% of the production each year until paid. The production payment would probably also involve an annual interest charge on the $600,000; however, for the sake of simplicity, we will omit this calculation from our example.

Both ventures hire drilling contractors on a turnkey basis, who agree to bring in the wells for $150,000. As we said, in both cases, the operators agree to cover the completion costs, if the drilling is successful.

Unfortunately, completion costs never become an issue for Fund #1. Drilling is completed by January 1, 1983, but 10 days later, the well is capped and abandoned as a dry hole. Fund #2, on the other hand, strikes commercially exploitable reserves, completes, and is ready for production by January 10, 1983. Thereafter, we will assume that it is extremely successful, and gross receipts from the operation of the well are $400,000 a year, until the reserves are depleted in 1991. Actually, the constant rate of production is for illustration purposes only, since production would undoubtedly diminish as time passes.

Of the $150,000 paid by Funds #1 and #2 to their respective drilling contractors, let us assume that $120,000 qualifies as intangible drilling and development costs, and $30,000 as tangible equipment costs, both of which are paid in 1982. That year, each venture also spends $25,000 on administrative expenses. Thereafter, Fund #2 continues to pay $50,000 a year for maintenance, administrative, severance and windfall profit taxes, and operating costs, exclusive of royalties. Fund #2 also incurs completion costs; however, these funds are provided by, and are allocated to, the operator and therefore do not affect our investors. For the sake of simplicity, we will also ignore the small depreciation and investment credit allowances on the tangible equipment costs.

Based on all these factors, the following charts illustrate the effects of both ventures on their participants. First, Fund #1:

	1982	1983	Total
Investment	$200,000	-0-	$200,000
Gross Income	-0-	-0-	-0-
Deductible Expenses			
Intangible Costs	$120,000	-0-	$120,000
Administrative Costs	25,000	-0-	25,000
Bonus Payments	-0-	$25,000	25,000
Tangible Drilling Costs	-0-	30,000	30,000
Total Deductions	$145,000	$55,000	$200,000
Depletion	-0-	-0-	-0-
Taxable Income (Loss)	($145,000)	($55,000)	($200,000)

In 1982 for their $200,000 investment, the investors in Fund #1 are entitled to deduct the $120,000 in intangible drilling and development costs, and the $25,000 in administrative costs, for a total tax deduction of $145,000. They cannot deduct the bonus payment of $25,000, or the tangible equipment costs of $30,000, until 1983, when the property becomes worthless. Then they are entitled to an additional deduction of $55,000. If we assume the investors are in the 50% tax bracket, the economic results of their unsuccessful venture would be as follows:

	Investment	Tax Deduction	Tax Savings	Cost of Investment (Investor Tax Savings)
1982	$200,000	$145,000	$ 72,500	$127,500
1983	-0-	55,000	27,500	(27,500)
Total	$200,000	$200,000	$100,000	$100,000

As you can see, while the participants in Fund #1 invested a total of $200,000 in cash, after taxes the actual cost of their attempt to strike oil or gas was half that amount, or $100,000. Still costly, but at least the tax benefits absorbed part of the blow.

Now, for the more fortunate participants on Fund #2 (for help in reading the chart that appears on the next page, refer to the explanation immediately following):

As you can see, the results in the first year, 1982, are the same for Fund #2 as they were for Fund #1. It is in 1983, and thereafter, that the changes occur. Naturally, there is no loss deduction in 1983 for the bonus payment or tangible equipment costs since, far from being declared worthless, the property has begun to operate and produce income. Now, the bonus and tangible costs must be deducted through cost depletion (if that method is used) and ACRS.

Fund #2

	1982	1983	1984	1985	1986	1987	1988	1989	1990	1991
Gross Receipts	-0-	400,000	400,000	400,000	400,000	400,000	400,000	400,000	400,000	400,000
Less Underlying Royalty (⅛)	-0-	50,000	50,000	50,000	50,000	50,000	50,000	50,000	50,000	50,000
Gross Income	-0-	350,000	350,000	350,000	350,000	350,000	350,000	350,000	350,000	350,000
Deductible Expenses										
Intangible Drilling Costs	120,000	-0-	-0-	-0-	-0-	-0-	-0-	-0-	-0-	-0-
Operative & Administrative Expenses	25,000	50,000	50,000	50,000	50,000	50,000	50,000	50,000	50,000	50,000
Total Expenses	145,000	50,000	50,000	50,000	50,000	50,000	50,000	50,000	50,000	50,000
Taxable (Loss) Income before Depletion	(145,000)	300,000	300,000	300,000	300,000	300,000	300,000	300,000	300,000	300,000
Depletion	-0-	56,000	52,500	52,500	52,500	52,500	52,500	52,500	52,500	52,500
Taxable Income (Loss)	(145,000)	244,000	247,500	247,500	247,500	247,500	247,500	247,500	247,500	247,500
Non-deductible Expenditures										
Bonus Payment	25,000	-0-	-0-	-0-	-0-	-0-	-0-	-0-	-0-	-0-
Tangible Drilling Costs	30,000	-0-	-0-	-0-	-0-	-0-	-0-	-0-	-0-	-0-
Production Payment	-0-	100,000	100,000	100,000	100,000	100,000	100,000	-0-	-0-	-0-
TOTAL CASH EXPENSES	200,000	150,000	150,000	150,000	150,000	150,000	150,000	50,000	50,000	50,000
Cash Invested	200,000	-0-	-0-	-0-	-0-	-0-	-0-	-0-	-0-	-0-
CASH AVAILABLE FOR DISTRIBUTION	-0-	200,000	200,000	200,000	200,000	200,000	200,000	300,000	300,000	300,000

From the gross recepits of $400,000, ⅛ ($50,000) must be used to cover the royalty payments to the landowner. That leaves the venture with a gross income of $350,000. To determine the taxable income, we deduct from the gross income the $50,000 per year operating and administrative expenses, and also the depletion allowance. Assume the venture qualifies for percentage depletion. The depletion allowance will be equal to 16% of the gross income in 1983, and 15% in 1984 and thereafter. Note that percentage depletion thus calculated does not exceed 50% of the taxable income from the venture in any year. We will assume it also does not exceed 65% of any of the investors' taxable incomes from other sources.

To determine the cash available for distribution to the investors and operator, the gross income is now reduced by the cash expenses, which include operating costs and the production payments to the landowner through 1988, when the full $600,000 production payment will be repaid. Cash available for distribution until 1989 equals $200,000.

Now turn your attention to the chart at the bottom of the page, which sets forth the results to the participants of the investment in Drilling Fund #2, assuming they are all taxed in the 50% bracket. Remember the special allocations of this venture: the investors are entitled to 100% of the first year losses (which consist of the intangible drilling costs), and 60% of the income, losses, and cash distributions thereafter. Except in 1982, the taxable income and distributions listed on this chart represent 60% of the figures set forth on the previous one.

	Investment	**Tax (Loss) Income**	**Tax Savings (Cost)**	**Distribution**	**Annual Benefit (Cost of Investment)**	**Cumulative Benefit (Cost)**
1982	200,000	(145,000)	72,500	-0-	(127,500)	(127,500)
1983	-0-	146,400	(73,200)	120,000	46,800	(80,700)
1984	-0-	148,500	(74,250)	120,000	45,750	(34,950)
1985	-0-	148,500	(74,250)	120,000	45,750	10,800
1986	-0-	148,500	(74,250)	120,000	45,750	56,550
1987	-0-	148,500	(74,250)	120,000	45,750	102,300
1988	-0-	148.500	(74,250)	120,000	45,750	148,050
1989	-0-	148,500	(74,250)	180,000	105,750	253,800
1990	-0-	148,500	(74,250)	180,000	105,750	359,550
1991	-0-	148.500	(74,250)	180,000	105,750	465,300

As you can see, the partially sheltered returns from the venture will eventually put the investors well ahead of the game—$465,300 worth by 1991. Don't forget, however, that these results were computed for illustration purposes only and are very optimistic. The results of an actual oil and gas venture depend upon all the economic and legal factors previously discussed. Never let the lure of a pot of gold come between you and careful analysis of the investment, or the good advice of an experienced, independent professional.

How to Evaluate an Oil and Gas Program

Oil and gas tax shelter offerings usually come in the form of a prospectus or offering circular. This prospectus is written primarily to comply with SEC and state securities law disclosure requirements, not to provide readily understandable information to the average investor. The prospectus will elaborate on the risk factors and potential conflicts of interest of the promoters, as well as provide technical geological reports and data, drilling cost estimates, economic forecasts, etc., all of which are hard to read and harder to understand. There is, however, certain information that is comprehensible and that it is important to analyze before investing. This includes: prior activities of the sponsor: proposed drilling activities; use of the proceeds of the offering; the financial terms of the investment; and potential future assessments.

Prior activities of the sponsor are the most important disclosure item in an oil and gas prospectus. In addition to setting forth a brief biography of the promoters, operators, driller and geologists, and sometimes the net worth of the general partner, driller, and operator, this section should detail the performance of prior drilling ventures in which they were involved. The track record should indicate the dates the prior drilling programs were organized; the amounts invested; the number of wells drilled and whether they were completed producers or dry holes; the total revenues distributed to the investors since inception of the programs; and, hopefully, the revenues distributed over the last few months. You should look at the bottom line and see how much the other investors actually received on their investments and over what period of time. By reviewing distributions made in the last few months you may be able to determine whether they are beginning to decline, are holding steady, or possibly are even increasing. The percentage of wells completed is not as important as the amount of money they generate. You should also determine whether the wells drilled in the earlier programs are in the same geographical area and are of the same type (exploratory or developmental) as the wells in your program. Operators and geologists tend to develop expertise in specific areas which may not translate well to other locations.

The proposed drilling activity section of the prospectus should generally indicate the number of wells and whether the wells to be drilled are wildcats or developmental or a mix of the two. You should understand what you are looking for, i.e., high-risk, high-return wildcatting; lower-risk, lower-return development drilling; or perhaps a bit of both. Generally, the more wells being drilled by the program the better, since this reduces your risk. You should refer to prior activities or request information on how the geologist and operator have fared with similar drilling activities in the past.

When you review a prospectus for an investment in a drilling program, it will usually contain a report by the geologist evaluating the prospects to be drilled, and perhaps outlining the potential commercial results if the drilling is successful. The report will generally include maps which indicate proposed drilling sites as well as the location of producing wells in the area. While the reports may be impressive and the theories set forth tempting, you should not base your investment solely upon them. We have yet to read a geological report in a prospectus that does not sound promising, and yet, many investments fail.

The use-of-proceeds section of the prospectus will show you how much of your invested dollars are actually going to be used for drilling activities and how much for promotional fees, etc. Naturally, the more you spend for drilling the better (85% or more of the proceeds should be used to drill).

Financial terms of the investment should be analyzed to see exactly what is expected of you and what you can expect. Some ventures will require the investors to pay for their investments in full in the first year; others will permit then to pay in installments over several years with the later installments secured by promissory notes, letters of credit, or other collateral. In the latter type of venture, the partnership will generally borrow using the investors' future payments as collateral and thus providing the funds for drilling and the deductions, which generally will exceed the cash contributed in the initial year. Naturally, interest will have to be paid on these loans and the investor will directly or indirectly bear the expense.

You should understand how the costs and revenues of the venture are to be shared. In some ventures the investors pay all drilling costs and the promoters will pay the completion costs, with revenues to be shared in proportion to the cash contributed to the venture. This, at first glance, may seem attractive since the promoter is putting his own money into the deal. However, the completion costs are required only after a well is drilled and determined to be commercial. Therefore, the promoter's investment is a much lower risk investment than yours. In other ventures the investors put in all the cash and the promoters take a small percentage of the revenues before the investors receive their money back ("payout") and then take a larger percentage of revenues later. Depending upon the relative percentages involved and, of course, the success of the venture, either type of structure may be acceptable as long as the investor retains a fair share of the profits.

One final item to look for in the prospectus is the possibility of additional assessments. Some ventures provide that they can call upon the investors for additional cash contributions if the venture requires them for completion costs or additional drilling. If the investor fails to meet this additional call, his share of the revenues will be automatically reduced.

Before moving on to coal, we should touch upon the economic outlook for oil and gas. The decontrol of gas is scheduled to begin in 1985, with some talk in Congress and by the Administration of accelerating that date. At present there is a great discrepancy in gas prices, ranging from $2.00 or less per thousand cubic feet for shallow, older wells, to $9.00 per thousand cubic feet for deep gas wells (15,000 feet or more). Naturally, if the price controls are lifted, we can expect the price of shallow gas to increase and that of deep gas to decrease. Therefore, the shallower wells may become more economical as we draw closer to deregulation.

Oil prices, on the other hand, are not regulated, and thus fluctuate with the market. Prices rose dramatically with the oil shortages and dropped nearly as sharply with the recent "glut." When oil prices decline, so does drilling activity, making more rigs and equipment available, and thus lowering drilling costs. Therefore, it may be economically feasible to take advantage of the opportunities provided by the fluctuations of oil prices.

CHAPTER X
Coal

The coal industry is fond of calling our continent "the Persian Gulf of coal." It is estimated that buried beneath our land are nearly 4 trillion tons—enough to fill the nation's energy needs for centuries. There is no question that America is coal-rich.

Yet, despite this abundance, oil and natural gas have dominated the twentieth century, even though domestic reserves of these minerals are dwindling fast. Each year, more and more of the oil we consume is imported. As our dependence on foreign sources continues to increase, so does our trade deficit and vulnerability to political and economic pressure. Americans glimpsed the implications in the gas lines of 1973.

The government is painfully aware of the problem. In his April, 1977 address to the nation on energy, President Carter urged that we "reduce our vulnerability to potentially devastating embargoes . . . protect ourselves from uncertain supplies by reducing our dependence on oil." He called for a return to coal, our most abundant resource, and stated that increasing coal production, from 485 million tons in 1977 to more than a billion tons by 1985, was a major goal of his administration.

Unfortunately, speeches alone will not win coal a leading role in America's energy drama. There are reasons why oil is the preferred mineral; problems that plague coal from mining to burning. Environmental issues are among the most serious. In July, 1977 Carter signed into law strict regulations prohibiting the coal industry from ever again employing what has been called the "rape, ruin, and run" strategy of strip or surface mining. Now, when mining companies rip up large areas of land to expose and empty coal seams, they must restore the land to its original shape and use when they are finished. This includes filling in holes, contouring the land, replanting grass and trees, and removing all wastes. Technology that has advanced enough to slice the tops off entire mountains now must find ways to put them back. In addition, strip miners are banned entirely from certain agricultural, scenic, and other prime or difficult-to-restore areas, particularly in the West. It is too soon to gauge the full impact of the legislation on the industry, but, obviously, it will mean greater time and costs and, at least initially, lower production and profits.

Air pollution is also a problem. Users of coal are under pressure from the government and environmentalists to utilize devices such as smoke-stack "scrubbers," to prevent dangerous amounts of sulfur-dioxide from entering the atmosphere. Many have balked at their cost, inconvenience and, often, ineffectiveness. To the coal industry, it simply means another deterrent to potential customers, who might otherwise consider conversion to coal.

Add to these and other environmental issues, labor problems, health and safety hazards, transportation problems, etc., and you will understand why increased production and usage of coal is easier said than done. Then consider another stumbling block engineered, oddly enough, by the IRS. At the same time President Carter was calling for increased coal production, his tax enforcers were busy removing one of the key tax incentives for private investment in the industry. We will consider the details of this apparent lack of policy coordination within the executive branch of government later, in the tax section of this chapter.

Despite the problems, the outlook for coal is not all bleak. If not our ideal non-renewable energy resource, is is still our most abundant. We know where it is and how to get it. It is affordable (a dollar's worth of coal produces more energy than a dollar's worth of oil at today's prices), and with the help of technology, it can be cleaned up and better suited to our current energy needs.

From an investor's point of view, as oil supplies continue to diminish, the demand for coal is likely to increase, as is the selling price, which is known to fluctuate with the price of oil and gas. During the 1973 embargo, coal prices skyrocketed, and provided owner-investors with windfall profits. Prices have settled down for the time being, but the profit potential is still solid, and the chance of another upsurge ever-present.

As in real estate, the effectiveness of a coal tax shelter, or its ability to provide deductions and profits, depends upon the economic success of the venture. We cannot—and need not—make you an expert on this tightly-knit and highly-specialized industry. We can introduce you to some of the major areas of concern—economic and tax—and help you determine the right questions to ask about any coal deal you consider.

Coal ventures, like real estate, involve the use of land. However, whereas real estate ventures are concerned with the rental value of structures erected upon the land, coal ventures are concerned with the extraction and sale of minerals that lie beneath its surface. This requires three phases of operation: the selection of a site and acquisition of mineral rights; the mining of the mineral; and the sale of the coal for a profit.

Selection and Acquisition

A coal tax shelter can be initiated by the owner of a mineral property, a mining company, a syndicator, promoter, etc. In any case, it must begin with the rights to extract the coal from a particular area of land. Mineral rights are usually granted by lease, for a fixed number of years, or until all the mineable and marketable coal has been removed. In return, the venture—usually a limited partnership—will pay the lessor royalties, based upon the proceeds from the mining operation, or the amount of coal mined (e.g., $4 per ton). In order to ensure the lessor a return from his property, the lease may call for a "minimum royalty payment" each year, regardless of the tonnage produced. If this payment is required in advance of mining, it is called an "advanced minimum royalty." Chances are, if you have heard anything at all about coal shelters, it relates to these payments, and to the much-publicized Treasury Regulations and IRS ruling limiting their deductibility. We'll discuss the action and its results fully when we treat the tax aspects of coal.

There are many things to consider when evaluating a coal property. As an investor, you will probably receive your information from the prospectus, which should contain a general description of the area and a mining engineer's assessment of the quantity, type, quality, and placement of the coal reserves. A venture can acquire the rights either to property that has been, or is currently being, mined, or to unexploited territory. There are advantages to stepping into an existing operation. Presumably, the venture will then be able to utilize some or all of the development work done by the previous owner—such as the installation of roads to move in machinery and haul out coal—

which, otherwise, would involve considerable time and start-up costs.

Incidentally, the issue of roads is a key consideration. Obviously, once the coal has been mined and sold, it must be transported to the buyer. Transportation takes on new dimensions when you are dealing with something as bulky as coal, routinely sold by the ton. The preferred mode is railroad or, if proximity to the buyer makes it economically feasible, trucking. It is essential that the mine have access to transportation lines with adequate facilities for loading and hauling the coal to desired locations. The offering memorandum should describe the transportation arrangements, including the availability, price, and capacity of equipment, trucks, and trains earmarked for your coal, and any contracts entered into with truckers or railroad companies. Look for mention of a "tipple," which is a large, expensive piece of machinery that crushes coal and loads it onto railroad cars. If the venture does not own one, it may be required to pay a charge, or to sell the coal to a tipple owner at prices slightly below the market. Access to a tipple is essential since without it, the venture may not be able to ship the coal in an economically feasible manner.

You will probably get your information about the coal itself from the engineer's report included in the prospectus. If a proper analysis of the property has been made—based upon adequate test borings—predictions about the quantity, location, type, and quality of coal should be quite accurate. This is not true of oil and gas reserves, which can be elusive, despite positive geological indications.

Mineable coal deposits are located in seams which often run in uniform patterns throughout a region. These can vary greatly in width, starting at about 18″ and running much wider, especially in the West. The seams may be located below the underground water table, and thus more difficult to mine; they may be "gassy," and thus potentially explosive; or they may lack a hard and thus relatively safe ceiling. Additionally, the seams may not be uniform or they may be split (divided by a layer of dirt), in which case the coal would have to be separated from the dirt before it could be used. These factors contribute to the expense and commercial feasibility of mining and marketing the coal.

One piece of coal property can contain many seams, each located at a different depth and composed of a different type or quality of coal. By "type" of coal we mean either "steam" coal, which is used by utilities and other companies as a source of power; or metallurgical, or "met" coal, which possesses certain properties essential to the production of steel. "Met" coal will generally command a significantly higher price in the marketplace. However, in times of low steel production, even relatively high quality "met" coal may have to be sold as "steam" coal, as most purchasers fulfill their basic needs through long-term contracts.

The quality of coal is in part determined by the amount of pollutants it contains. The higher the sulfur and ash content, the "dirtier" and less desirable the coal. Although the sulfur content can be partially reduced by a washing process prior to use, this means an additional step and expense, and entails a lower margin of profit.

The BTU rating of the coal is also an indicator of quality. Basically, BTU's (British Thermal Units) are a measure of the energy that will be produced by burning the coal. The higher the rating, the better the quality of the mineral.

It is important for the coal to be of high quality, not only because it will command a better price, but also because higher-quality coal is in demand, even when coal supplies are plentiful, whereas low-quality coal may not be marketable when production levels are high. Generally, coal is considered good quality if its sulfur content is lower than 1%, its ash content lower than 5%, and its BTU rating higher than 13,000. The offering memorandum should furnish this information. It should be carefully analyzed, not only in terms of the current market, but with regard to the future as well.

Mining

Once the property has been selected and the mineral rights acquired, the venture can begin the actual business of mining coal. The mining operation may be directed by the general partners themselves, or an independent mining contractor may be employed. As with real estate and all business ventures, the competence and experience of the operator are crucial to success. Check his track record in similar kinds of ventures. Also consider whether he has the freedom to become involved in potentially competing ventures. The coal market is changeable. A better offer could lure an operator away from his responsibilities to your venture. Of course, guarantees of performance can be obtained and may be quite effective; in the case of financially responsible operators. Still, as a backup, it is best to have a syndicator with the ability and incentive to step in, should it become necessary.

Coal mining can take one of two forms, depending upon the location of the reserves. If the seams run relatively close to the earth's surface, the "strip" and "strip and auger" methods can be used. Strip mining entails removing the earth's cover (overburden) and digging out the coal with large and expensive, but relatively unsophisticated machinery, such as bulldozers and front-end loaders. Often, this includes an auger, which drills into a horizontal seam from the surface, spewing out coal as it goes. Strip and augering can be relatively simple and inexpensive, depending upon the amount of overburden involved. Unfortunately, strip mining can also be devastating to the landscape. As we said earlier, strict legislation has recently been passed, requiring mining ventures to restore stripped land to its original contour once the operation is completed. While this adds considerable expense and effort, it is intended to provide a comfortable balance between environmental and energy needs. Surprisingly, many in the coal industry are glad this issue, which floundered about in the past, has finally been resolved. At least they now know what is expected of them and can move forcefully ahead to work within the new guidelines.

If the coal is located too far beneath the earth's surface to be strip mined, it must be reached by tunneling, or "deep mining." Deep mining is environmentally less objectionable; however, it is more expensive and complicated, and poses its own kinds of problems, including mining disasters and health hazards to the miners. Deep mining also requires expensive and elaborate equipment.

In both deep mining and surface operations, it is essential for the venture to be adequately equipped at all times, since without equipment, neither coal nor profit can be produced. Typically, as coal prices begin to rise, equipment becomes more difficult to obtain. Depending upon the size of the operation, mining equipment can run in the hundreds of thousands to many millions of dollars. As a result, the cost of the equipment is usually paid for with borrowed funds and the equipment itself pledged as security for the loan.

In some cases, the partnership will acquire the necessary

equipment itself, either through purchase or lease. Frequently, however, the venture will employ a mining contractor who owns or leases the equipment himself. Either way, adequate reserves must be set aside for repairs, replacements, and carrying costs of the equipment, in case income from the operations is not sufficient. The general partner, or mining contractor, as the case may be, must have the ability to maintain and repair the equipment, which by nature is complicated and difficult to replace. They must also accurately estimate the cash reserves that may be needed to carry the loan payments through lean periods brought on by breakdowns, acts of God (such as the flood a few years ago that severely curtailed coal production in Kentucky and West Virginia), and labor problems (such as the prolonged United Mine Workers' strikes in 1978 and again in 1981).

Labor, by the way, is not a factor to be dealt with lightly in the coal mining industry. Labor problems are notoriously intense, emotional, and characterized by the volatile natures and iron wills of both sides. Many mine workers are affiliated with a union, usually the United Mine Workers Union (UMW), which is the largest and most vocal. Some mining operations are non-union, but are still affected by union activities, either through comparable wage and benefit demands, or by direct pressure from striking miners to cut off the supply of coal from non-union, non-striking mines. Interruption of income by a prolonged strike or labor dispute could be disastrous for the venture, since certain fixed expenses, such as the minimum royalty and loan payments, must be met. If arrangements are not made for a moratorium on these payments until production is resumed, or if adequate reserves of coal are unavailable for shipping, the venture risks losing both its equipment and mineral rights. For this reason, when evaluating a coal venture it is wise to consider the expiration date of the current labor contract and the prospects for a strike, including any history of wildcat strikes in the area. Also, with the help of a professional, examine the provisions made in the loan and lease agreements, if any, to defer fixed payments in the event of a problem.

The operating expenses of a coal venture will generally include the costs of such items as labor, transportation, management, access road building and maintenance, equipment repair and maintenance, coal brokerage or sales commissions, state severance taxes imposed on coal removed from the land, licensing fees, the "black lung" tax, and the costs of complying with strip mining legislation and government mining regulations. These expenses should be measured against competitive mining ventures and the projected selling price of the coal to determine whether a bottom-line profit will exist.

If the venture is not taking over an existing mining operation, be sure provisions are made for adequate working capital. It can take weeks or months to obtain the necessary permits to open a new mine. Only after the permits are obtained can haul roads be constructed and mining of coal begin. Even after the first coal is mined and sold, 30 to 45 days may elapse before the first check from the purchaser of the coal arrives. During this period, overhead expenses and loan payments, as well as the weekly payroll of the work force, must be met. Many a small-scale coal venture has failed due to a lack of working capital to sustain it until full production could be achieved.

Marketing

The final phase of a coal mining operation is marketing. The selling price of coal is influenced by many factors, including, of course, the type and quality of coal, and the supply and demand of the market. Coal prices, as we mentioned, are also known to fluctuate with those of oil and gas and so are affected by developments in the oil and gas industry.

Frequently, coal ventures attempt to minimize the effects of market fluctuations by entering into sales agreements prior to mining. These are called "end-user" contracts and usually involve large buyers, such as utilities, steel companies, or coal merchants. Foreign markets such as those in Western Europe are also a possibility. End user contracts generally specify the quantity and quality of coal to be delivered, the price (often subject to fluctuations in labor and mining costs), and the time of delivery. While they can offer substantial protection against an adverse market, their effectiveness can be weakened if the end user has the right to terminate easily. They will also serve little purpose if the commitments made are unrealistic in terms of the capabilities of the venture. These aspects of the contracts should be carefully checked, as should the arrangements made for dealing with strikes, acts of God, and other contingencies.

If a venture owns the mineral rights to relatively high-quality coal, it may prefer to forego end user contracts and take a chance on the open (or "spot") market. If the market is a good one, rising coal prices could mean substantially greater profits. On the other hand, a poor market could mean low profits, or no profits at all.

Tax Aspects of Coal Shelters

Unlike real estate, but like oil and gas, coal tax shelters generally do not offer excess tax deductions over a period of years. You will see in the illustration that closes this section that the losses available to offset an investor's income from other sources usually occur in the first year of operation. Still, in the years that follow, if the venture is well-structured and economically sound, investors in coal can expect sizeable returns, a good portion of which will be tax-free. The following are the major tax elements involved:

Advanced Minimum Royalties

As we mentioned earlier, most coal ventures structured as tax shelters acquire the mineral rights to coal property by lease, in return for royalty payments geared to the amount of coal mined, or the proceeds derived from its sale. Essentially, the equivalent of rent, these royalties are normally considered ordinary and necessary business expenditures, and are deductible in the year paid or accrued. Sometimes, however, coal leases contain special provisions for making the royalty payments, with varying tax results. For example, some leases require all or a portion of the royalties to be paid in advance, before the coal is mined or sold. Many also require a minimum royalty payment to be made each year, regardless of the tonnage produced. Advanced royalties are credited against payments due when the coal is eventually mined.

Generally, advanced royalties are deductible only in the year the coal to which they relate is actually sold. However, an exception is made for advanced minimum royalties which, according to the Treasury Regulations, may be deducted when paid or accrued, even if no coal has yet been mined or sold. This enables a venture paying advanced minimum royalties to obtain deductions in years when no income is produced (i.e., in the first year of operation). Of course, these deductions may be used by investors to offset income from other sources.

This tax benefit is small compared to that available to coal ventures before they were assaulted by the Treasury, beginning in the latter part of 1976. Prior to that time, the Regulations simply stated that advanced royalties (not necessarily limited to minimum royalties) could be deducted when paid or accrued. The only real limitation was the economic reality of the advanced payments claimed; there had to be enough coal in the ground to make it reasonably possible for the royalties paid in advance to be recouped. As a result, many coal ventures at the time were structured so that all or a substantial portion of the anticipated future royalties were paid in the first year, thus generating enormous first-year deductions. Often, non-recourse financing was used to make the payment, further enhancing the benefits. While, theoretically, the investors would pay more taxes in the later years when there would be no royalty payments to offset income from the venture, the incentive to those seeking immediate tax relief was powerful.

October 29, 1976, was the beginning of the end. Proposed Regulations were issued indicating that advanced royalties would only be deductible in the year the coal to which they related was actually sold. Only advanced *minimum* royalties could still be deducted, apparently without restriction, in the year paid or accrued. This meant that the coal leases of shelter ventures had to include minimum royalty provisions. This added pressure, but left plenty of room for substantial front-end deductions. Coal ventures were structured so that several years' (or all) of the minimum royalty payments were made in advance. Borrowed funds could still be used, although now a portion or all of them had to be personally guaranteed by the investors, to satisfy the at-risk provision. There was still good incentive for investing in coal, at least for a while.

On December 19, 1977, the ax fell again on coal. The Treasury finalized the proposed Regulations, adding provisions that severely restricted the early tax benefits available to coal ventures. First, they added a definition of a minimum royalty provision, specifying that it must call for substantial uniform payments over the life of the lease or 20 years, whichever is shorter. Second, they made the deductibility of advanced minimum royalties subject to a certain restriction contained in another section of the Code. In a related ruling, the IRS interpreted this restriction to mean that, regardless of when a prepaid or advanced minimum royalty payment is made, it can only be deducted over the period to which it relates. In other words, if a 10-year lease requires a minimum royalty payment of $20,000 per year, and the venture pays all $200,000 in the first year, it can still deduct only $20,000 that year, and $20,000 each year thereafter. Although coal ventures can still produce first-year losses, they are no longer the tax shelters they once were.

Obviously, the Regulations in force before 1976 regarding advanced royalties spurred investment in coal. One has to wonder why—in light of President Carter's pledge, less than 9 months before, to increase coal production and usage—these effective tax incentives were eliminated by a department of his own executive branch of government.

One other point to consider: the Regulations provide that advanced minimum royalties are deductible only by the owner of an "operating interest" in coal reserves. A coal lease is generally considered to provide an operating interest, unless it substantially restricts the lessee's right to mine the coal. The advice of tax counsel on this matter is recommended.

A Note of Explanation

At this point, it might be helpful to clarify a phrase that relates not just to royalties, but to all deductible expenses. We have repeatedly referred to items as deductible "when paid or accrued." The distinction depends upon the accounting method selected and regularly used by the taxpaper or venture. If the "cash receipts and disbursement method" is used, items will generally be deductible in the year they are actually paid. If the "accrual method" is used, they will be deductible in the year the obligation to pay them becomes fixed, regardless of whether or not money changes hands. An accrual method venture, therefore, can get the benefit of a deduction (say for a minimum royalty payment), by simply giving a promissory note as evidence of its obligation. Subject to the at-risk provisions, the note can even be non-recourse. Obviously, the accrual method offers greater potential for leverage and so is used by many tax shelter ventures. Those that choose cash basis may try to increase their leverage by using borrowed funds to pay expenses.

Depletion

For a complete explanation of the depletion deduction and the methods for computing it, refer to page 26. Here is a brief recap, and a look at those aspects of the deduction relevant to coal ventures.

The depletion deduction is to mineral property what the ACRS deduction is to business or investment-related property: an allowance that permits an investor to recoup his investment. In the case of mineral ventures, specifically coal, it allows the owner of mineral rights to deduct the cost of acquiring the rights to mine and, as we shall see, often more, as his coal is being mined.

The depletion deduction is available only to the owner of an "economic interest" in the coal reserves. According to the Regulations, "an economic interest is possessed in every case in which the taxpayer has acquired by investment any interest in the mineral in place. . . ." For tax purposes, an "interest in the mineral in place" generally means the investor has the right to share the proceeds derived from the sale or disposition of the coal. While most coal leases provide this right, and satisfy the acquisition "by investment" requirement as well, often the final determination of whether or not an economic interest exists rests with the structure of the deal, not the substance. Therefore, rather than risk losing the depletion allowance, an investor should clear this point with tax counsel.

The depletion deduction for coal and other mineral ventures can be computed using either the "cost depletion" or "percentage depletion" methods, whichever yields the greater allowance. Under cost depletion, the deduction for each ton of coal mined is computed by dividing the amount paid for the mineral rights by the estimated number of tons of coal acquired. For example, if 400,000 tons of coal are acquired for $800,000, the deduction per ton is $2.00 ($800,000 divided by 400,000 tons).

Under percentage depletion, the Code permits a deduction equal to 10% of the gross income from the mineral property. However, the deduction cannot exceed 50% of venture's taxable income. Gross income means, the total income derived from the mining processes—which include extracting, transporting, and processing the coal (cleaning, breaking, sizing, and loading)—minus royalties and rental payments. Taxable income for percentage depletion purposes equals gross income, minus the deductible items incurred in connection with the mining processes, such as exploration and development costs, operating expenses, transportation costs, administrative and interest charges, depreciation, and state and local taxes. Therefore, if a venture has a gross income of $300,000, and a taxable income of $50,000, under the percentage depletion method the depletion deduction for the year would be $25,000, computed as follows:

10% × $300,000 (gross income)
Equals $30,000
50% of $50,000 (taxable income)
Equals $25,000

which is thus the maximum depletion deduction allowed.

Most coal tax shelters will use the percentage depletion method, since it generally yields the greater depletion deduction.

Exploration Expenditures

All expenditures paid or incurred during the year for the purpose of ascertaining the existence, location, extent, and quality of minerals (i.e., geological surveys, core drilling, etc.) are fully and currently deductible, at the taxpayer's election, provided they arise before the venture reaches the "development stage." For tax purposes, the development stage will be considered reached when a sufficient quantity and quality of coal has been disclosed to justify commercial exploitation. However, if and when the venture achieves commercial production, the benefits of the deductions taken for exploration expenditures will be subject to recapture, in one of two ways. The venture may either include all or a portion of them in the gross income for the year commercial production is achieved; or forego depletion deductions in an amount equal to the benefits previously claimed.

Development Expenditures

Development expenditures are those arising after the existence of commercially exploitable quantities of mineral have been confirmed, but before the mine achieves commercial production. These include the costs of making the mineral accessible, i.e., road building, tunneling, and driving shafts. Expenditures that occur in the process, but which are already subject to the depreciation deduction, i.e., the costs of acquiring or improving mining equipment, may not also be claimed as development expenses.

The venture has its choice of deducting development expenditures currently, in the year they are paid or incurred, or over the period of time the coal is mined.

"Ordinary and Necessary" Business Expenses (Operating Expenditures)

Once the venture reaches the production stage, as in all businesses, the "ordinary and necessary" expenses incurred in the coal mining operation will be deductible. These expenses generally include, in addition to royalty payments, items such as labor, equipment maintenance, transportation, tippling, coal processing (i.e., washing), land reclamation, state severance taxes, management fees, fees paid to contract miners (if applicable), and selling commissions and expenses. Certain other fees paid to the organizers of the venture for guarantees and covenants not to compete, may also be considered deductible ordinary and necessary expenses, if reasonable in amount.

ACRS and Investment Tax Credit

If the venture purchases its own equipment, the ACRS deduction and investment tax credit will apply. In general, equipment used in mining coal will be considered "5-year" property for purposes of ACRS. This means the entire investment may be written off over 5 years, on an accelerated basis, and a full 10% investment credit is available if the property is new. If the property is used, only the first $125,000 will qualify for the investment credit. Of course, if the property (i.e., mining equipment) is subsequently sold or otherwise disposed of, the entire gain realized will be subject to recapture at ordinary income rates to the extent of the ACRS deductions previously taken. Similarly, if property for which investment credit has been taken is prematurely disposed of, the investment credit will also be subject to recapture.

If borrowed funds are used to purchase mining equipment, the interest on the loan is deductible, as are the rental charges for any equipment which is leased.

Sale, Exchange, or Involuntary Disposition of Coal Properties

If a venture sells its interest in a coal property or loses it, perhaps as a result of failure to meet minimum royalty payments, the gain, if any, will generally be taxed at capital gains rates, provided the property has been owned for at least 12 months.

In addition, there is a special provision of the Code [Section 631 (c)] that permits a venture to dispose of its right to mine the coal while retaining a so-called "royalty" interest in the property. In effect, the venture subleases the mineral rights, often in return for annual royalty payments, and perhaps a sizeable down payment. Again, provided the coal property has been owned for at least 12 months, the royalty income will be subject to tax at the more favorable capital gains rate. Additionally, since the venture retains an economic interest in the property, it is permitted to claim depletion deductions to offset the royalty income. However, according to the provision, only cost depletion may be used. If the venture is itself a lessee, as is usually the case with coal shelters, the royalties it in turn pays to its lessor may not be deducted outright. Instead, they can be added to the cost of the property when figuring the depletion allowance.

Section 631 (c) provides an interesting alternative for coal ventures; a way to continue receiving income from the property at capital gains rates, without the burden and risks of a mining operation.

An Illustration

On January 1, 1981, the Mae Mining Company was organized to acquire by lease the mineral rights to 1,000 acres of previously undeveloped land in Kentucky, containing approximately 1,000,000 tons of high-quality steam coal. Under the terms of the lease, the venture must pay the lessor a royalty of $4.00 per ton of coal mined and removed from the land. Regardless of the number of tons produced, beginning on January 1, 1981, a minimum royalty payment of $200,000 must be made, in advance of mining, on the first of each year. Naturally, the minimum royalty will be credited against the $4.00 due on each ton of coal mined.

The participants in the venture invest a total of $150,000 in 1981, and each personally guarantees the $200,000 promissory note, delivered to the lessor as payment for the 1981 minimum royalty. The note is payable in 4 equal annual installments of $50,000 with 10% interest. In addition, that year the venture spends $20,000 for exploration expenditures, which it elects to deduct currently, and $114,000 for access-road building and other development costs, also to be deducted in 1981. A contract miner is engaged, who agrees to supply the necessary equipment and work to mine at least 100,000 tons of coal annually, beginning in 1982. An end-user contract is signed with a local utility company that agrees to purchase up to 100,000 tons per year at $32.00 per ton. Mining, processing, tippling, transportation, and management costs, exclusive of royalties, are figured at $27.00 per ton. Based on these figures, the overall tax results of the transaction are as follow on the chart on the next page.

From the chart you can see that in 1981 the combination of the minimum royalty payment, the exploration and development expenditures, the interest on the note, and the lack of any income from the mining operations results in a net loss of $354,000, which the investors can divide and use to offset their income from other sources.

In 1982, however, the mine is in full operation, producing 100,000 tons of coal, which at $32.00 per ton furnish a gross income of $3,200,000. After deducting the mining and other costs of $3,120,000, the venture is left with $80,000 of taxable income and, theoretically, the same amount of cash. From this taxable income, the yearly allowance for depletion is deducted; it is computed by taking 10% of the gross income, up to a maximum of 50% of the taxable income. Ten percent of $3,200,000 is $320,000. However, 50% of $80,000 is $40,000, which is thus the maximum depletion deduction in 1982. This amount is further reduced by the $20,000 in development expenses claimed in 1981, which must now be recaptured. The net result for tax purposes is a taxable gain of $60,000 ($80,000 taxable income minus $20,000 depletion allowance).

There is still presumably $80,000 in cash available. Fifty thousand dollars must go toward the annual payment on the note, leaving $30,000 for distribution to the investors. As you can see from the chart, starting in 1986, when the note is fully repaid, distributions will jump considerably.

Remember, these results are for illustration purposes only, and thus present optimum tax and economic possibilities. Naturally, the actual results of a coal deal will depend upon the success of each particular venture, as well as the limitations imposed by the partnership at-risk provision and provisions affecting distributions. As always, the assistance of experts is strongly recommended in evaluating this type of investment.

	1981	1982	1983	1984	1985	1986 & thereafter
Tons mined	-0-	100,000	100,000	100,000	100,000	100,000
Gross income at $32 per ton	-0-	3,200,000	3,200,000	3,200,000	3,200,000	3,200,000
Expenses						
Mining Costs at $27 per ton	-0-	2,700,000	2,700,000	2,700,000	2,700,000	2,700,000
Royalty at $4 per ton	200,000	400,000	400,000	400,000	400,000	400,000
Exploration Expenditures	20,000	-0-	-0-	-0-	-0-	-0-
Development Expenditures	114,000	-0-	-0-	-0-	-0-	-0-
Interest on Notes	20,000	20,000	15,000	10,000	5,000	-0-
TOTAL EXPENSES	354,000	3,120,000	2,115,000	3,110,000	3,105,000	3,100,000
Taxable Income (Loss) before depletion deduction	(354,000)	80,000	85,000	90,000	95,000	100,000
Depletion Deduction	-0-	20,000	42,500	45,000	47,500	50,000
TAXABLE INCOME (LOSS)	(354,000)	60,000	42,500	45,000	47,500	50,000
Payment on Notes	-0-	50,000	50,000	50,000	50,000	
CASH AVAILABLE FOR DISTRIBUTION		30,000	35,000	40,000	45,000	100,000

Other Solid Mineral Properties

The tax aspects of coal ventures are generally applicable to ventures involving other solid minerals (e.g., gold, silver, copper, zinc, bauxite, etc.), except for the capital gains provision of Section 631 (c), which applies only to coal, iron, and timber. If the commercial exploitation of other minerals becomes as economically feasible and potentially rewarding as coal, it is probable that ventures involving them will also be structured as tax shelters.

PART IV
Other Major Shelters

CHAPTER XI
Equipment Leasing

In some ways, equipment leasing as a tax shelter is similar to real estate. Both types of ventures involve the rental of property, both depend heavily upon ACRS deductions and leverage, and both spread their excess losses over a period of years. However, the tax benefit period of an equipment leasing venture is generally much shorter. Only a few years after investing—as ACRS deductions begin to decline or disappear and interest payments give way to amortization—investors will find themselves taxed on more income from the venture than they actually receive. This early appearance of so-called phantom income makes equipment leasing unsuitable for those seeking long-term tax deferrals. As we shall see, it is further not geared for those seeking spectacular returns, such as could result from a successful oil deal. Basically, equipment leasing can be a relatively conservative method of deferring tax liability for a short period of time, while possibly earning a moderate profit.

It is only in the last 2 decades that equipment leasing has emerged as a widely accepted method of acquiring property. Today, it has grown into the multi-billion-dollar industry, involving a vast array of "equipment" ranging from computers to jet aircraft, boxcars to cable TV, oil tankers, shipping containers, medical equipment, farm machinery, and more. When used as a tax shelter, it usually involves the following elements: equipment with a high purchase price, paid for largely with borrowed funds; one party or investor group (the "lessor") willing to assume the burdens and risks of property ownership and, often, to accept a lower return on investment in exchange for early tax benefits; and one party (the "lessee") willing—or forced—to sacrifice the tax benefits of ownership to be free of the down payment, burden, and risks.

In a simple tax shelter leasing transaction, the investor group (usually an individual, limited partnership, or subchapter S corporation) purchases the equipment using invested capital plus a sizeable loan, either from the seller or a financial institution. Since equipment leasing is subject to the "at-risk" limitations, a portion (or all) of the loan will probably be personally guaranteed by the investors to enable them to take advantage of all the initial tax benefits. Prior to or simultaneous with the purchase, the property is leased to a user, at a rental rate designed to cover the loan payments and, ideally, to provide some excess cash for distribution to the investors.

An owner-investor should know exactly what it is the lessee is trying to avoid or accomplish by leasing. *His benefits can be your risks*. In that context, we will approach the economics of equipment leasing.

One of the simplest motives for leasing is the possibility of obtaining the use of the property at a lower price. Often, in return for a financially sound lessee and initial tax benefits, an investor group will be willing to accept a lower rate of return on its cash investment than the interest rate available from a lender. Thus, the effective annual cost of using the property is lower than it would be if the lessee purchased the property using borrowed funds.

A party might also choose to lease rather than purchase equipment because it wants to avoid, or is unable to raise, a down payment. Or perhaps it is a new or high-risk company that cannot secure a loan. An owner-investor must always question the credit-worthiness of the lessee. That factor may be the single most important reason for the success or failure of the venture.

If a lessee is unable to meet its rental payments and defaults on its lease, the investor group could be forced to go through lengthy and sometimes prohibitively expensive foreclosure proceedings to repossess the property. In anticipation of such problems, it is important that the group obtain a "perfected security interest" in the property (similar to a mortgage interest), which would entitle it to a priority claim to the property before any other creditors. Even then, repossession could be followed by a frantic effort to locate a new lessee or buyer. For, all the while, there is the pressure of the purchase loan—for which, you will remember, the investors are personally liable. Even disregarding their liability, if they want to keep the property, they will have to continue making the payments, or risk seeing the lender exercise its own security interest and foreclose. Foreclosure or premature sale of the property would bring the rules of recapture into play, terminating any tax deferral and probably resulting in an economic loss.

There are several reasons why it might be difficult to sell the equipment or to find a new lessee. These should be considered, not only because of a possible default, but also because many equipment leasing ventures depend upon lease renewals or eventual sale of the property to recoup the cash investment of the participants. This is especially true if the initial lease is not a "full-payment" lease, which means it is not sufficient either in duration or rental rate to completely repay the loan and return a profit to the investors.

Obsolescence is a major obstacle to lease renewals and sale of the equipment. Especially in technologically intensive fields such as computers and medicine, "generations" of advances could occur before the initial lease runs out. Specialized equipment that appeals only to a limited market also could be difficult to re-rent, as could equipment that is hard to move, maintain, or repair.

Just as the viability of the lessee and the nature of the equipment are crucial, so are the terms of the lease agreement, for they govern the rights, duties, and relationship of the different parties. One must assume the lessee has negotiated the lease to afford itself maximum protection. Thus the lease should be scrutinized by a professional representing the investor's interests, to be sure it contains no troublesome provisions. For example, the lessee should not have the right to terminate prematurely or to assign the lease to another party who is financially less responsible.

Depending upon the type of equipment and length of the lease, the responsibility for maintaining, repairing, replacing parts, and insuring the property may rest either with the lessor or lessee. Generally, in a long-term situation, the obligation will rest with the lessee. Even then, in the interest of preserving the value of your property, it is essential that provisions be made for the use of skilled technicians and quality replacement parts.

If the equipment should prove defective, the risk of loss, repair costs, and potential damages could be substantial. The lessor could bear the burden of defects, either through expressly stated warranties, or through warranties that are implied. If the equipment is defective and causes loss of business or other economic damage to the lessee, not only could the lease be terminated but the lessor could be held responsible for any damages occurring, unless there are specific disclaimers in his behalf. In this situation, the protection of limited liability is very important. Furthermore, the investor group should be certain to obtain the warranties of the seller and manufacturer upon purchase. If they are financially sound, the warranties could be helpful in avoiding the adverse consequences of defective equipment.

As in most tax shelter situations, investors in equipment leasing are placed in a passive role, dependent upon the ability, experience, and integrity of the syndicator and manager. Presumably, the offering memorandum will provide some insight into their backgrounds and past performances in similar types of ventures. The investor should feel confident that they will be able to handle the potential problems and carry out the functions of an equipment leasing venture, such as profitably selling or re-leasing the equipment in the event of a default, early termination, or expiration of the lease, and enforcing warranties in the event of a defect. They should also have the responsibility to make periodic inspections to make sure the lessee complies with the terms of the lease concerning maintenance of the property. This is the best way to ensure that the equipment will be returned in good condition and will have economic value at the end of the lease term.

These are the general economic considerations of equipment leasing. Of course, they should be supplemented by the help of a professional who understands the nature and risks of the specific kinds of business and property involved. Some ventures are more complicated than others and some, like cable TV, require substantial services in addition to equipment. Cable TV ventures, a fairly common leasing shelter, usually involve the construction of a cable system in a specific area and the installation of equipment in each subscriber's home, in return for an installation fee and a monthly "subscription" charge. The venture or its managers normally bear the responsibility of operating and maintaining the system. Because of the technical nature of the business, their skill and experience in choosing a location (a populated area with many potential subscribers is best) and successfully installing, operating, and marketing the system is particularly important.

Cable television, as well as many other types of equipment used in leasing ventures, often is subject to the rules, regulations, and restrictions of government regulatory agencies, such as the Federal Communications Commission or, in the case of railroad cars, the Interstate Commerce Commission. This might include limitations on the rental rates that may be charged. When investing, it is always wise to check out the major effects of these regulatory provisions on the equipment under consideration.

Before moving on to the tax aspects, we should mention one type of venture that has arisen in recent years which combines many of the tax and economic aspects of both equipment leasing and oil and gas investments. In this type of venture the investors will purchase the tangible equipment necessary to complete and produce an oil and gas well. The equipment generally consists of tubing, casing, valves, and tank batteries (storage tanks). This equipment will either be leased to the drilling venture or provided in exchange for a percentage of the revenues generated from the well. In this manner, investors can participate in oil and gas wells with substantially lower risk than if they had participated in the drilling activities, since their money is not spent until the well has been drilled and tested. Naturally, their return is not as great as the drilling partners', nor are their first-year tax deductions. However, the combination of investment tax credit and ACRS deductions over the years can still make this type of venture attractive from a tax point of view.

Tax Aspects

Equipment leasing ventures generally derive their tax benefits from the ACRS deduction; to a lesser extent, the investment tax credit; and, with certain limitations, the interest deduction. These, together with normal operating expenses, such as maintenance, salaries, and insurance, usually provide deductions and credits in the early years of the venture that exceed income. As we said, however, in a relatively short time, a cross-over point will be reached and the investors will begin to be taxed on "phantom income," or income they do not receive. This is, perhaps, the most serious drawback of equipment leasing shelters. Investors should be aware of this problem and plan to deal with it, before investing.

ACRS and Recapture

Under the Economic Recovery Tax Act of 1981, all personal property (i.e., equipment) falls into one of four categories. Equipment is classified for tax purposes as either "3-year," "5-year," "10-year," or "15-year" property. Cars, light-duty trucks, research and experimentation equipment, certain horses, and special tools are classified as 3-year property. At the other end of the spectrum, the 15-year class consists exclusively of certain types of property used by public utilities. The 10-year class is also composed largely of public utility property, as well as railroad tank cars and certain amusement park structures. Most other personal property falls into the 5-year class, which is the catchall for property not included in the 3-, 10-, or 15-year classes.

The percentage of the cost of an asset which may be written off each year under ACRS is determined by two things. One is the recovery class the property falls into, and the other is the year the property is placed in service. The law provides 3 tables indicating what percentage of the cost of the property may be deducted each year. One table is for property placed in service in 1981 through 1984. A second table applies to property placed in service during 1985, and a third table applies to property placed in service after 1985. The tables are reproduced on the following page for 3-, 5-, and 10-year property:

1981–1984

	Class of Property		
	3-year	5-year	10-year
Recovery Year		[Recovery Percentage]	
1	25	15	8
2	38	22	14
3	37	21	12
4		21	10
5		21	10
6			10
7			9
8			9
9			9
10			9

1985

	Class of Property		
	3-year	5-year	10-year
Recovery Year		[Recovery Percentage]	
1	29	18	9
2	47	33	19
3	24	25	16
4		16	14
5		8	12
6			10
7			8
8			6
9			4
10			2

1986 and after

	Class of Property		
	3-year	5-year	10-year
Recovery Year		[Recovery Percentage]	
1	33	20	10
2	45	32	18
3	22	24	16
4		16	14
5		8	12
6			10
7			8
8			6
9			4
10			2

Here is an example of how the ACRS deduction is computed. If a computer (5-year property) is purchased for $100,000 and placed in service in 1982, the ACRS deduction for that year will be $15,000 (15% of its cost). During 1983, 22% ($22,000) may be written off. In 1984, 1985, and 1986, the ACRS deduction will be $21,000 per year. However, if the same asset is purchased and placed in service in 1986, the write-offs would be: 1986—$20,000; 1987—$32,000; 1988—$24,000; 1989—$16,000; and 1990—$8,000.

The ACRS deductions indicated in the tables are allowed regardless of when the property is placed in service during the year. In other words, for a taxpayer in an existing venture, using a full calendar year, the same ACRS deduction will be allowed for a $100,000 piece of equipment whether it is purchased and placed in service on January 1 or December 31. However, a limit is imposed in the case of a taxable year of less than 12 months—for example, if a partnership is formed in the middle of a year. The amount allowed is determined by multiplying the first-year ACRS percentage in the table by a fraction, the numerator of which is the number of months in the short taxable year and the denominator of which is 12. For example, if a partnership is formed in July of a given year and has a December 31 year-end, only half [6 months ÷ 12 months] of the first-year ACRS deduction will be available. It remains to be seen whether enterprising tax shelter promoters will be allowed to organize partnerships with few or no assets early in the year, and then later admit investor partners and purchase equipment, while claiming a full ACRS allowance.

In addition to the ACRS allowance, beginning in 1982, taxpayers will be permitted to expense (completely deduct in the year of acquisition) a limited portion of the cost of personal property which would otherwise be deductible only through ACRS. In 1982 and 1983, the amount of cost which may be expensed is $5,000 per year. During 1984 and 1985, the first $7,500 of cost may be expensed. For 1986 and later years, the first $10,000 of cost may be expensed. This additional deduction is not pro-rated according to the time the property is placed in service or as a result of a short taxable year; it is permitted in full no matter when the asset is acquired. However, if the election to expense is made, the amount expensed may not also be included in the cost recovered through ACRS. Furthermore, no investment tax credit is allowed on the expensed portion of the cost of the asset; only the balance of the cost is eligible for the credit, assuming the asset otherwise qualifies.

As far as ACRS recapture, the standard rules apply to equipment leasing ventures. When equipment or other personal property is sold or otherwise disposed of, any gain will be taxed at ordinary income rates, to the extent of all ACRS deductions previously taken.

Investment Tax Credit

The investment credit is generally available to the purchasers of personal property involved in equipment leasing ventures. The credit, which is fully explained in Chapter III, can offer substantial tax savings, since it is not merely a deduction which reduces income subject to tax, but a direct credit against taxes that are due. Unfortunately, there is a significant restriction on the use of the credit by non-corporate owners (including partners of a partnership) and shareholders of a subchapter S corporation who lease the property to another party. In an apparent attempt to limit the tax shelter potential of equipment leasing ventures, the Code prohibits non-corporate lessors from claiming the investment credit unless:

- the property in question was manufactured or produced by the lessor; or
- the term of the lease (including renewal provisions) is less than 50% of the useful life of the property and,
- in the first 12 months of the lease, the business expenses of the lessor (including maintenance, salaries, repairs, etc., but not including depreciation or interest) exceed 15% of the income from the property.

This eliminates the use of the credit when the lessee assumes all the burdens of maintenance, repairs, and insurance, as in a "net lease" situation. Thus, those situations that provide the greatest economic protection for the lessor might not provide investment credit. Fortunately, if the credit is unavailable to the investors, the Code allows it to be assigned to the lessee, presumably in return for higher rent.

The Interest Deduction

Generally, the interest paid in connection with the purchase of property that is leased will be fully deductible, unless it is considered "investment interest," in which case the deduction could be limited. In an equipment leasing situation, interest will be considered "investment interest" if either of the following occurs:

- the sum of the "ordinary and necessary" business deductions of the lessor, exclusive of interest, taxes, and depreciation, is less than 15% of the rental income for the year; or
- the lessor is guaranteed a specific return on his investment, or against economic loss.

In either case, the interest deduction will be limited to $10,000, plus the net investment income for the year. Net investment income equals the investor's income from investment property (as opposed to business operations), such as dividends, interest, short-term capital gains, etc., minus the investment expenses for the year, which include property taxes and ACRS.

Classification as investment interest is not uncommon in equipment leasing ventures and could substantially alter the anticipated tax results. However, it should be noted that if any portion of the interest deduction is not allowed in a given year because of this limitation, it generally may be carried forward and used in a subsequent year.

Equipment Leasing and At-Risk

Equipment leasing is subject, to the "at-risk" limitation, which was discussed fully in Chapter V. As a result, in order to claim the investment credit, if otherwise available, and utilize the excess deductions that may be available in the early years of such ventures, investors may be forced to personally guarantee all or a portion of the loans made with respect to the purchase of the property. This will not present a problem to the investors as long as the lessee continues to make rental payments sufficient to cover the loan payments. However, should the lessee default or otherwise terminate the lease, the investors could be called upon to repay the loan to the extent of their guarantees.

Classification of the Transaction

In many respects, the business arrangements of a leasing transaction are similar in structure and effect to a sale of the property by the lessor to the lessee with the purchase price paid in installments. This is particularly true when most of the risks, burdens, and benefits of ownership fall upon the lessee. The danger in a tax shelter situation is that, although the parties call it a lease and treat it as such, the IRS and courts will view the transaction as a sale, for tax purposes. Gone would be such important tax benefits as the ACRS deduction and investment tax credit, if the lessor was no longer considered the owner.

Fortunately, the IRS will issue an advanced ruling as to whether they consider a transaction a lease or sale. To receive such ruling, the following conditions must be met:

- the lessor must make and maintain throughout the term of the lease (including renewal options) a minimum unconditional at-risk investment equal to at least 20% of the cost of the property;
- the fair market value of the property at the end of the lease term (including renewal options) must equal at least 20% of the cost;
- the estimated remaining useful life of the property at the end of the lease term (including renewal options) must be at least 1 year, or 20% of the total estimated useful life, whichever is greater;
- at the time the property is purchased, the lessee may not have a contractual right to buy it at less than fair market value, nor may it have the right, at the time the property is first placed into service, to cause it to be purchased by another party;
- the lessee may not furnish or pay any part of the cost of the property, or improvements to it (except for ordinary maintenance and repairs);
- the lessee may not lend the lessor any of the funds to purchase the property, or guarantee any loans made in connection with the purchase; and,
- the lessor must demonstrate that it expects to make a profit from the transaction, exclusive of tax benefits.

We should also note that the IRS usually will not rule with respect to property that is considered of "limited use," which means property that probably will not have any other lessees or buyers at the end of the initial lease term.

While the above guidelines do not have the effect of law, they do touch upon the issues that would undoubtedly be raised by the courts, should they have to decide the status of a transaction for tax purposes. If an advanced ruling is not obtained, at the very least, the advice and opinion of tax counsel on these matters should be sought.

Ownership of the Property

As we discussed with respect to real estate, at the request of the lender or for convenience purposes, property may frequently be owned on behalf of the investors by a trust, or nominee corporation. The danger in these situations is that the IRS and courts will rule that the nominal owner is entitled to certain major tax benefits. Once again we must warn that if a nominee or trust is involved, an advanced ruling, or the advice of counsel, on the tax consequences should be sought.

Sale of the Property

In the event of a sale of property utilized in an equipment leasing venture, gain will be taxed at ordinary income rates to the extent of any ACRS deductions previously taken. The balance of the gain should be eligible for long-term capital gains treatment, provided the property has been held for the required 12 months.

An Illustration

On June 1, 1981, Beverly W. purchased a new computer for $100,000. She paid $20,000 in cash—$10,000 on June 30 and $10,000 on January 1, 1982. The $80,000 balance was also paid on June 30, 1981, from the proceeds of a loan by the manufacturer, which Beverly personally guaranteed. As a concession to aid sales, the manufacturer agreed that the loan must be repaid over 7 years with interest at a below-market 10%. Payments were set at $15,945 per year ($1,328.75 per month), and it was agreed that only interest would be payable until January 1, 1982, at which time amortization would begin.

Simultaneous with the purchase, Beverly leased the computer

to a corporation for a 6½-year term at an annual rental rate of $17,000, payable $1,425 per month. The lessee, who was granted a 3-month rent concession, agreed to bear all the costs of maintenance, insurance, and repairs. As a result, a net lease was considered to exist, triggering the investment interest limitation, and preventing Beverly, a non-corporate owner, from utilizing the investment tax credit.

The economic and tax results of the transaction over the 6½-year term of the lease are as follows:

	Rental Income	Interest Payment	ACRS	Taxable Income (Loss)	Amortization of Loan	Cash Flow	Cash Contribution
1981	4,275	4,000	15,000	(14,725)	-0-	275	10,000
1982	17,100	7,625	22,000	(12,525)	8,320	1,155	10,000
1983	17,100	6,755	21,000	(10,655)	9,190	1,155	
1984	17,100	5,794	21,000	(9,694)	10,151	1,155	
1985	17,100	4,732	21,000	(8,632)	11,213	1,155	
1986	17,100	3,559	-0-	13,541	12,386	1,155	
1987	17,100	2,263	-0-	14,837	13,682	1,155	
					64,942	7,205	20,000

In 1981, although the lease commenced on June 30, only 3 months' rental was paid, because of the rent concession. Interest, however, was calculated for 6 months at 10%. Amortization of the loan did not begin until 1982. The ACRS deductions are computed on the basis of the percentages prescribed by statute. If Beverly placed the computer in service in 1982, she could expense $5,000 of the cost that year and recover the remaining $95,000 of cost through ACRS. Because Beverly is not able to claim the investment credit, it would be advisable for her to expense whatever portion of the cost she can.

You can see from the chart just how quickly the crossover occurs in an equipment leasing venture. Basically, this is because of the short ACRS life of the equipment and the short term for amortization of the loan. By 1986, Beverly will be paying taxes in ever-increasing amounts on more income than she actually receives. Assuming a 50% tax rate, the results of the investment to her in the first 6½ years will be as follows:

	[A]	[B]	[C]	[D]		
	Cash Invest-ment	**Taxable Income (Loss)**	**Tax Savings (Cost)**	**Distri-bution**	**Net Benefit (Cost) [A-C+D]**	**Cumulative Benefit (Cost)**
1981	10,000	(14,725)	7,362.50	275	(2,632.50)	(2,632.50)
1982	10,000	(12,525)	6,262.50	1,155	(2,582.50)	(4,945.00)
1983	-0-	(10,655)	5,327.50	1,155	6,482.50	1,537.50
1984	-0-	(9,694)	4,847.00	1,155	6,002.00	7,539.50
1985	-0-	(8,632)	4,316.00	1,155	5,471.00	13,010.50
1986	-0-	13,541	(6,770.50)	1,155	(5,615.50)	7,395.00
1987	-0-	14,837	(7,468.50)	1,155	(6,313.50)	1,081.50
TOTAL	20,000		13,876.50	7,205		

Although at the end of 6½ years the equipment has cost Beverly $20,000, it has saved her $13,876.50 in taxes and earned her $7,205 in distributions from the rental activities. Thus, through the end of 1987, Beverly has actually received $1,081.50 more than she invested to purchase the equipment through tax savings and distributions. Keep in mind, however, that the lease expires at the end of 1987 and Beverly is personally liable on the loan, which has a remaining balance due at the end of 1987 of $15,058. Whether or not she ends up with a profit from the transaction, rather than merely a tax deferral or an economic loss, now depends largely upon whether she can re-lease or sell the equipment.

CHAPTER XII
Movies, Books, Records, Artworks, and Magazines

Prior to the Tax Reform Act of 1976, motion pictures were popular as tax shelters, because of their great potential for leveraging depreciation deductions and investment tax credits into large front-end tax benefits, with little or no risk to the investor. The appeal of these ventures was greatly diminished when the "at-risk" rules were enacted. As a result, investors in these properties can no longer use non-recourse financing to increase allowable tax benefits.

We should note at the outset that the future of movie, book, record, and artwork deals is very uncertain from a tax point of view. Through various rulings and other actions which we will shortly discuss, the IRS has indicated that it is scrutinizing these activities. Perhaps rightly so. There is no question that many of these ventures are both highly speculative and highly leveraged, and thus lend themselves to abuse. The IRS seems determined to limit their tax shelter potential, either through restrictions on the use of specific allowances, application of the at-risk rules, or both. This is not to say that a well-structured, legitimate movie, book, record, or artwork investment cannot still offer substantial tax benefits, and even return a nice profit. Just be aware that many key tax issues are being challenged by the IRS and could at any time be resolved to the detriment of the investor. For this reason, it is absolutely crucial to consult a tax expert when considering one of these deals.

Apart from the at-risk factor, movie, book, record, and artwork shelters have many economic and tax considerations in common. All involve the purchase of the materials and rights needed to reproduce and market a specific property. In a movie deal, the investors acquire the negative (from which prints will be made) of a previously unreleased film, together with the copyrights necessary to commercially exploit it. In a book deal, the investor purchases the plates, negatives, and copyrights needed to produce and exploit a previously unpublished book. A record deal involves the purchase of a master recording and the copyrights to a previously unreleased record, while an artwork deal involves the purchase of the master (e.g., a lithographic plate) of an original work of art, along with the rights to reproduce and sell it, often in limited quantities.

To acquire these properties, the investor will usually be required to provide a cash down payment, along with a promissory note to the seller or producer acknowledging an obligation to repay the balance of the purchase price, generally from the proceeds of the property. In a sense, the seller acts as the lender, although it is also possible to obtain independent financing, especially in movie deals, when the venture has retained a major distributor to market the film. A date is set, perhaps 7 to 10 years later, for the repayment of the balance of the note, should the proceeds from the property prove insufficient. Of course, the seller will retain a security interest in the property as collateral for the loan and the investor will be personally liable for repayment in order to satisfy the at-risk rules.

Since the investor's obligation to repay the full purchase price may be contrived to inflate the price to drive up tax benefits, the IRS, in a series of recent rulings, has reiterated that the burden is on the taxpayer to prove that the stated purchase price is, in fact, equal to the "fair market value" of the property. If this is not proven, the stated cost might be disallowed for ACRS, investment credit, and interest deduction purposes, with significant adverse tax results.

The value of artistic, literary, and musical properties is more difficult to quantify than the value of tangible property, such as a piece of equipment or a building. Usually, the promoter of a deal will provide an appraisal of the property by an "independent" expert in the field. It is up to the investor to verify his independence and credentials as well. Calling in another expert can never hurt. When the appraisal is reviewed, be sure it sets forth the basis for its conclusions, as well as an analysis of the actual cost of producing the property. If production costs are strikingly lower than the stated value of the property, it could mean the latter is unrealistic. The economic performance of similar types of property, especially those by the same producer, writer, musician, or artist, is also a good indicator of value. You should be aware that the IRS has its own panel of experts to evaluate these properties and the Economic Recovery Tax Act of 1981 added a provision imposing a penalty of up to 30% if the appraised value of any property exceeds 150% of what the true value is determined to be (more about this in later chapters).

When acquiring any of these properties, it is also important to obtain the right to exploit them in as many markets as possible. Frequently, the rights purchased cover only U.S. distribution or, in the case of movies, do not include television rights. If there are restrictions on the rights you obtain, get an expert opinion about the possible economic consequences.

Once the property has been acquired, its commercial success will depend to a large extent on the effectiveness of the production, marketing, and distribution programs. Theater dates must be arranged for movies and presumably television rights will be sold; books must appear on bookstore shelves; records in record stores; and artworks in galleries, mail order catalogues, and other distribution channels. Promotion and advertising must be effective and well timed to contend with the ever-present competition from other producers, publishers, musicians, and artists seeking their share of the market.

Since it would be difficult, time-consuming, and probably, ineffective and expensive for an investor to direct these activities himself (or even to personally locate a representative), a tax shelter offering will generally make the services of a distributor available, (unfortunately, if the selected distributor defaults or fails to perform, the investor could be left on his own to find a replacement). The skill and track record of the distributor in similar ventures should be carefully evaluated, since his expertise could mean the difference between success and failure. Everyone is undoubtedly aware of what good publicity and high exposure can do for property of this sort. Remember, as in all tax shelter deals, only if the property is commercially successful can you hope for a return equal to, or greater than, your investment.

For his services, the distributor will generally receive a share of the income or receipts from the property, possibly with an upfront fee. Sometimes, he will agree to advance the costs of production, promotion, advertising, and distribution, in which case he will probably insist on being repaid out of the first available proceeds from the property. He may not be the only one with priority claims on the profits. The seller too will demand a share, as repayment on the note. This is an important point to consider when analyzing one of these deals. Once everyone takes his piece of the pie, will a phenomenally successful property be required, in order to allow the investor to recoup his investment, much less show a profit?

Even under the best of circumstances, the odds of a huge success are not great. Public acceptance of movies, books, records, and artworks is highly subjective and difficult to predict. Because of the speculative nature of these deals, they are best suited to high-bracket taxpayers, who can afford the investment and, as we shall now see, the tax risks they involve.

Tax Aspects

Because movie deals were, for many years, the most popular of this type of investment, most of the tax law in the area has developed around them. There have been some rulings with respect to books, records, and artworks, but mainly just indications that the IRS plans to treat them in much the same manner as movies. It is obvious that the Service has little use for any of these shelters and will continue to contest them vigorously, as it has for years. The attack is mainly centered on 2 key allowances—the investment tax credit and now the ACRS deduction. Of course, the valuation (basis) of the property for both ACRS and tax credit purposes is the IRS's main weapon.

Investment Tax Credit

The IRS has long been trying to limit the availability of the investment tax credit to movie shelters and, more recently, to book, record, and artwork deals. Their position has been that most of the costs of producing a movie, i.e., expenses for screenplay, wardrobe, set design, actors, directors, cameramen, etc., are "intangible" costs, and thus are not eligible for the credit. (Remember, investment credit is only available for tangible property with a useful life of at least 3 years.) Prior to the Tax Reform Act of 1976, the Treasury position was set forth in Regulations that also listed as "intangible" many of the costs of producing books, i.e., manuscript, illustration, research, clerical, and other such expenses. While records and artworks were not specifically dealt with, it was safe to assume that they too would suffer the impact of the Regulations.

Had the position of the Treasury been upheld, it would have meant the elimination of a significant tax benefit for movie investors. Fortunately for the taxpayer, however, Walt Disney Productions took the issue to court and won. The decision was that the costs of producing a motion picture are tangible, and thus are eligible for investment credit. The Treasury Regulation was ruled invalid in that respect.

The decision of the court was codified by the 1976 Tax Reform Act, which stated that, with certain exceptions and limitations, the costs of producing movies and television films and tapes could qualify for investment credit. Still, the IRS refused to let go. They seemed determined to limit the tax benefits from these ventures one way or another. Apparently, they have shifted their attack on movie shelters to another front. A little-publicized private ruling indicated that they intend to construe the provisions of the Tax Reform Act very strictly. Stubbornly, they insist that the Reform Act position—that movies are to be treated as tangible property—applies only for investment credit purposes. For all other purposes, such as determining whether property qualifies for accelerated cost recovery, they will continue to argue that the costs are intangible, and thus not eligible.

As for books, records, and artworks, which were not specifically dealt with by the Act, it is probable that the IRS will continue to challenge their use of investment credit on the grounds that the bulk of their costs are intangible. While there is certainly legal precedent to support the opposing position, should it come to a court battle, the time and expense of fighting the issue might not be worth the victory.

While the Tax Reform Act generally allowed the use of investment credit for movies and television films and tapes, it also included certain restrictions. Only new property of this type is eligible for the credit and then, only to the extent of the "ownership interest" in it. Congressional Committee reports indicate that an investor's "ownership interest" is meant to equal his capital at-risk. Thus, the investment credit for a motion picture apparently is limited to 10% of either the qualified cost of the property, or the amount the investor is at-risk, whichever is lower. The Economic Recovery Tax Act of 1981 added a provision (discussed in Chapter III) limiting the basis of property for tax credit purposes to the amount the taxpayer is at-risk with respect to this property. It is possible, although unlikely, that this provision does not apply to movies but does apply to books, records, and artworks.

Qualified cost, you will recall, is the portion of the cost of property normally eligible for investment credit. Generally, for movies, the investor is limited to either 6⅔% of the qualified cost (provided he uses this percentage with respect to all his film properties) or the percentage based on the useful life of the movie, which for this purpose is considered to equal the time it takes for depreciation deductions to total 90% of the cost. The latter method probably won't offer any additional benefits, since the income forecast method of depreciation (explained later in this chapter), which is commonly used by movie ventures in lieu of ACRS, usually reaches the 90% level in less than 7 years.

It should also be noted that only those portions of the cost of producing a movie or television film or tape attributable to the United States (i.e., American actors, sets, film processing, etc.) are eligible for investment credit, unless at least 80% of the costs are domestic, in which case all will be allowed. If the 6⅔% method is chosen, the tax credit is not subject to recapture as with the 90% method.

Some ambiguity was created with respect to movies as a result of the 1981 Act. If the taxpayer elects to use the ACRS allowance for a movie, it is possible that the normal tax credit rules might apply (see Chapter III) rather than the special 6⅔% and 90% rules set forth above. The normal rules apply to books, records, and artworks (subject, of course, to the IRS argument that they are intangible property and thus do not qualify for the tax credit).

Since books, records, and artworks are not bound by the Reform Act restrictions on investment tax credit, they are also not assured of the privileges. Undoubtedly, more challenges and changes are to come. For this reason, when considering one of these investments, it is especially important to consult a tax expert about the current status of this area of the law.

Depreciation and ACRS

It is obvious that the IRS is also trying to limit the use of depreciation deductions by these types of ventures. Again, a major issue is whether or not the costs of the property involved are intangible. For, although the Code permits a deduction for the depreciation (now ACRS) of both tangible and intangible property, only tangible property (with a useful life of at least 3 years) may use the accelerated methods or ACRS. By asserting that the bulk of the costs of movies, and, by implication, books, records, and artworks, is intangible for depreciation purposes, the IRS may be attempting to pressure investors into using the straight-line method, rather than risk a challenge. While there is certainly legal precedent to support the taxpayer's position, again the fruits of victory must be weighed against the effort and expense of litigation.

In addition to the "intangible" issue, the IRS is also questioning the cost basis for computing depreciation (now ACRS). Their position is that the cost basis for depreciation or ACRS cannot exceed the fair market value of the property. Obviously, this could substantially reduce the deduction. Whether the IRS position will be upheld remains to be seen. Meanwhile, an investor can protect himself by making sure he has sufficient data, in the form of appraisals, etc., to support his claim that the fair market value of the property equals the cost.

There are certain other items to be aware of with respect to depreciation and ACRS.This type of property would generally be considered 5-year property for ACRS purposes. However, most movie deals will elect not to use ACRS and instead will use the income forecast method. The income forecast method was devised for properties like these, in recognition of the fact that their flow of income is often quite uneven. (This is not necessarily true of artworks.) Commonly, income is highest in the year of release, then rapidly diminishes thereafter. The idea of income forecast is to match the depreciation deductions to the income produced by the property. This is done by multiplying the depreciable cost (cost minus salvage value) by a fraction determined as follows: the denominator is the estimated total income to be earned from the venture during its useful life; the numerator is the income from the property for the year. For example: the owner and the distributor of a film with a depreciable cost of $1,000,000 estimates that the total income from it will be $1,200,000. In the year of release, the income is $600,000. Using the income forecast method, the depreciation deduction that year will be $500,000, computed as follows:

$$\$1{,}000{,}000 \times \frac{\$\ 600{,}000\ (1)}{\$1{,}200{,}000\ (2)} = \$500{,}000$$

It is important for the distributor or other experts to accurately estimate the income, and to be able to support their claims. If a prior year's estimate proves incorrect, future years' depreciation deductions will have to be adjusted to reflect the error.

Distribution, Marketing, and Promotional Fees

The distribution, marketing, advertising, and promotional fees and expenses incurred by movie, book, record, and artwork ventures are generally fully deductible as ordinary and necessary business expenses, unless the transaction is classified as a joint venture or partnership between the investor and the distributor, in which case these items might be considered non-deductible partnership distributions to the distributor. Generally, a joint venture exists when parties join together with the intention of carrying on a business and sharing its profits. Whether or not one is considered to exist depends upon the structure and facts of each situation, and the latest case law and Regulations. Again, the advice of tax counsel is recommended. If the arrangement between the investor, distributor, and, possibly, the seller is considered a joint venture, the rules of partnership taxation would apply. The IRS might contend that the payments for these expenditures should be deductible in later years, if at all, since to allow the deduction in the year paid or incurred would not clearly reflect the income of the venture.

An Illustration

In July 1982, Jenna H. purchased the master recording of "Disco Sounds for Latvian Americans," and all the copyrights necessary for commercial exploitation. A $5,000 down payment was required on the total cost of $50,000, with the balance secured by a recourse promissory note. The agreement provided that 80% of the proceeds from the property, after distribution fees were deducted, must go toward repaying the note. The note had an outside due date of 10 years, and an annual interest rate of 6%.

Jenna entered into a distribution agreement with Arthur M., a distributor recommended by the seller. The distributor was to supervise production, promotion, and sale of the records, in exchange for 50% of the gross (total) receipts generated. (Let us assume, for illustration purposes only, that the IRS does not challenge either the investment credit or the fair market value of the recording and that it is eligible for the full 10% tax credit.) It was decided that the income forecast method would be used to compute depreciation, and at the end of 1982 the following estimates were made:

Year	Actual Earnings	Estimated % of Total Income	Fraction
1982	$32,000	40	32,000/80,000
1983	16,000	20	16,000/80,000
1984	12,000	15	12,000/80,000
1985	8,000	10	8,000/80,000
1986	4,000	5	4,000/80,000
1987	3,200	4	3,200/80,000
1988	2,400	3	2,400/80,000
1989-91	2,400	3	2,400/80,000

The salvage value of the master at the expiration of the useful life is estimated to be $2,000, and is subtracted from the $50,000 cost, to arrive at a basis for depreciation of $48,000. Using the above chart to compute the depreciation deductions, and taking into account all the preceding information, the tax and economic results of the investment over the next 10 years are as follows on the chart on the next page.

Footnotes

[1] Gross receipts represent the proceeds available from exploitation of the record, before deducting debt service and distribution fees.

[2] Interest is computed at a rate of 6% per year on the unpaid balance of the loan (in 1982 only a half year's interest is paid since the property was purchased in July. For the purpose of this illustration we will omit imputed interest.) As you recall, interest is payable from 80% of the proceeds from the record after distribution fees have been deducted. Any amount remaining from the 80% after the interest has been paid will be used to amortize the loan. (Amortization appears later on the chart as a non-deductible expense.) Beginning in 1987, the proceeds from the venture will be insufficient to fully cover the interest payments. In that case, the unpaid balance of the interest will be payable on the due date of the loan. A schedule of interest and amortization payments appears on page 192.

[3] The distributor is entitled to a fee equal to 50% of the gross receipts from the property. The payment we will assume to be fully deductible as an ordinary and necessary business expense.

	1982	1983	1984	1985	1986	1987	1988	1989–91
Gross Receipts [1]	32,000	16,000	12,000	8,000	4,000	3,200	2,400	2,400
Deductions								
Interest [2]	1,350	2,013	1,750	1,567	1,470	1,280	960	960
Distribution fee [3]	16,000	8,000	6,000	4,000	2,000	1,600	1,200	1,200
Depreciation [4]	19,200	9,600	7,200	4,800	2,400	1,920	1,440	1,440
TOTAL DEDUCTIONS	36,550	19,613	14,950	10,367	5,870	4,800	3,600	3,600
TAXABLE INCOME (LOSS)	(4,550)	(3,613)	(2,950)	(2,367)	(1,870)	(1,600)	(1,200)	(1,200)
Investment Credit [5]	5,000	-0-	-0-	-0-	-0-	-0-	-0-	-0-
Amortization of Loan [6]	11,450	4,387	3,050	1,633	130	-0-	-0-	-0-
CASH DISTRIBUTIONS TO JENNA [7]	3,200	1,600	1,200	800	400	320	240	240

[4] Depreciation is calculated using the income forecast method, by applying the fractions set forth in the chart on page 189 to the depreciable cost of $48,000.

[5] Investment credit equals 10% of the $50,000 cost.

[6] Refer to the schedule of interest and amortization payments on the next page for calculation of the non-deductible amortization payments.

[7] Any funds remaining after payment of the distributor's fee and interest and amortization on the loan, will be available to Jenna as cash distributions.

If we assume that Jenna is taxed at the 50% level, the results of her investment over the next 10 years will be as follows on Chart II on the next page.

It is apparent that Jenna is substantially ahead of the game by 1991, with a cumulative economic benefit of $17,675. However, at this point the note is due, and the limited success of "Disco Sounds" has left an unpaid balance on the note of $24,350. If Jenna fails to pay that amount, the seller will foreclose on its security interest, and reclaim the master and accompanying copyrights. This means there will be a gain on foreclosure equal to the difference between Jenna's adjusted cost (cost minus depreciation deductions), which now equals $2,000, and the unpaid balance of the loan. Because of the rules of recapture, this $22,350 gain ($24,350 minus $2,000) will be subject to tax at ordinary income rates unless the seller collects the balance due on the note from Jenna.

Of course, as we emphasized earlier, there is a good chance that the structure of Jenna's deal and the tax benefits arising from it will be challenged by the IRS. Obviously, a motive for profit, other than tax savings, could easily be missing in this type of investment.

Magazine Tax Shelters

Certain provisions of the Code have made magazine tax shelters a popular investment during the last few years. Basically, two sections of the Code are involved. One section permits the taxpayer to deduct all expenses incurred to establish, maintain, or increase the circulation of a newspaper, magazine, or other periodical. The second provision permits a taxpayer in the publishing business to defer reporting prepaid subscription income until the year he is obliged to furnish or deliver the newspaper,

CHART I
Interest And Amortization Payments

	Cash Available For Payment [80% Gross Income Less Distribution Fees]	Interest Due	Interest Paid	Amortized Payments	Balance Due on Loan at End of Year
1982	12,800	1,350	1,350	11,450	33,550
1983	6,400	2,013	2,013	4,387	29,163
1984	4,800	1,750	1,750	3,050	26,113
1985	3,200	1,567	1,567	1,633	24,480
1986	1,600	1,470	1,470	130	24,350
1987	1,280	1,460	1,280	-0-	24,350
1988	960	1,460	960	-0-	24,350
1989–91	960	1,460	960	-0-	24,350

CHART II

	[A] Cash Contributed	[B] Taxable Income (Loss)	[C] Investment Credit	[D] Tax Savings	[E] Cash Distribution	[F] Annual Benefit [D + E-A]	[G] Cumulative Benefit
1982	5,000	(4,550)	5,000	7,275	3,200	5,475	5,475
1983	-0-	(3,613)	-0-	1,806	1,600	3,406	8,881
1984	-0-	(2,950)	-0-	1,475	1,200	2,675	11,556
1985	-0-	(2,367)	-0-	1,184	800	1,984	13,540
1986	-0-	(1,870)	-0-	935	400	1,335	14,875
1987	-0-	(1,600)	-0-	800	320	1,120	15,995
1988	-0-	(1,200)	-0-	600	240	840	16,835
1989–91	-0-	(1,200)	-0-	600	240	840	17,675
TOTAL	$ 5,000			$14,675	$ 8,000		$17,675

magazine, or periodical. Together, these two provisions permit a limited partnership engaged in the magazine business, to generate excess tax losses during the first year as a result of expenses incurred relative to increasing circulation, while at the same time deferring the recognition of income until later years when the magazines are delivered to subscribers. Again, the experience and track record of those publishing and marketing the periodical is essential to the success of the venture, since this is a very competitive business with a high mortality rate. Naturally, when evaluating this type of transaction it is important to know the background of the parties involved. This is particularly vital since ventures like these are structured to comply with the at-risk rules by having the investors assume part of the liability to subscribers who have prepaid their subscriptions.

CHAPTER XIII
Research and Development Shelters

One of the up-and-coming types of tax shelters today is the Research and Development (R&D) shelter. R&D shelters are formed to research and develop new technology, processes, and products that can range from jet planes to genetic engineering, from computers to cancer cures. The allure of an R&D shelter, in addition to the tax benefits that are described below, is that an investor has the opportunity to get in on the ground floor of the development and ownership of a new product, invention, or breakthrough, and to share the profits which may result.

R&D shelters usually take the form of limited partnerships, with the limited partners contributing the capital needed to fund the research project, and the general partner or "sponsor" supplying the research project, as well as any work in progress. The ventures are often initiated by a company in need of additional funds to begin and/or complete the research or development of a potentially commercial product or technology. The sponsor company, or an affiliate, will usually perform and supervise the research activities on behalf of the partnership. If a commercially exploitable product results, the partnership will then transfer its rights to the product to the sponsor, in return for royalty payments based on a percentage of the sales.

Analyzing R&D shelters from a business point of view is difficult, since they often involve products and technologies which are complex, technical, and unfamiliar to the average investor and his advisors. The determination of whether a product can be developed from a technological point of view is one that should be made with the assistance of an expert in the field. Naturally, the background of the sponsors should also be checked and their experience and track record in similar ventures analyzed. It is also important to consider whether they have budgeted the project properly. Have they allowed sufficient funds not only to complete the research, but also to market the product? A marketing feasibility study by independent consultants in the field should be available. This will identify the potential market for the product being developed and estimate its potential sales. If the potential market is too small or already saturated by competitors with greater financial and marketing capabilities, this could add additional risks.

Some R&D ventures involve heavy research into areas where technology is young and relatively untested commercially,—for example, genetic and medical research projects. Other ventures are more oriented to the improvement of existing products or technology. Naturally, the former involve greater risks, but could also be considerably more profitable.

Also from a profit point of view, you should examine the split between the investors and the sponsor. If the investors are providing virtually all of the cash, while the sponsor is contributing only a project in the earliest stages of development, the investors should be entitled to a greater share of the revenue. This would not be the case if the sponsor had already sunk large amounts of capital into the project. Also be aware that there will usually be a considerable lag between the time an investment is made and the time profits are generated, even by a successful product. Medical products, for example, may require years of testing before they can be marketed.

The limited partnership will usually employ the sponsor company to license and/or market the product, in return for royalty payments to the partnership. Some ventures give the sponsor the option to buy out the partnership at some point in time. This type of arrangement should be approached with caution, since the sponsor obviously will not exercise the option unless it is beneficial to him. In other words, the investors could be bought out for a small percentage of the true potential value of the product.

In many R&D ventures, stock or the right to purchase stock (warrants) of the sponsor company are often distributed to investors. If the stock is, or becomes, publicly traded and the product is successful, the investors are in a position to profit from any favorable stock market reaction to the product, even before profits are generated. However, if the success of the company depends solely on the success of the product, the stock will not be of much value if the project fails.

Tax Aspects of R&D Shelters

After you have carefully examined the economics of an R&D deal, you should then be sure that the tax structure is sound and will, in fact, deliver the anticipated benefits. The main tax objectives of R&D ventures are to provide investors with tax deductions in the early years, and, hopefully, long-term capital gains treatment of any eventual profits. The foundation for the tax deductions was laid by a provision of the Code enacted in 1954 to encourage research activity. This provision permits taxpayers to deduct "research or experimental expenditures which are paid or incurred by them during the taxable year, in connection with a trade or business." The Treasury Regulations promulgated with respect to this provision define the phrase "research and experimental expenditures" to mean costs in the laboratory sense, including those incidental to the development of a pilot model, plant process, product, formula, invention, etc. This also includes the improvement of any existing property of the same nature, as well as the costs of obtaining a patent. Research and experimental expenses do not include expenses for the testing or inspection of materials or products for quality control, efficiency surveys, management studies, consumer surveys, advertising and promotion, or, generally, the cost of acquiring property which is subject to the ACRS or depletion allowances. It also does not include the cost of acquiring another person's patent, model, process, or product.

In most R&D shelters, the partnership does not perform the research itself, but enters into a research contract with the sponsor, or perhaps another party. The fact that a third party performs the research should not jeopardize the tax deductions, as long as the research is performed at the partnership's risk; in other words, as long as there is no guarantee that the research will be successfully completed. If there is such a guarantee, the deductions could be questioned.

The Code also states that R&D expenses must be paid in connection with the taxpayer's "trade or business." This does not present a problem since, in 1974, the Supreme Court held that a limited partnership, newly formed for the purpose of developing a product, meets the trade or business requirement and qualifies for the R&D deduction.

Many R&D deals are structured to give investors the maximum deduction in the first year, sometimes in excess of their actual cash contributions. This can be accomplished by the delivery of a recourse note to the research contractor, or by borrowing from a bank, using the investors' future payments as collateral and paying the contractor in advance of the research. If the pre-payment covers research to be performed much beyond the close of the year, the IRS could argue that the deduction should be allowed only when the research actually occurs. The partnership should have a valid business purpose for the pre-payment, other than merely to accelerate losses; for example, the research contractor needs the funds to meet its obligations for material and personnel.

Another important benefit of R&D deals is the potential for the profits generated to be taxed at the more favorable long-term capital gains rates. If the research results in a patentable product, this can be accomplished by having the partnership transfer all rights to the patent to a third party (usually the sponsor) in exchange for royalties based upon gross sales. The Code provides that long-term capital gains treatment will be available with respect to the sale of patents. If the product is not patentable, obtaining long-term capital gains treatment is more difficult. One possible method is to provide for the purchase of the limited partners' interests in the partnership by the sponsor, which generally results in capital gains treatment. However, if the sale and price are prearranged, the investors may not be considered at-risk for tax purposes, and may not be able to use the deductions. Still another possibility is for the partnership to hold on to the product or technology for more than 12 months, then sell all of its rights to the property. Again, however, the IRS may contest the favorable tax treatment and the outcome of such a dispute is uncertain.

The Economic Recovery Tax Act of 1981 added a tax credit for R&D expenditures incurred after June 1981 equal to 25% of the increase in R&D expenditures over the average expenditures for the preceding taxable years. (Certain transitional rules apply in the first 2 years.) However, the credit is generally not available to tax shelters because it does not apply to start-up ventures, as does the R&D deduction. Furthermore the credit may only be used to offset taxes due on income arising from the venture.

Before moving on, we should consider some of the tax risks involved in R&D deals. First of all, the IRS can be expected to question whether the sponsor has an expressed or implied obligation to buy out the investors, regardless of whether the project succeeds or fails. If such an obligation exists, the investors might not be considered at-risk. The SEC and the Financial Accounting Standards Board (FASB) are already looking into some R&D deals with this in mind.

Second, if the partnership is acquiring technology, warrants, or stock from the sponsor, and is also paying the sponsor to do the research, the IRS may seek to recharacterize certain research payments as non-deductible payments for stock, warrants, or existing technology. Third, the IRS could argue that the partnership and the sponsor are really a joint venture, and that the payments to the sponsor are really contributions to the venture. That would mean that the R&D deductions would have to be shared by the investors and the sponsor on the basis of their interests in the revenues generated. Finally, the IRS could argue that the partnership is merely providing financing to the sponsor—acting as a lender—and thus is not entitled to any deductions at all. These elements, along with the structure of any deal, should be considered by a tax expert before you invest.

CHAPTER XIV
Energy Tax Shelters

The Energy Tax Act of 1978, the Crude Oil Windfall Profit Tax of 1980, and, to some extent, the Economic Recovery Tax Act of 1981 have spawned a new breed of tax shelters—"energy shelters," based on tax incentives instituted by Congress to reduce America's dependence on oil and gas.

You will recall from Chapter III that an "Energy Tax Credit" is now available for the cost of constructing certain facilities, or buying equipment that qualifies as "energy property." Generally, the credit is equal to 10% of the cost of the property, but it may be as high as 15% on equipment which produces energy from the sun or wind (such as photovoltaic cells or windmills). Energy tax credits can mean that a substantial portion of the initial cost of energy property can be recovered through tax savings in the year the property is placed in service.

For example, in the case of a windmill costing $100,000 and qualifying for both the energy credit and the investment tax credit, the owner of the equipment could reduce his taxes by as much as $25,000 in the year the windmill begins to produce energy. In addition, another $100,000 could be deducted via ACRS over a five-year period.

The Code lists the following types of energy property as qualifying for the energy tax credit:

(1) alternate-energy property (e.g., boilers using fuels other than oil and gas products);

(2) solar, wind, or geothermal energy property;

(3) specially defined energy property (generally equipment designed to reduce the amount of energy consumed in any commercial or industrial process);

(4) recycling equipment;

(5) shale oil equipment;

(6) equipment for producing natural gas from geo-pressurized brine;

(7) qualified hydroelectric generating property;
(8) cogeneration equipment;
(9) qualified intercity buses;
(10) ocean thermal equipment (equipment used to convert ocean thermal energy into electrical or other useful energy); and
(11) biomass fuel property (biomass is any organic substance other than oil or gas—crops, sewage, etc.).

In addition to the above properties, a special credit was added by Congress to encourage the production of gasohol. That credit can equal up to $0.40 per gallon for alcohol and alcohol-blended fuels, provided that they are not produced from petroleum products.

As with all tax shelters, the promise of substantial tax savings should not blind an investor to the economic risks of energy shelters. In many cases, the technology in this area is simply not advanced enough to generate power economically. This means that many projects which qualify for the credit, such as plants designed to produce ethanol from sugar cane, may be too costly to build on a commercial scale. Few if any partnerships are in a position to raise tens or hundreds of millions of dollars to construct such facilities, regardless of the amount of tax credits they generate. Furthermore, conventional lending sources, such as banks and insurance companies, are often wary of lending money to projects that have not yet been proven commercially feasible.

Still, with the growing concern about fuel costs and consumption, energy shelters should continue to proliferate. One type already showing promise is the small scale hydroelectric (SSH) facility. The technology for such facilities has, by now, been basically established. An energy tax credit of 11% and an investment tax credit of 10% can be applied against virtually the entire cost of building such properties. And, perhaps most significant of all, the Public Utilities Regulatory Policies Act of 1978 (PURPA) exempted SSH facilities from the rate-setting controls of federal and state public utility commissions. PURPA also *requires* utility companies to purchase electricity generated by these facilities.

On the down side, a number of lawsuits have been filed challenging the rules adopted by the Federal Energy Regulatory Commission (FERC) implementing PURPA, and it may be years before the issues are resolved. In addition, obtaining the required license from FERC to construct an SSH facility can be a long and expensive process. Finally, financing for such facilities is not easy to obtain, and even a relatively small SSH can cost millions of dollars.

Another up-and-coming energy shelter is the "Energy Management System," which involves the use of specially designed equipment to reduce energy consumption, or the waste of heat, in an existing "commercial or industrial process." Unfortunately, the Regulations promulgated by the IRS took a very restrictive position as to what type of energy management property could qualify for the energy tax credit. They indicated that the property must be used in connection with an industrial or commercial "process which includes chemical, physical or mechanical action to produce a desired result." This seems to eliminate equipment used in an office, for retail sales, or for residential purposes. The fact is, the tax rules for this type of equipment, with respect to the energy tax credit, investment tax credit, and ACRS, are currently complicated and unresolved. The advice of tax counsel should be sought when venturing into this area.

With respect to the economics of these ventures, many are structured to earn profits based on a percentage of the energy costs saved by the consumer. For example, a venture will install the energy-saving equipment on the premises of a user, free of charge. The user, in turn, agrees to split any energy cost savings with the venture. Because the field is relatively young, it is difficult to accurately predict the amount of savings that will result. It is also difficult to monitor the savings and collect the venture's share. Before investing, check the track record of the sponsors, with a special eye to the ultimate economic results to investors in similar types of deals.

Quite often, there is a time limit imposed on tax benefits enacted by Congress, particularly when they are intended to stimulate investment in a particular industry or segment of the economy. Depending upon subsequent developments, these incentives may or may not be extended. Energy tax credits for solar, wind, geothermal, ocean thermal, hydroelectric generating property, biomass property, and intercity buses are currently scheduled to expire at the end of 1985. Credits for all other energy property, unless extended by Congress, will expire at the end of 1982.

CHAPTER XV
Farming, Cattle, and Timber

Historically, farmers have been granted certain tax benefits and incentives, some to simplify their record-keeping burdens and others to encourage land improvements and other such activities. For example, farmers may deduct currently certain expenditures that in non-farming operations would have to be capitalized and deducted through depreciation. Such allowances have made farming ventures an effective way of deferring tax liability from one year to the next and, in some cases, of converting ordinary income to capital gains when the tax deferral ends.

Naturally, it didn't take long for high-bracket taxpayers to recognize the shelter potential of farming and to begin investing, or "farming" on a part-time basis in the hopes of deferring tax liability on income from non-farm sources. Obviously, this was not what the IRS and Congress intended, and so the 1976 Tax Reform Act took several steps to limit the availability of tax benefits to so-called passive farmers. Broadly, the Act included farming as an at-risk activity and also restricted the current deductibility of many prepaid costs. Although this had decidedly adverse effects, investors can still derive significant tax benefits from these ventures.

The Code defines farming as "the cultivation of land or the raising or harvesting of any agricultural or horticultural commodity including the raising, shearing, feeding, caring for, training, and management of animals." We will turn first to the latter part of the definition, for it encompasses some of the most popular types of farming shelters: ventures involving cattle and horses.

Cattle tax shelters generally take one of two forms: "feeding" operations or "breeding" operations. In a feeding operation, basically the investor purchases young cattle for the purpose of fattening them up, then selling them to a slaughterhouse, anticipating a profit. Usually, the whole transaction takes less than eight months. A breeding operation, on the other hand, encompasses a period of years during which time a small herd is increased in numbers through breeding. The larger herd is then sold, again presumably at a profit.

Feeding and breeding ventures vary greatly in tax objectives and results. Basically, cattle feeding is purely a deferral device; feeding shelters are designed to enable the investor to defer his tax liability from one year to the next, by incurring deductible expenses in connection with the feeding and maintenance of the herd in one tax year, and realizing income in the next when the herd is sold. Breeding, on the other hand, in addition to deferring taxes, offers the possibility of converting ordinary income to capital gains.

Now, let us look more closely at each type of venture.

Cattle Feeding

Commonly, the promoter of a feeding venture acts as an agent for the investor and arranges for the purchase of the cattle and the necessary feed. The transaction is highly leveraged, with the investor providing as little as 5% to 10% of the cost, the balance being obtained through loans from lending institutions, the seller, the operator or, perhaps, the promoter. Frequently, the loans will be in whole or part non-recourse, depending upon the amount of losses available and how much the investor is willing to risk. The cattle are generally kept for a period of four to eight months in a commercial "feedlot," where they are fed and maintained by the "feedlot" operator until ready for sale.

The profitability of a cattle feeding operation depends upon the ability of the venture to dispose of the cattle at a price which exceeds their cost, including the cost of feeding and maintaining them during the period preceding the sale. Even in a stable market, however, the profit margin in cattle ventures is not very high, especially in tax shelter situations where the investor has the added burdens of interest charges on loans, and management and syndication fees. Since the price of cattle and feed is subject to frequent fluctuation—often determined by the location of the feedlot—the timing of the sale and the placement of the cattle could make the difference between profit and loss. Many ventures will attempt to soften the potential effects of price fluctuations by purchasing cattle at different stages of development and placing them in feedlots in different geographical areas of the country. This could help prevent a situation in which all the cattle come on the market at the same time (perhaps when demand or prices are low), and could also diminish the effect of geographical disparities in price. Additionally, it would lessen the risk of total loss as a result of natural disasters, such as disease, or man-made catastrophes, such as the bankruptcy or insolvency of a feedlot operator.

Speaking of the feedlot operator, one should remember that he has complete control of the property. His skill and experience are paramount and should be thoroughly investigated when analyzing this type of investment. (That goes for the promoter and syndicator as well.) Frequently, in exchange for a share of the profits, the feedlot operator, promoter, or syndicator will offer the investor a guarantee against economic loss. In that case, the financial ability of the guarantor becomes important, as does the effect of the guarantee on the at-risk loss limitation, which applies to cattle ventures.

From a tax shelter point of view, cattle feeding operations can generate excess deductions, by permitting the investor to deduct, in one year, the cost of feeding and caring for the animals, as well as the interest charges on the loans. In the following year, when the cattle are sold, the income is taxed at ordinary income rates, unless, of course, the investor takes further steps to defer his tax liability. Often, cattle ventures will offer investors the opportunity to continue the deferral by perpetually reinvesting the proceeds of the sale.

Prior to the Tax Reform Act of 1976, the deferral aspects of cattle feeding operations were much more significant for year-end tax planning purposes than they are today. The cost of feeding cattle could be fully prepaid at year-end, giving rise to an inflated deduction, even though the feed was not consumed until the following year. Investors would also often prepay interest on the loans and deduct the prepaid charges at year-end.

The 1976 Tax Reform Act required participants in most cattle feeding tax shelters to deduct the cost of feed only when it is consumed, and the interest charges only in the period to which they relate. This prevents an investor from coming into a venture late in December and obtaining substantial tax benefits, but it does not eliminate the deferral for an investor who enters a venture earlier in the year. Most of the feed will then be consumed within the year, the cattle will be sold in the next, and the income will be successfully shifted.

In addition to these restrictions, the 1976 Reform Act also

imposes a special restriction on most farming corporations, and on farming partnerships with a corporation as a partner. Now, these types of ventures must capitalize (deduct through ACRS), rather than deduct when paid, all expenses, except interest and taxes, incurred prior to the sale of the cattle. If you are entering a cattle partnership—feeding or breeding—it is essential to know whether a corporate partner exists that could bring this restriction into effect.

Cattle Breeding

As we said, in breeding tax shelters the objective is not only to defer tax liability (usually for a longer period than in feeding operations), but also, when the tax is finally paid, to pay it at the more favorable long-term capital gains rate. The investors in a breeding operation acquire a herd, again in a highly leveraged transaction that could involve a loan of up to 90% of the cost. How much of the loan is non-recourse again depends on the amount of losses available and how much the investor is willing to risk. In this case, the herd consists mainly of cows and heifers (cows who have not yet borne calves), with a small number of hardy bulls to "service" them. The care of the herd and the breeding operations are supervised by a rancher. All of these activities are arranged by the promoter.

Each year, the cows are bred and should produce a calf crop of 75% to 85%. The male calves and non-reproductive females (culls) are sold (usually to feedlot operator) and the proceeds are funneled back into the breeding operation. Frequently, the investors will be required to contribute the balance of funds needed to maintain the herd. After about 5 to 7 years, the herd should increase sufficiently in number to be sold, assuming the price is right.

As in a feeding venture, the operator, in this case the rancher, has complete control of the property. He is responsible for handling the potential trouble areas of a breeding operation, such as the mortality rate of the animals, the effects of disease and weather, the rate of reproduction, and increase in feed and maintenance costs. Guarantees against loss may be available from the rancher, but it is still essential to check his track record in similar types of ventures. In both feeding and breeding operations, the help of an expert should be sought to analyze not only the economics of the transaction and the projections, but the parties involved as well.

From a tax point of view, in addition to deductions for feed, management, and maintenance costs, and interest on the loans, a breeding operation will utilize ACRS and investment credit on purchased (as opposed to raised) animals. For ACRS purposes, cattle are considered 5-year property. Naturally, because cattle are also considered personal property, if the animals are sold, the gain will be subject to recapture as ordinary income, to the extent of any ACRS deductions taken. Investment credit will also be recaptured if the purchased animals are prematurely sold.

ACRS and investment credit will not be allowed on raised cattle, since these animals have no cost basis. However, they do present an important tax advantage. If raised cattle have been held for at least 24 months, any gain on their sale should be taxed at the more favorable capital gains rate. This is how the conversion of ordinary income to capital gains occurs. The investor uses the deduction attributable to raising the cattle to offset ordinary income from other sources, then sells the raised cattle at long-term capital gain rates.

Horse Racing and Breeding

The Economic Recovery Tax Act of 1981 increased the attractiveness of horse racing and breeding ventures. Under ACRS, racehorses over the age of 2, and breeding horses over the age of 12, are considered 3-year property. Younger racehorses and breeding horses are classified as 5-year property. The tax considerations are similar to cattle breeding except that there is no tax credit available for horses. The theory of breeding and racing is that the best racehorses produce the best racehorses. Therefore, the objective is to mate quality horses and race the offspring, or sell them to those who will race them, then begin the breeding cycle again. Naturally, the general partner or manager should be experienced and have a successful track record (in this case, literally) in all aspects of the operation, from breeding to training to racing.

Other Farming Activities

The tax deferral and other benefits attributable to cattle ventures are also available, to a limited extent, in farming ventures involving field crops, orchards, groves, vineyards, poultry, etc. These ventures used to be much more effective, due to the tax incentives traditionally awarded farmers. Prior to the Tax Reform Act, many items that would normally have to be capitalized, such as seed costs and the costs of developing orchards and vineyards, could be deducted immediately when paid. Additionally, the Code permitted, with certain significant limitations, the current deduction of fertilizer costs, soil or water conservation expenses, and the costs of clearing land.

When it became apparent that these advantages were being used by part-time farmers for whom they were not intended, the Tax Reform Act moved to restrict them. In addition to imposing the at-risk limitation on farming, the Act provides that the costs of developing orchards and vineyards must be deducted through depreciation, and the costs of seed, fertilizer, and other such farm supplies can only be deducted when used. Also, the restriction, discussed in the cattle section, concerning corporations and partnerships with corporate partners now applies.

Despite these limitations, through the use of leverage, farming ventures can still be attractive, especially if farmland, which generally will increase in value, is acquired as part of the investment. As always, the ability and experience of the farm manager is of key importance and his track record should be evaluated. So should the risks of farming, which include weather, water (or the lack of it), labor conditions (e.g., the grape pickers), crop disease, insects, and fluctuations in the market. In this technical and unfamiliar field, the advice of an expert is indispensable.

Timber

Timber ventures, which are not widely available as tax shelters, are in some respects similar to farming and in others to mineral ventures. Like farming, they involve resources that are replaceable. Like mineral ventures, they are eligible for the cost depletion allowance. Other deductible items should include management fees, costs of estimating the inventory of uncut trees, property taxes, salaries and, of course, interest charges. Usually, timber is a long-term investment, requiring large amounts of invested capital, and offering only limited potential for leveraging tax write-offs. However, when the timber is sold, a large portion of the income should be taxed as capital gains.

The major business considerations of timber ventures are the cutting, sale, and transportation of the trees. Accessibility is vital to success. As always, effective management is essential, as is professional assistance in evaluating the projections and parties involved.

PART V
Miscellaneous Shelters, Tax-Sheltered Income Investments, and Tax-Reduction Techniques

CHAPTER XVI
Miscellaneous Shelters

Professional Sports Franchises

One of the more exotic and attractive tax shelters—especially to sports buffs—is the ownership of a professional sports team. Usually, these investments take the form of a limited partnership, since large amounts of invested capital are required. Generally, when a group acquires a team, whether basketball, baseball, football, hockey, etc., they are purchasing the following assets: (1) the franchise, granted by the league, which is the right to operate the team in a specified area, to participate in the college player draft and to share TV, radio, and other league revenues; (2) the right to use a specified arena or stadium, usually pursuant to a lease with the arena's owners; (3) sports equipment; and (4) player contracts.

The revenues earned by the team are mainly derived from ticket sales, TV and radio revenues, and concessions, such as parking, food, drinks, programs, and novelty items sold at the games. The expenses include rent for the arena; interest on debts; equipment costs; franchise fees; travel expenses; advertising promotion costs; salaries of the manager, coaches, trainers, scouts; and, most significantly, the often astronomical salaries of the players.

The profitability of the team depends upon its ability to draw the fans, which may in turn depend upon the record of the team and the presence of big name superstars who remain uninjured. Even with a winning team and big name players, however, teams could and often do operate in the red, as a result of lack of fan interest, or because expenses are too high. One of the hidden expenses to watch for in a sports venture is the cost of litigation which often results from disputes between players and teams, and teams and leagues. These costs can be quite significant.

The tax advantages of owning a sports team arise not only from the deductibility of operating costs, but the manner in which the costs of acquiring the team, which are usually quite substantial, can be deducted. Although the costs of the franchise are generally not deductible, the costs of acquiring the arena lease can be written off in equal amounts over the life of the lease. Equipment costs are subject to ACRS. Player contracts, which are not eligible for ACRS, may be depreciated on a straight-line basis over the generally short useful life of the player. When acquiring a team, the purchaser will want to allocate as much of the cost as possible to player contracts, because of this relatively short life. On the other hand, the seller will try to allocate the cost to the franchise, since this will result in gain for him taxed at capital gains, rather than ordinary income, rates.

The Tax Reform Act of 1976 imposed certain restrictions on the sale of sports teams, mainly with respect to player contracts. According to the Act, it will be presumed that not more than 50% of the cost of the team is allocable to these contracts, unless proven otherwise. The 1976 Reform Act also tightened up the rules of recapture, in the case of a sale of the team, to encompass any depreciation deductions previously taken on player contracts which are no longer in effect at the time of sale because of retirement of the player or other circumstances. As with other personal property, any gain derived from the sale of player contracts will, by reason of recapture, be taxed at ordinary income rates, to the extent of any depreciation taken.

On the risk side, when considering a sports venture, you should investigate the operating history of the team and league, and be aware that the dynamics of the team and its profitability can change drastically from year to year along with its ever-changing personnel.

Commodity Straddles

Until recently, many tax-oriented investors seeking to defer capital gains from one year to the next invested in commodity straddles. Perhaps the most popular commodity for tax deferral purposes was silver, since, unlike wheat, corn, soybeans, sugar, cocoa, etc., it is not usually subject to the wide fluctuations in price caused by weather and crop conditions. As we shall see, recent judicial and legislative actions have all but eliminated commodity straddles as tax shelters. But first, a brief look at how they used to work.

Basically, commodity straddles involved the purchase and sale by an investor of contractual rights to accept, in the case of a purchase, and deliver, in the case of a sale, a specified quantity of a commodity, on a specified date, for a specified price. These contractual rights are known as "futures contracts," or simply "futures." A straddle existed when the investor simultaneously entered into a contract requiring delivery of the commodity to him in one month and another contract requiring him to deliver a like amount of the commodity in another. By simultaneously assuming positions on both the buy and sell sides of the market, the investor assured himself of a potential gain on one contract and a corresponding loss on the other, no matter which way the price of the commodity fluctuated. That gain and loss could be timed according to his tax needs.

The actual cost of the transaction was only a small amount in commissions paid to the commodity broker. By maintaining a proper balance of buy and sell contracts, the risk of economic loss was small enough so that the brokerage houses would probably require only a minimal amount of cash for the futures, with the rest being purchased on margin (using borrowed funds secured by the contracts).

We have greatly simplified the structure of straddles and minimized the risks that could exist, especially if the price spread between the contracts fluctuated inconsistently. Unfortunately for tax shelter investors, in a pre-1981 case involving a commodity straddle, the tax court held that the losses in that case would be disallowed since the venture was not "engaged in for profit." This ruling put other investors in similar ventures in jeopardy. Subsequently, the 1981 Economic Recovery Tax Act eliminated any future commodity straddles as tax shelters.

All Savers or Tax Exempt Savings Certificates

The Economic Recovery Tax Act of 1981 included a provision allowing taxpayers to earn up to $1,000 interest ($2,000 for married couples filing joint returns) tax-free, during their lifetimes, by purchasing special, tax-exempt savings certificates. To qualify, a certificate must be issued after September 30, 1981, and before Janury 1, 1983, and must have 1-year term of maturity. The interest rate ("investment yield") on the certificate must equal 70% of the average 1-year U.S. Treasury Bill yield. The certificates must be available in $500 denominations, and issued by a qualifying institution such as a bank, savings and loan association, credit union, etc. If the certificate is redeemed, or pledged as collateral for a loan prior to the end of the 1-year term, the interest exemption will be forfeited for that certificate.

Individual Retirement Accounts (IRA's)

To the benefit of taxpayers, the Economic Recovery Tax Act of 1981 greatly liberalized the rules regarding Individual Retirement Accounts, better known as IRA's. IRA's are trusts, or custodial accounts, set up with banks, savings and loan associations, credit unions, or any other qualified organizations or individuals, including some brokerage houses. Any individual who is receiving compensation for services can set up an IRA, even if he or she is already participating in a pension, profit-sharing, or Keogh plan. As much as $2,000 can be placed in the account each year (or 100% of your earned income if it is less than $2,000). That amount is *tax-deductible* for the year it is paid, provided it is deposited before you file your tax return for that year.

In addition to the deduction, any interest earned on money placed in an IRA is *tax-free* until the year you begin to withdraw the funds. Withdrawals can be made without penalty when the taxpayer reaches the age of 59½, (or earlier in the case of death or disability). They *must* begin when the taxpayer turns 70½ and will be taxed at ordinary income rates. The withdrawal can be made in full or in installments and will be taxed when taken. Hopefully, they will occur when the taxpayer is retired and in a lower tax bracket.

In the case of married couples, if both people work, each can establish an IRA with a $2,000-per-year limit. This would bring their total deduction to $4,000 if they file a joint tax return. If only one spouse works, two IRA's can still be established, but the maximum combined deposit per year is only $2,250, with not more than $2,000 going into one account.

Gifts to Charity

Gifts to charities have been utilized for many years to reduce the tax liability of high-bracket taxpayers. Now, the Economic Recovery Tax Act of 1981 has made the charitable contribution deduction available also to lower-bracket taxpayers (i.e., those who claim the standard deduction). For the years 1982 and 1983, such taxpayers can deduct 25% of charitable contributions of up to $100. (This makes the maximum deduction $25 [25% of $100]). In 1984, the limit on charitable contributions will be $300 (the maximum deduction will therefore be $75 [25% of $300]). In 1985, 50% of all charitable contributions may be deducted, and in 1986 100% of all donations to qualified charities will be tax-deductible. As of now, this special provision is set to expire after 1986, and, as with higher-bracket taxpayers, there are limits to the total amount of the deductions that can be claimed. Generally, for most qualified charities, deductions cannot exceed 50% of the donor's adjusted gross income.

Many high-bracket taxpayers who itemize their deductions utilize charitable contributions as tax-deferral devices. For example, artworks, or other valuables that have appreciated in value over the years, can be contributed with the amount of tax deductions computed on the basis of the fair market value, not the original cost of the object to the donor. However, again there are limitations on the amount of deductions that can be claimed in these kinds of situations, based on the type of property donated, its use by the charity, and how long it was owned before the donor gave the gift.

Another way of providing leveraged tax benefits using the deduction for charitable contributions is for the taxpayer to buy the property on installment (i.e., paying part in cash and the balance over a period of years). If the property is then contributed to a qualifying charity, the taxpayer can claim a deduction for the full value—the total price—even though he has only made a partial cash payment. Naturally, the later payments will still have to be made, but the tax benefits in the first year can be substantial.

Gifts, Clifford Trusts, and Other Income-Shifting Techniques

As we have seen, there is a certain element of economic risk involved in all tax shelter investments, since they are business enterprises and thus subject to the vagaries of the business world. Obviously, it would be ideal if one could reduce taxes without being subject to the uncertainties of the economy. Certain tax-planning techniques are being utilized to accomplish this by shifting income from high-bracket taxpayers to lower-bracket ones, without removing the assets involved from the family group. The simplest method is to give a gift of income-producing property or money to a lower-bracket taxpayer, perhaps a child or retired parent. As a result, the income earned on the property would be taxed at lower rates. However, the asset given as a gift can no longer be under your control. The Economic Recovery Tax Act of 1981 raised the amount of gifts that can be given tax-free in any year to $10,000 per recipient, or $20,000 per recipient in the case of a husband and wife giving a gift jointly.

Another way of accomplishing the same objective without giving up complete control of the asset is to set up what is known as a "Clifford Trust." A Clifford Trust is generally a trust set up for at least 10 years. The interest earned on the property transferred to it is distributed to the beneficiary (the individual designated by the grantor as the recipient of the benefits of the trust). The trust must be irrevocable for the 10-year term and cannot be controlled by the grantor. At the end of the 10 years the property reverts back to the grantor. The advantage is that during the 10-year period the income earned is not taxed at the grantor's tax rates, but rather at the (hopefully) lower rates of the beneficiary.

A recent court case highlighted another related tax-planning technique. Assume a taxpayer makes an interest-free loan to a member of his family in a lower tax bracket. The loan is repayable on demand and there is no pre-arranged plan to cancel the debt. The lower-bracket taxpayer invests the money and earns the interest, paying taxes at a lower rate than his benefactor would have paid. Perhaps the beneficiary uses the proceeds of the trust to pay for college or graduate school, deferring repayment of the loan until his needs for the funds have passed.

Municipal Bonds

As we mentioned earlier in the book, municipal bonds are not really tax shelters, since they generally do not provide tax deductions. They do, however, provide tax-free income. A municipal bond, as you will recall, is essentially tangible evidence of the obligation of a municipality, town, village, port or housing authority, state, political subdivision, etc., to repay a loan made by a taxpayer. The term of the bond (i.e., loan) varies from short-term (a few months or years) to longer-term (40 to 50 years). The face value of the bond is payable when the term of the bond expires (reaches maturity).

The income earned on municipal bonds is the interest paid on the loan by the municipality. Generally, the interest rate is determined by the market conditions prevailing at the time the bond is first issued. If interest rates are generally high at the time, the interest rate on the bond will be high as well. However, the rate is also affected by the credit rating of the municipality or agency that issues the bond.

Naturally, if the credit rating of the municipality is not great, it will have to offer a higher interest rate in order to attract investors. Bond issues are rated generally by two independent services—*Moody's* and *Standard and Poor's*—on the basis of quality and financial stability of the municipality. The ratings run from Triple A for the top of the line, down to C and D for the lower end of the quality scale.

In addition to the interest rate payable, income can be earned on municipal bonds by virtue of the price paid for the bonds. For example, if you purchase a bond with a face value of $5,000 for $4,500, with a 10% interest rate, your effective return is really greater than 10% because you are earning 10% of $5,000, or $500 yearly, on a $4,500 investment. Another advantage is that bonds, like stocks, are generally freely traded on the over-the-counter market, offering investors easy liquidity, not often available in conventional tax shelters. However, the market value of the bond will, to a large degree, depend upon its interest rate as compared to the prevailing one, as well as the remaining term of the bond and, of course, its rating.

The fact that bonds are freely tradeable gives them certain tax shelter potential in the more traditional sense, as a result of what is referred to as "swapping." If a bond you purchased is now selling for a lower price (perhaps due to a rise in interest rates, while your rate remains fixed), you could sell the bond at a capital loss and use the loss to offset other capital gains. With the proceeds of the sale you could purchase a different type of bond with a similar return and thus be in essentially the same economic condition, but now with a substantial tax loss to claim.

CHAPTER XVII
Additional Considerations

The tax shelter investments we have discussed are the major ones available today but by no means are they the only possibilities. Many types of business operations can be structured to maximize tax allowances and generate deductions to offset income from other sources. Furthermore, just as new legislation will inevitably eliminate or reduce existing possibilities, so will it undoubtedly create new ones. It seems safe to predict that as long as the government uses the tax system to stimulate segments of the economy, as well as to raise revenues, there will be opportunities for tax shelter.

In this final chapter, we will consider some general items that relate to most existing shelters and probably also to those yet to come. These factors could greatly influence the short- and long-term outcome of your investment, and should not be overlooked in the initial analysis and evaluation.

Activities Not Engaged in for a Profit

We have repeatedly stressed the importance of choosing economically viable ventures. This is partly because a business failure could cause you to lose your investment and, through recapture, many of the tax benefits you may have claimed. In addition, unless you really stand to make a profit on the investment other than through tax savings, you could find many of the anticipated tax benefits flatly disallowed. This is because the Code distinguishes between those ventures engaged in for profit and those not engaged in for profit, such as hobbies and ventures engaged in purely for the tax benefits. While taxpayers involved in the former may deduct expenses even though they exceed income from the activity, those involved in the latter may only deduct expenses to the extent of income from the venture, except for certain specified allowances, such as real estate taxes and interest. In essence, this means ventures not engaged in for profit cannot generate excess deductions to offset income from other sources.

While this section of the Code was originally intended to restrict hobby-type activities, it is broad enough to cover other questionable endeavors, such as those whose prime objective is to generate tax benefits. The determination of whether a true profit motive exists is purely subjective, but certain guidelines do exist. For example, the Code provides that if gross income from an activity exceeds deductions for 2 out of 5 consecutive years, the activity will be presumed to have been engaged in for profit. Unfortunately, many tax shelter ventures are unable to meet this requirement since, in the early years of operation, deductions usually exceed income. Therefore, they must depend on a series of factors which, according to the Treasury Regulations, are collectively considered when making a profit motive determination. They are as follows:

[1] *The manner in which the activity is carried on*—i.e., is it a businesslike manner, with the maintenance of proper books and records, and the adoption or abandonment of techniques apparently with the intention of improving profitability?

[2] *The expertise of the investor or his advisors*—i.e., has extensive study or expert consultation been undertaken to learn the accepted business, economic, and scientific practices of the activity, and are they being followed?

[3] *Whether a significant amount of non-recreational time is devoted to the venture by the investor or his representatives.*

[4] *Whether the business assets can be expected to appreciate in value over time.*

[5] *The success of the investor in similar types of ventures.*

[6] *The operating history of the venture*—i.e., do the losses exceed the income for a longer period of time than is customarily required to bring such an operation to profitable status?

[7] *The amount, if any, of occasional profits earned from the activity in relation to the amount of money invested*—i.e., even if profits occur only occasionally, if they are large enough a profit motive may be presumed.

[8] *The financial status of the investor*—i.e., is this his main source of income?

[9] *Whether the activity has elements of personal pleasure or recreation, which could make it less of a business, and more of a hobby or leisure activity.*

While no one factor will decide the profit motive issue, each will contribute to the final determination. In recent years, the IRS has had some degree of success in attacking tax shelter deductions based upon the "not for profit" issue. Therefore, when entering a tax shelter venture with remote profit potential, coupled with significant tax benefits, it would be wise to consider this list and consult an expert about your chances of being subject to the "not for profit" limitation.

Minimum Tax on Tax Preferences

In an attempt to equalize what Congress termed an unfair distribution of the tax burden resulting from various special deductions and deferrals available to high-bracket taxpayers, these taxpayers are now subject to two additional taxes on these so-called items of tax preference. These two taxes are known as the "add-on minimum tax" and the "alternative minimum tax," both of which can have significant consequences for tax shelter investors.

The "add-on minimum tax" is payable by the taxpayer in addition to his regular income tax and is generally equal to 15% of the total of his tax preference items for the year, to the extent that they exceed the greater of $10,000 or one half of the taxpayer's tax liability for the year. The items of tax preference most often subject to the "add-on minimum tax" are as follows:

[1] The amount by which the ACRS deduction for property (other than real estate) that is subject to a lease exceeds the deduction that would have been allowed if the straight-line method of depreciation were used. For the purposes of computing what the straight-line allowance would have been, salvage value is disregarded and the following useful lives are used: 5 years for 3-year cost recovery property; 8 years for 5-year property; 15 years for 10-year property; and 22 years for 15-year public utility property.

[2] The amount by which the ACRS deduction for real estate exceeds the deduction that would have been allowed if the straight-line method were used. For this purpose, a 15-year useful life is assigned, and again salvage value is disregarded.

[3] For pre-1981 ventures, the amount by which accelerated depreciation deductions for real estate or leased property (as in equipment leasing ventures) exceed the deductions that would have been allowed using the straight-line method.

[4] The amount by which the annual depletion deduction (when

percentage depletion is used) exceeds the adjusted basis of the property.

[5] The excess of the deductions allowable for intangible drilling costs attributable to producing wells, above the amount that would have been deductible if the costs were not currently deducted, but instead deducted over a 10-year period, or through the cost depletion method.

In the case of these and other such items the add-on minimum tax would be calculated as follows: Let us assume that an oil venture, in which Ann H. has 10% share, has generated excess intangible drilling costs in 1982 of $150,000. Ann's share of this tax preference item is therefore $15,000. Let us assume that she has no other tax preference items for the year and that her regular tax liability is $12,000. The computation of her "add-on minimum tax" would be as follows:

Tax preference items	$15,000
Minus the greater of	$10,000
(or ½ of tax liability, i.e. $12,000 × ½ = $6,000)	
Equals tax preference items subject to minimum tax	$5,000
"Add-on Minimum Tax Rate" 15% = $750 additional tax	

While the 15% additional tax may not in itself seem significant, it does reduce the benefits available from affected shelter, and should be considered in the analysis of any venture.

The "alternative minimum tax" is imposed on what is called "alternative minimum taxable income," and then only to the extent that the tax exceeds the sum of one's regular income tax and the add-on minimum tax.

The alternative minimum tax rate is as follows:

Tax Rate	Amount of Alternative Minimum Taxable Income
0%	$0–$20,000
10%	$20,000–$60,000
20%	$60,000 and above

The alternative minimum taxable income is generally equal to the gross income of the taxpayer, less any deductions, plus the 60% long-term capital gain deduction, and certain other itemized deductions in excess of 60% of the taxpayer's adjusted gross income. An example of how the alternative minimum tax is computed is as follows:

Suzanne G. recently sold her interest in a real estate shelter she entered in 1975, for a $100,000 long-term capital gain. She has $68,300 of other income. Her taxable income is thus $108,300 ($68,300 + 40% of 100,000) and her regular tax on this, let us assume, would be $45,468. The alternative minimum tax is computed as follows: $68,300 + $60,000 ($100,000 × 60%), or $128,300 of alternative minimum taxable income. The tax is $0 on the first $20,000, 10% on the next $20,000, or $4,000, and 20% on the next $68,300 or $13,760, for a total alternative minimum tax of $17,760. But since this does not exceed her regular tax of $45,468, Suzanne has no alternative minimum tax due.

Estate Considerations

We demonstrated earlier that both sale and foreclosure are less-than-ideal ways of disposing of tax shelter property or investments. As you recall, in either case, many of the early tax benefits, arising, for example, from ACRS deductions, intangible drilling costs, and investment tax credit, could be subject to recapture, often resulting in taxable gain greater than the actual cash received. Taxable gain is measured by the difference between the investor's adjusted basis and the amount received, or deemed to have been received, from the sale or foreclosure.

Many practitioners say that the best way to dispose of a tax shelter investment, at least from a tax point of view, is to die owning it. That is because the beneficiary would not be saddled with your adjusted basis (reduced by depletion or ACRS deductions), but instead could use the generally higher fair market value of the property. Thus, when the beneficiary sold the property, the gain would be measured by the difference between the fair market value and the amount received for the sale. Assuming the property was sold at, or close to, its fair market value, there would be little or no taxable gain on the transaction, and all or most of the income tax liability initially deferred by the investor would be permanently avoided.

You should, however, consider that if you bequeath your tax shelter property after the so-called cross over point has been reached—that is, after taxable income from the venture begins to exceed cash distributions—all you may be leaving your beneficiary is a tax headache. Without having enjoyed the early benefits of the shelter, he may be gaining nothing but your deferred tax bill.

These are some of the main estate considerations of tax shelters, discussed in a very general manner. The tax laws and consequences in this area are much more complicated and should be thoroughly reviewed with an expert.

Tax Audits

Undoubtedly, a question in the mind of every tax shelter investor is—and certainly should be—Will I be subjected to and can I survive an audit? Generally, an audit is an examination conducted by the IRS of the tax return and, possibly, the supporting books and records of a taxpayer, to determine whether his return complies with the requirements of the tax laws. This process could result in a challenge by the IRS, and the disallowance of some or all of the tax deductions and other benefits claimed by the investor, and the payment of additional tax.

An audit may focus either on the return of an individual, or that of a venture, i.e., a partnership tax return. It may be conducted right at the place of business where the books and records are kept, in which case it is referred to as a "field audit," or it may be carried out at the office of the IRS, either in person or by mail, in which case it is called an "office audit." Of the two, the field audit is generally more extensive.

Usually, when a partnership or other venture with more than one investor is involved, the IRS will audit the partnership return, books, and records, than seek to recover a share of any deficiency from each of the investors. In this case, as in the case of an individual audit, the burden is on the taxpayer to prove that the items reported on the return are correct. For this reason, it is essential that you have access to the books and records necessary to substantiate the claims. This is especially important in the case of individual investments, such as book, record, and cattle deals, etc., when an independent company may have control of the necessary documents.

After the examination has been completed, the IRS agent will issue a written report stating and explaining any adjustments he determines should be made. If the taxpayer agrees with the determination or any compromise offered by the IRS, he simply pays the difference and the matter should be closed. If, however, an agreement is not reached, the taxpayer will receive a "30-day letter" from the IRS, setting forth the adjustments they propose. The taxpayer may then continue to press his claim through further administrative channels within the IRS, or choose to litigate the issue in court. Naturally professional assistance is essential through all stages of these proceedings, from the initial audit on. Settlement conferences may prove effective, since the IRS is often as anxious to avoid burdensome litigation as you are.

Sometimes, however, settlement is not possible, in which case the IRS will send the taxpayer a "notice of deficiency," or "90-day letter," stating that an underpayment of tax has been found. The taxpayer now has 90 days from the date of the notice to take one of two actions. He may either file a petition in Tax Court, the tribunal in which questions of tax liability are resolved without the taxpayer first having to pay the disputed tax; or he may pay the tax allegedly due, file a claim for a refund, then sue for the refund in the United States Court of Claims or a Federal District Court. Advice of counsel is again essential in deciding where and how to litigate, since different issues may be governed by different legal precedents, depending upon the forum chosen.

While the prospect of an audit and litigation is certainly nothing to relish, it does not necessarily mean a deficiency will be found or that you will lose the issue in court. Normally, the chances of an audit are not great, since only a small percentage of returns are selected and, of those, an even smaller percentage are litigated. Unfortunately, your chances rise as a tax shelter investor. In selecting returns for audit, usually with the help of computer technology, the IRS has indicated an increased focus on tax shelter ventures.

If you are audited and a deficiency is successfully asserted against you by the IRS, the Economic Recovery Tax Act of 1981 has made the results even more costly than before. Not only must you pay the deficiency, but you must also pay interest on that amount at a rate equal to the prime rate. If the deficiency is due in part to overvaluation of property, an additional penalty will be assessed. The Valuation Penalty applies if the value claimed for property (e.g., for ACRS or tax credit purposes) exceeds 150% of the value finally determined to be correct. The penalty will be imposed only if the property was acquired within 5 years of the year in question and the deficiency is more than

$1,000. The penalty will equal 10% of the deficiency if the overvaluation is between 150% and 200%; 20% if the overvaluation is between 200% and 250%; and 30% if the property is overvalued by more than 250%. This penalty, together with potential negligence or fraud penalties (ranging from 5% to 50%), should serve to deter promoters and investors from inflating the value of property to increase tax deductions.

The IRS focus on tax-oriented ventures is not likely to diminish. For this and countless other reasons, it is essential to consult a tax expert before investing.

Changes in the Tax Laws

No matter how carefully a tax shelter venture is structured to conform with existing tax laws, it still faces the possibility that the laws could be changed, as a result of legislative action or judicial interpretation. Any changes, of course, could dramatically alter the tax benefits available to investors. While you can learn of major proposals, developments, and changes in the tax system from the newspapers and financial periodicals, an expert should be consulted for a more complete analysis of how they affect your particular tax situation or investment.

The following is a look at some of the more significant proposals affecting tax shelters that have recently been or are currently being considered by Congress.

Subchapter S Corporations—Subchapter S corporations could acquire more of the attributes of partnerships for tax purposes. Distributions would be tax-free to the extent of the stockholder's basis for his stock. Excess losses in any year would be allowed to be carried over to later years, and the treatment of stockholders would be liberalized, with the limit on their number being raised to 35 and the prohibition against earning excess passive income generally eliminated.

Promoters of Abusive Tax Shelters—Promoters of abusive tax shelters would be subject to a penalty equal to the greater of $1,000 or 10% of the gross income derived, or to be derived, from the venture. The promoters of abusive shelters would also be subject to court injunction to prevent continued activity in the area.

Partnership and Subchapter S Audits—The tax treatment of partnership or subchapter S income, losses, deductions, etc., would, for audit purposes, be determined at the partnership or corporate level, in a unified proceeding, rather than in separate proceedings for each partner or stockholder.

Undoubtedly, other tax proposals will be considered by Congress. These proposals will be subject to extensive debate and scrutiny before being approved, if ever, by the Committee, the full House, the Senate Finance Committee, the Senate, and finally the President. Naturally, during this process, changes in the provisions can be expected. Again, we say, check the status of new legislation, as well as proposed effective dates, before investing.

State and Local Tax Considerations

All along, we have been mainly concerned with the federal income tax consequences of tax shelter ventures. The investor should also be aware that the benefits from these investments can help reduce his state and local tax liability, just as in the later years, income from the ventures can increase his state and local tax burden. However, if the investor resides or earns most of his taxable income in one state, the tax benefits of a venture organized in another may not be available to offset his state and local income taxes. Because these taxes can be quite substantial, this factor could be significant in the evaluation of a shelter investment. Additionally, if a venture is organized, or does business, primarily, in another state, the venture and/or its investors could be required to file tax returns and submit to taxation in that state. Therefore, prior to investing, the laws of the states involved should be considered.

One last point related to state and local issues: if a business venture carries on its operations in a state other than the one in which it was organized, it may be required to formally qualify to do business in that state. Failure to do so could result in the imposition of fines, or other penalties or restrictions. Again, familiarity with the laws of the states involved is essential.

To Invest or Not to Invest

Throughout our discussion of tax shelters, several major investment objectives have consistently emerged. These are:

(1) Deferral of tax liability;
(2) Conversion of income subject to taxation at ordinary in-

come rates to income subject to taxation at more favorable long-term capital gains rates;

(3) Cash returns from the investment; and,

(4) Appreciation in value of the assets acquired.

But what about the results of the investment as a whole? How do you determine whether a tax shelter will, in the long run, be more profitable than simply paying your taxes and investing your remaining capital in a less risky area?

The concept of deferring tax liability to a later date will result in economic benefit to the investor, if he is taxed at a lower rate when he eventually pays the piper, and/or if he successfully invests his tax savings so that he is earning money on dollars that would originally have been paid in taxes. If the tax dollars saved, and the income earned from them, and from the venture itself combine to exceed the costs of the investment and any tax liability arising from it, obviously the investor will be ahead of the game. Ideally, the investor had the foresight to create a fund out of his tax savings and earnings to meet future tax liability from the venture, especially when phantom income is involved.

But how can you assess these variables in advance? The amount the investor will earn on the tax dollars he saves can be estimated by assuming those dollars will be invested in a manner consistent with his other available cash, i.e., in savings accounts, Treasury Bills, municipal bonds, stock, etc. On this basis, you can anticipate, for example, that he will earn between 12% and 15% annually on the tax savings from his shelter. Add to this the projected annual cash return from the venture, and the estimated growth in the value of the assets (strictly an educated guess), which will be distributed if they are sold or if the mortgage is refinanced, and you will have the projected positive return on the investment. Usually, these types of economic projections or forecasts will be provided by an accounting firm representing the syndicator. When analyzing them, it is important to carefully examine the assumptions upon which they are based, to be sure they are reasonably related to actual market conditions, and not just the hopes, dreams, or guesses of the syndicator.

Once the positive aspects of the investment have been determined, the cost must be figured and subtracted from the benefits to arrive at the bottom-line profit or loss. To determine the cost, start with the after-tax price of the investment, i.e., the cash invested less the tax dollars saved. Next, determine the tax that will eventually be due on phantom income and other income generated by the venture (i.e., profits from operations and proceeds from the sale of the venture). Then, reduce the positive results of the investment by these costs.

To complete the analysis, compare the bottom line to what would have happened had you paid your taxes and invested the remaining cash in a manner consistent with your normal portfolio. The results should make it obvious whether or not the tax shelter investment is worth the risk.

Summing Up: How, Where, and When to Invest

Just as a tax shelter must be properly structured and economically viable, so must it be well-suited to the needs and goals of the investor. Shelter should be chosen largely on the basis of his economic situation—present and future—and his investment objectives. Obviously, an investor who expects to earn substantial income for many years will not benefit optimally from a venture offering a short-term tax deferral, whereas another investor heading toward retirement might. Age and health thus become very real factors bearing upon earning potential and estate considerations.

The first step, then, is to assess your situation and determine your objectives. Take into account your financial needs and resources; the effects of such factors as the maximum tax rate and minimum taxes on preference items; the future burden of phantom income and the provisions you must make to meet it; the growth potential of the investment; the lack of liquidity; and the risks associated with the type of venture under consideration. Once you determine what you can and cannot live with, the field of suitable investments should be considerably narrowed.

You can generally gain access to shelter investments through your lawyer, accountant, stockbroker, business advisor, banker, and acquaintances in the business community. Remember, however, that a person recommending a deal might be receiving a commission from the syndicator, and could have strong economic incentive to analyze the investment in a most favorable manner. In addition to checking his past association with the people in control of the deal, the advice of an independent financial advisor could prove invaluable. Remember also that there are two aspects to every tax shelter deal. While your financial advisor may be quite competent to analyze the tax consequences, especially with the more exotic shelters, his experience on the business side may be limited. A talk with someone experienced and knowledgeable in the area could round out the analysis.

As for when to invest, the days of slipping into a tax shelter just hours before the new year are over. As a result of the Tax Reform Act of 1976, year-end investments ordinarily will not offer substantial tax benefits, nor will they leave you a wide selection of investments from which to choose. Maximum tax benefits will generally be available by investing early in the year. Psychologically, that will also allow you time to properly analyze the investment, without the pressure of "getting into something" before the year ends.

And so we have come full cycle: back to a proper analysis of the investment. We reaffirm and close with what we have emphasized throughout this book—a tax shelter investment must be sound business investment. Failure as a business will inevitably mean failure as a tax shelter.

Glossary

The terms defined in this glossary are the major ones that appear consistently throughout the book. The definitions are meant to clarify our usage of the terms and may not, especially in the case of tax terminology, conform to the technical legal definitions.

Accelerated Cost Recovery System, or ACRS—the method for computing the annual tax deduction allowed for the cost of tangible business or investment-related property.

Accelerated Depreciation—methods of computing the depreciation deduction that usually allow for greater deductions in the early years of the venture, e.g., the "declining-balance method" and the "sum-of-the-years-digits method." (See "Depreciation Deduction")

Adjusted Basis, or "Tax Basis"—the figure, based upon the cost of an investment or property, used to determine gain or loss upon disposition of the property and the amount of allowable deductions each investor may claim.

Amortization—repayment of loan principal.

Depletion Deduction—the annual tax deduction allowed to the owner of mineral property for the actual or theoretical decline in value of the property due to extraction of the mineral.

Depreciation Deduction—the annual tax deduction allowed for the actual or theoretical decline in value of business or investment-related property due to wear, tear, or obsolescence. (See also "Straight-Line Method" and "Accelerated Depreciation")

Investment Tax Credit, or "Investment Credit"—a tax allowance, usually generated by the acquisition of business or investment-related property, which is subtracted directly from the amount of tax dollars otherwise due.

Leverage—the use of borrowed funds to acquire business or investment property or to finance a business venture.

Limited Liability—a legal status inherent to certain types of business organizations, such as limited partnerships and corporations, which limits an investor's responsibility for the debts and obligations of the venture to the amount of money he has invested or committed.

Non-recourse Loan—a loan for which none of the participants in a venture is personally liable. Generally, the lender agrees to accept only the property of the venture as security for the loan.

Phantom Income—"paper" profits from a venture that result in taxable income that exceeds the actual amount of cash generated by the venture. Phantom income usually arises when money is expended on items that are not tax deductible, such as amortization of a loan.

Recapture—the taxation of all or a portion of the gains from disposition of property at ordinary income rates by reason of prior depreciation or ACRS deductions taken.

Salvage Value—the estimated value of a depreciable asset at the end of its useful life.

Straight-Line Method—the method of computing the annual depreciation or ACRS deduction by which the depreciable cost is deducted in equal annual amounts over the useful life or recovery period of the property.

Tax Deductions, or "Deductions"—tax allowances that reduce a taxpayer's taxable income before his tax liability is computed. Tax deductions usually result from the expenditures of money in connection with a business or investment.

Index

ABOUT THE AUTHORS

Robert Tannenhauser received a B.A. degree from Syracuse University, a J.D. from Brooklyn Law School and an L.L.M. in taxation from New York University. He is currently a practicing tax attorney and partner in a New York law firm.

Carol Tannenhauser holds a B.A. from Syracuse University and an M.A. in communications from New York University. She is a freelance writer.

The Tannenhausers live in New York City with their son David.